MOUNTJOY:
ELIZABETHAN GENERAL

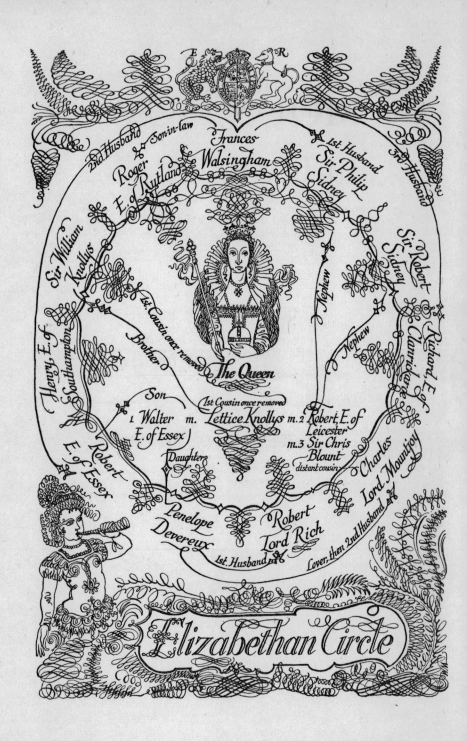

Elizabethan Circle

MOUNTJOY:
ELIZABETHAN
GENERAL

BY

CYRIL FALLS

ODHAMS PRESS LIMITED
LONG ACRE, LONDON

First published 1955

CONTENTS

ILLUSTRATIONS

TO THE
WARDEN AND FELLOWS OF
ALL SOULS COLLEGE
OXFORD

PREFACE

WHILE engaged in writing *Elizabeth's Irish Wars,* published in 1950, I became deeply interested in the personality and qualities of Charles Blount, Lord Mountjoy and Earl of Devonshire. He was one only of the long line of the Viceroys of Queen Elizabeth I in Ireland. He was, however, the last and the most important. In three years of hard, hot, and at first indeterminate fighting he brought to a victorious conclusion a war which had gone ill for the Queen's Government, had cost it dear in men and money, and had gravely perturbed it. In the process he defeated a dangerous Spanish invasion. He was, in a modern phrase, the "supreme commander" in one of the greatest of Elizabethan military achievements. His viceroyalty filled upwards of a quarter of the book mentioned above, which was devoted to all the Irish wars of the reign.

His life, from 1563 to 1606, was short, but even so *Elizabeth's Irish Wars* treats only a small proportion of it, and that only the military facet. It does not reveal his character, except as a soldier. It does not deal with his earlier or later career. He was, with his friend Lord Southampton, one of the two most prominent leaders of the Essex party after Essex himself. He was the lover of his chief's sister, fighter in other phases of war by sea and land, bookman and patron of poets, finally one of the great figures and ruling spirits of the first few years of King James I. Here, it seemed to me, was a rich life. I made up my mind to reconstruct it and hoped to add something of value to the historical writing on the first Elizabethan age, writing which, for all its abundance, is short of serious biographies.

I also decided that, so far as I found the necessary material available, I would include a study of his mistress, Lady Penelope Devereux, later Lady Rich, finally and briefly Countess of Devonshire. This decision was reached not only because she was

A*   9

a romantic figure, immortalized by the enchanting verses of Sir Philip Sidney, praised by other poets, celebrated far and wide for her beauty, bound to Charles Blount by a deep and enduring passion, but also because of her influence on her lover, an influence which at one moment bore him to the brink of disaster. Penelope was a politician, and a dangerous one. She not only fought in the front rank under her brother's standard but —at least so he averred in a weak moment when facing a traitor's death—urged him on with the taunt that his friends said he had lost all his valour. It seems clear that she used her power over her lover to push him forward in her brother's cause. The story of Charles and Penelope is highly dramatic, and it is one story.

No sooner had I begun than I realized how ambitious I had been. In the absence of family papers men and women make as a rule only comparatively rare appearances in correspondence until they become important figures; then many people write to them and preserve their letters, while others write about them. This I found to be the case with Charles Blount. That he served in the decisive fighting against the Invincible Armada is attested only by a few words in his Admiral's despatch, though fortunately we know the part played by his ship. His action in the Islands Voyage must be sketched from a few references to his ship in that expedition. Most of his intermittent service in the Low Countries and Brittany is recorded by rare mentions of his name. Even when these occur it has to be borne in mind that captains of companies in those days were often absent from their commands, as he is known to have been. Moreover, other Blounts served in these campaigns and one of them was named Charles, so that it has to be decided whether the reference applies to the hero or not. When he reaches Ireland, on the other hand, his actions, and often his thoughts, can be followed, sometimes from day to day, always from week to week, for well over three years; but by then the year 1600 has already been reached.

Others must judge how far I have succeeded in my aim with respect to the lean years. I am confident that I have at least produced a portrait of him, and of Penelope too, which leaves them better-defined figures than they were before. Yet I will admit that I had hoped to find more material for his youth than I did.

My treatment of the Irish viceroyalty follows what appear to be reasonable lines: I have, as compared with my book on the Irish wars, increased the detail of events, military operations in particular, in which he took a personal part, and ruthlessly cut down that of the problems and campaigns of subordinates who acted partly on their own initiative and were not under his eye. With them I have confined myself to results. Yet I have tried to make it clear that policy and strategy were dictated by him. Correspondence from England poured upon him, yet it touched strategy little. Sometimes a political matter, such as the treatment of an Irish magnate, was involved, but the great bulk of the letters he received were concerned with administration, chiefly complaints of expense and orders to root out corruption. Otherwise he was left to himself. He was a masterful commander who delegated as little as he could, and he had the Queen's confidence.

Mountjoy was an admirable soldier. Yet, new to high command, he began with stumbling and disappointment, though with no serious rebuffs. He was groping in the green Irish maze, where facts were as doubtful as the paths through the bogs, where you might ride through a defile with half a dozen troopers one day in safety and be met by a storm of musketry the next, where the best measures of protection on the march were tested by men who appeared from nowhere after wading "as familiarly through rivers as water-spaniels", where the most loyal of noblemen and chiefs had codes of behaviour not well comprehended in Dublin Castle and wholly incomprehensible to Whitehall, where a campaign might depend on which side had the pastures for grazing, and where nonetheless you might have to face a drilled and disciplined force trained and equipped on the same lines as your own. He learnt all this quickly and thereafter acted with the confidence created by familiarity.

He became so deeply imbued with the principle of surprise and so determined in his pursuit of it that the word might have served as his motto. He planted garrisons so skilfully and combined them so well with his field army that one rebel leader or another was always in trouble, "while he kept all the rest like dared larks in continual fear, as well of himself as of the garrisons adjoining". A chain of garrisons is a necessity in fighting an enemy practising guerrilla warfare, but ruinous if formed at the expense of mobility, badly planned, or overdone. The manner in which he picked up and concentrated his garrisons for major operations in itself stamps him as a very able commander. His greatest initial achievement, however, was in the field of pure leadership. "Being a nurse to this army as well as a general", he pulled it together and made it capable of facing a foe whose recent successes had discouraged it. As one of his captains, whom I later quote at some length, wrote of him, he "cast the coward out of her Majesty's army, that sometime troubled it very much".

His policy and action during the first eighteen months of his viceroyalty can be appreciated only if we realize as clearly as he did the sword of Damocles suspended above his head. He dared not allow himself to be drawn into deep commitments with his field army while the Spanish threat remained. He took considerable risks, but not the supreme risk of getting tied down in Ulster. The Spaniards were never off his mind. Though he might expect strong reinforcements if they landed, he must keep a mobile force ready to intervene at once. When they did land his real grandeur of will and spirit was revealed.

I am deeply indebted to Mr. A. L. Rowse for having on more than one occasion copied with his own hand extracts from manuscript sources for me. I feel myself to lie under an even greater obligation for the ideas and advice from the deep store of his knowledge of the first Elizabethan age which I have derived from innumerable conversations during the past three years or so. One learns a lot of history from talking to him for three years. I have to thank Mr. John Buxton for calling my attention (before the publication of his remarkable book on Sir Philip Sidney, which appeared only just before this went to press) to dedications and references to both Charles and Penelope in late Elizabethan and early Jacobean poets, some of the references being obscure and easily overlooked. The Warden of All Souls, Mr. John Sparrow, found for me the books from Mountjoy's library in the Bodleian.

C. F.

I

THE ANCIENT HOUSE

WHEN the boy Charles Blount sat for his portrait he insisted,
so the tale goes, that the artist should depict him holding a
trowel and, so that there should be no doubt about the meaning
of the tool, should inscribe on the painting, "Ad reaedificandam
antiquam domum". It sounds unlikely in a boy and the fact that
he was not the heir to his ancient house might create further
doubt, even though the teller claims to have had the story from
his own lips.[1] Yet younger sons have restored family fortunes,
and the reign of Queen Elizabeth I encouraged youth to aim
high. The symbolism is to the point. Charles Blount was ambitious, eager for place and power; his house was ancient and
honourable; it was also in sore need of restoration.

The Blount family can be traced to a distant past. If we start
with the first famous representative on whom Charles had to
look back, we shall at the same time record its alliance with an
illustrious family of Spain, against whose soldiers and sailors
Charles fought and with whose ambassadors he sat to make peace
after the long war. In 1367 Sir Walter Blount accompanied
Prince Edward, the Black Prince, and his brother John of
Gaunt, Duke of Lancaster, to Spain, on the expedition in support of Pedro the Cruel, the deposed King of Castile. This
Anglo-Spanish military pact was followed by a matrimonial
alliance. In 1372 Don Pedro's daughter, the Infanta Constantia,
came to England to be the bride of John of Gaunt. She was
accompanied by a lady of high rank, Donna Sancha de Ayala.
Sir Walter Blount, John of Gaunt's henchman, married Donna
Sancha, the Duchess's lady-in-waiting. It is tempting to suppose
that she brought him a fine dowry; for in 1374 he purchased

[1] Moryson, Vol. II, p. 260.

from his half-brother the Mountjoy estates in Derbyshire. Seven years later he added the considerable Bakepuiz estates in Derbyshire, Leicestershire, and Hertfordshire. His wife had a pedigree long even for a land of long pedigrees and through her mother, whose name she bore, traced back to the royal houses of Aragon and Leon.

At the Battle of Shrewsbury on 23 July, 1403, Sir Walter, so the story goes, wore the arms of King Henry IV, John of Gaunt's son. He was killed in the fight. Shakespere in *1. King Henry IV*, makes a stirring tale of the tradition that he had sacrificed himself "semblably furnished like the King himself", to take the blows of knights determined to single out the King and kill him at all hazards. Shakespere also tells how Sir Walter had served as the King's envoy and attempted to reason the rebels into submission. The portrait is one of a gallant and honourable man, deep in the King's trust:

> *Here is a dear and true industrious friend,*
> *Sir Walter Blount.*

The son of Sir Walter and Sancha de Ayala, Sir Thomas, was Treasurer of Normandy. Thomas's son, another Walter, fought at Towton on the victorious Yorkist side and became the first Lord Mountjoy, Lord High Treasurer of England, and a Knight of the Garter. He also received from Edward IV the forfeited lands of Thomas Courtenay, Earl of Devonshire, killed at Towton in the Lancastrian ranks. Within the first lord's lifetime his eldest son was killed at Barnet, and his son died in childhood, shortly after inheriting the title as second lord. Next came the child's uncle, Sir John, third lord, who married a member of the Berkeley family. Their son William succeeded as fourth lord.[1]

So far the characteristics of the family are a taste for war and for making its way, getting the most out of the rival royal houses, Lancaster and York, the Red Rose and the White, just as the hero of this narrative was to make his way under the Tudor Rose. Another characteristic now appears: a taste for letters, for learning, for the exercise of the intellect, and for the society of men who practised them, also to be prominent in Charles.

[1] Croke, Vol. II, pedigrees, pp. 173-204; Harl., XXVI; D.N.B.

William Blount, fourth Lord Mountjoy, was in Paris in 1496 as a youth in his teens at a time when Erasmus, aged about 29, was giving lectures in order to keep body and soul together. William came to listen and at once attracted the brilliant young lecturer. The boy was evidently endowed with exceptional physical beauty, charm, and intelligence. A warm attachment, sentimental and emotional as well as intellectual, was established between the two. The letters of Erasmus contain many proofs of their affection, sometimes expressed in glowing language. "You would have seen me in Italy", he writes to Robert Fisher in 1499, "if Lord Mountjoy had not carried me with him into England. Whither would I not follow so humane, so kind, so amiable a young man"! A letter to William himself begins: "Salve, vero nomine Monjoie (Hail, by your true name, My Joy)".[1]

The visit to England gave Erasmus great pleasure. Mountjoy took him to the house of his father-in-law, Sir William Saye, at Bedwell, Hertfordshire. Child marriages were less common than formerly, but still survived. They amounted in effect to unbreakable betrothals, and, though Mountjoy had been married for two years, his wife remained in the custody of her father. (She was to die young, leaving only two daughters, and the line was to be carried on through Mountjoy's second wife, daughter of Sir Henry Keble, Lord Mayor of London.) Erasmus, who at that stage was far indeed from despising worldly pleasures, felt that England was the place for him.

"Your friend Erasmus gets on well in England. He can make a show in the hunting field. He is a fair horseman . . . The English girls are divinely pretty—soft, pleasant, gentle, and charming as the Muses. They have one custom which cannot be too much admired. They kiss you when you arrive; they kiss you when you go away; and they kiss you when you return. Go where you will, it is all kisses, and, my dear Faustus, if you had once tasted how soft and fragrant those lips are, you would wish to spend your life here".[2]

Mountjoy afterwards took Erasmus to the royal palace of

[1] Preserved Smith, p. 59; Froude, p. 54; Croke, Vol. II, p. 210; Allen, Tome I, Ep. 79. For the year Smith is followed. He gives the first visit of Erasmus to England as occurring between June and December, 1499.

[2] Froude, p. 42.

Eltham, where they saw Prince Henry, later to become King Henry VIII. After the hunting, the kisses, and the Court came graver entertainment. Erasmus stayed at Oxford. Then or earlier he met Thomas More, Colet, Fisher, Linacre, and Grocyn. He was delighted with his visit and with his company.

Mountjoy became page to Prince Henry and seems to have acted as junior tutor to him. When his master ascended the throne Mountjoy wrote to invite Erasmus to England and enclosed a letter from the King. Erasmus arrived in October, 1509—this was his third visit, the second having begun in 1505—On this occasion he grumbled. He was somewhat grasping and felt that too little was being done for him, though Mountjoy engaged himself to pay him a pension of £60 a year, quite a handsome allowance. Yet one grumble affords a useful piece of information: Mountjoy was absorbed in military affairs, "and moreover, though one of the old nobility and liberally disposed towards men of learning, he is not rich according to the standard of the English peerage". Perhaps he was over-spending and had started that habit in the family. He certainly accompanied the King to the Field of the Cloth of Gold in 1520, and that was a very expensive entertainment.[1]

In 1521 Mountjoy wrote to urge Erasmus to enter the lists against Luther. The letter drew a historic reply, which explains the difficult situation of Erasmus. In essence, he said that he had objected to the outcry against Luther because the Church was chaotic and he had hoped that good would come of Luther's attacks; he himself had not dreamt of quarrelling with the ruling powers.[2]

Mountjoy's son Charles was a scholar like his father and likewise enjoyed the friendship of Erasmus, who about 1531 dedicated to him a new edition of the *Adages*: "It must be your special care, dear Charles, to be a true son of your accomplished father, the true heir of his excellence, not to degenerate from his culture, and to prepare yourself to inherit his virtue even more than his advantages". Blount answered the dedication with a letter which drew from Erasmus the comment that, if the young man could write such Latin unaided, it was time for

[1] Rutland, p. 45.
[2] Froude, p. 274.

Erasmus to lay down his pen.[1] The man of learning in correspondence with the son of a munificent patron may be forgiven
a touch of graceful exaggeration. This does not imply that
Charles Blount, fifth Lord Mountjoy, was less than an accomplished man and a humanist. Another of his father's friends,
Leland, dedicated poems to him. He was extravagant, but it is
reasonable to conclude that he spent his money nobly.[2]

That can hardly be said of his son James, the sixth lord.
Though he also had intellectual interests, he was the most
disastrous figure in the line. On the accession of Queen Elizabeth in 1558 he was one of thirty-one noblemen directed to
attend upon her when she reached London from Hatfield. Next
year he appears as Lord Lieutenant of Dorsetshire, living at
Canford. Thereafter almost every trace of him is concerned
with his calamitous business enterprises, his gullibility, and his
weakness.

Light is thrown on the financial embarrassment of Mountjoy
by his shedding of lands between the years 1561 and 1563. On
6 December, 1561, he and his wife Catherine, daughter of Sir
Thomas Leigh of St. Oswalds, obtained a licence in the Hanaper
to alienate a whole batch of estates in Yorkshire, including St.
Oswalds, and Lincolnshire, to Robert Savile. On 16 December,
1561, the same thing occurred in respect of lands in the parish
of St. Giles-in-the-Fields, Middlesex, passed to Thomas Doughty
and Henry Heron. Then, by an extraordinary coincidence in
view of the future relations of the families, manors at Burnham,
Essex, were passed to Richard, Lord Rich, and to his son and
heir, Robert Rich, on 1 January, 1562. And on 1 April, 1563,
the year of Charles's birth, the couple alienated twelve messuages,
a curtilage, a barn, and twelve gardens in the parish of St. Giles-
in-the-Fields to Ralph Faulkner and James Powell.[3] In the case
of all except the Essex manors, the alienation was made jointly
by Lord and Lady Mountjoy, and these possessions were undoubtedly part of the unfortunate lady's dowry or settlement.
It is not possible to say whether they had to be disposed of
owing to the family's previous extravagance or to the beginning

[1] Froude, p. 407.
[2] Lodge, p. 363; C.S.P. Dom., 1547-80, pp. 185, 137, 139.
[3] C.S. Rolls, Elizabeth, Vol. II, pp. 370, 373, 381, 599.

of the present lord's mining ventures; but they must have been due to one or the other, or both.

A summary of Mountjoy's mining affairs must be prefaced by a note to the effect that the Government was constantly striving to make England independent of the Continent to the greatest possible extent in the mining of inorganic resources and to a lesser degree in metallurgy, so far as that existed. This consideration helps to account for the otherwise surprising names which appear in the record.

The story begins with a letter from Mountjoy to Sir William Cecil, the future Lord Burghley, on 22 May, 1566, in which he speaks of the progress of his copperas and alum works. Copperas and alum! The words were a knell in the Blount family. The story continues for a generation, its complexities baffling, but from the point of view of the son's biography not worth great expenditure of time or space. Mountjoy begged the Queen to advance him £6,000, and undertook to deliver within two years 150 tons of alum and the same weight of copperas, "as good as the Danish". Cecil leased to him a tenth part of the alum which had been assigned to him by the Queen. By 1572 Sir Humphrey Gilbert had taken a hand and was offering Lady Mountjoy £400 or £500 a year for mining land which had been settled upon herself and her children. Just afterwards Mountjoy made a report to the Earl of Leicester as well as Cecil about the mines.[1]

At a date unknown, about this time, Mountjoy addressed an obscure petition to the Queen to give her approval to a scheme which was to free him from debt, redeem land worth £600 and repay a loan of £1,000 within two years. It sounded a fine prospect, but there was an ominous hint that he might have been rash when he committed a trust to two men named Carleton and Hastings. Suggestions of a scandal follow. In 1582, after the death of Mountjoy, the Lord Chancellor appointed two lawyers to examine these men on behalf of his son William, the seventh baron. The interrogatories alleged that they, while commissioners in trust for Mountjoy, mortgaged for his debts lands in Yorkshire; induced him to transfer the mortgage to Canford in Dorset; sold the Yorkshire lands and with the proceeds redeemed his manor of Puddleton and had it passed into their own name;

[1] C.S.P. Dom., 1547-80, pp. 139, 272, 278, 288, 436, 441.

and then got Canford and Puddleton passed to the Earl of Huntingdon. It was alleged that some of the lands had been sold at a sixth of their value. The ugliest allegation was that the appointment of Carleton and Hastings as commissioners for the settlement of Mountjoy's debts had been obtained by the persuasion of Huntingdon—and Hastings, who bore his family name, must pretty certainly have been a relation. In this examination appears, as that of an interested party, the name of the seventh lord's younger brother Charles, at that time aged nineteen. Five years later Huntingdon is found bewailing to Burghley the cost of his law-suit with the Blounts. It must be said that Huntingdon, a grim Puritan who beggared himself as "a very faithful servant of the Crown", is an unlikely figure of a cheat.[1]

One last piece of evidence is found in a letter written in 1579 by a westcountryman, Piers Edgcombe, to Burghley, asking him to interest himself—and, needless to say, subscribe to—mining ventures. "I have to my charge", he writes, "dealt some ways with the Lord Mountjoy for his help at sundry times, and to my own hindrance as yet, howbeit I find good disposition in his L. to recompense me as he may, and therewith to farther his L. benefit in like manner". Edgcombe, too, had his scheme for dealings in Mountjoy's mining land and promised a profit to Burghley—or "Boureleyghe", as the name appears in a fine example of the waywardness of Elizabethan spelling. And Mountjoy was to be kept in the dark. "I deal wholly with the L. Mountjoy for the land", runs the postscript, "saving some part excepted to himself; for the rest, he knows not how I deal, nor shall do".[2]

This sixth Lord Mountjoy is said to have gone in for the unpromising, if fascinating, expedient of alchemy to restore his fortunes. Camden's statement receives a shred of confirmation in the diary of a friend who borrowed from Mountjoy a book on magic. To add to the disaster, his heir, Charles's elder brother William, hastened his death by debauchery.[3]

Such was the spectacle on which Charles Blount had to look

---

[1] C.S.P. Dom., Add., 1566-79, pp. 64-5; Rowse, p. 291.
[2] Lansdowne MSS., 29.
[3] Camden, p. 117; Carnsew, G. 30.

back as he surveyed his lineage. He was wise enough to turn his eyes forward more often than back. Behind him shone glory: of statesmanship, arms, and the culture and learning of the Renaissance; then fell the shadow of decay and dissipation of the family substance. In four generations had appeared two extravagant, if cultivated and high-minded men, a weak gambler, and a wastrel. What estate could stand up against such a combination?

His own tastes resembled those of his great-grandfather and grandfather, the friends of Erasmus; but he had to earn what they had enjoyed. A great love for a great beauty, the affection of a group of friends who included some of the highest and most outstanding of his generation, the pleasure of books and scholarship were to be enjoyed by him. None of them modified his determination to succeed in life. That determination was inflexible and was checked by no obstacle. Some apparently thought him not over-scrupulous about the means he employed. In a private letter to Cecil he once remarked that his honesty was the only occupation he hoped to make his living by, but admitted that this was not the common opinion. In fact, none of the allegations of sharp practice so common in that age are to be found in the evidence that has come down about him. Yet there can be no doubt that his first aim was to get on, that is, to acquire place, power, and wealth.

II

THE QUEEN'S FAVOURITE

CHARLES BLOUNT was born in 1563, the second son of James, Lord Mountjoy. His birthplace is unknown. His parents often lived at that time at Canford Manor, which had been left to his father by Gertrude, Marchioness of Exeter, on condition of building certain almshouses. The greater part of the original house was pulled down in 1765.[1] Charles's mother, whom, as has been revealed, his father involved in misfortune, was Catherine, sole heiress of Sir Thomas Leigh of St. Oswalds, Yorkshire. As in 1566 his father was reporting to Cecil on the mining work, Charles must have been familiar with the sorry business from the time when he was old enough to understand anything about it. He attended the University of Oxford, but there is no record of college, and he came down "not well grounded". He was entered of the Middle Temple in 1579.[2] Young men of family often became members of an Inn of Court without any intention of practising as lawyers. He became a Master of Arts in 1589.

It is related that, at about the age of twenty, he went to Whitehall to see the Queen at dinner. The Queen saw him, and he was apparently worth seeing at that time, though his portrait in his prime does not make him appear strikingly handsome. He was, we are told, tall, with brown hair, "a sweet face, a most neat composure". Another writer describes his eyes as "great, black, and lovely". The Queen asked who he was and was told that he was brother to William, Lord Mountjoy. Charles realized that she was talking about him, and blushed. He could not better have furthered his career. A blush upon a face so young and charming, a blush caused by her own gaze, was attractive to

[1] Heath and Prideaux, p. 47.
[2] Moryson, Vol. II, p. 265; Foster, Early Series, Vol. I.

21

Queen Elizabeth. She called him up, held out to him her hand to kiss, gave him gracious words, and told him that she had at once seen noble blood in him. Perhaps it was the blood which had flooded his cheeks. "Fail you not to come to the Court", said she, "and I will bethink myself how to do you good".

It was an extraordinary slice of fortune. Though Charles had intelligence and courage and was "a good piece of a scholar", he was both bashful and poor. Unless the Queen had made the advance and given him the invitation his chances of going to Court would have been small. It was not the only path to his goal, but it was straighter and smoother than others. A professional soldier like Vere, who lived in the field, might at any moment find himself subordinated to a courtier like Blount, younger, far less experienced, and of no better blood.[1]

At this time Robert Earl of Leicester, the Queen's chief favourite earlier in her reign, the man whom it had been confidently expected she would marry, had been married for some six years to Lettice, daughter of Sir Francis Knollys and widow of Walter Devereux, Earl of Essex. The Queen had been enraged by this marriage and had never forgiven Lettice. Though the new Lady Leicester was her kinswoman, it has been said that there was no woman whom she disliked more heartily. She had forgiven Leicester. He was always first in her favour. No one could replace him. Even after his command in the Low Countries, on the whole unsuccessful and in the course of which she had occasion to reprove him bitterly, she entrusted to him the army raised to meet the expected Spanish invasion in Armada year. Yet their relationship had changed. For sentimental converse she turned to younger men, one of whom was a handsome, bold-faced, glib-tongued, westcountryman named Walter Ralegh. Now there had appeared at Court a greater charmer and one who seemed to hold out promise of a glorious future, Robert Devereux, Earl of Essex, Leicester's stepson. The whisper ran that he had been brought there as Leicester's candidate for the office of favourite, against Ralegh.

The relations between Elizabeth and her favourites have been discussed at great length. The subject may be interesting,

---

[1] Naunton, p. 57. Naunton is a delightful collector of fragments. It is not possible to vouch for his reliability, but the substance can be accepted.

but is hardly edifying. Let it suffice to say that, while there exists no conclusive evidence, the overwhelming probability is that none of them, not even Leicester, was ever physically her lover. Her anger when one of them married—an anger directed more against the woman than the man—is typical of the reaction of one remaining in a state of virginity from policy and against natural inclination, of an amorous old maid, jealous of young people's happiness in enjoying each other. In all probability the majority of those, nearly all political and religious opponents, who ascribed lovers to her did not believe their own charges. The prophecy made by her to her first Parliament, though qualified by later words, was to prove true: "And in the end, this shall be for me sufficient, that a marble stone shall declare that a Queen, having reigned such a time, lived and died a virgin".[1]

Yet love and dalliance, hints of love, gestures of dalliance, were her pastime. The word "love" itself was bandied about. It was a perfect word just because it was imprecise. "My love to your Majesty"—a phrase anyone might use, but not quite of the same significance from everyone's lips or pen. Essex played upon the theme. "Madam, As in love there can be nothing more bitter than unkindness—"; "Most dear Lady, whom I love and trust more than I do all the world"; "While your Majesty gives me leave to say I love you, my fortune is, as my affection, unmatchable . . . it is not in your power, as great a Queen as you are, to make me love you less". These were dutiful, conventional, words to people at large, to the Court, to the Queen. To the Queen, yes, but to the woman did they not carry the suggestion of something a little warmer?

It was all an enchanting game with a strict code of rules. Nothing was made clear to the partner in the window embrasure any more than to the recipient of the letter. He or she was not even permitted to know whether there were anything to make clear. The unveiling, or even the pretence, of more than a hint of amatory sentiment, when one of the partners was the Virgin Queen, would have been crude and a breach of the rules. What cynics do not perceive, because the cynic is generally myopic, is the fact that these young adventurers, pushing their fortunes in

Neale: *Elizabeth I and her Parliaments*, 1559-81, p. 49.

the sun of the Queen's smiles, realized as clearly as the sober Burghley that they served a great queen. Only fools ever doubted that.

Skill and nerve in sport have always been popular and courtly traits. Charles Blount, a country boy who had ridden from early childhood, was an expert in the tiltyard. One day, after he had done well in the tilting, Elizabeth sent him a token, a gold queen, richly enamelled, from a set of chessmen. Next morning his servants fastened it to his sleeve with a crimson ribbon. He was not shy about displaying it. He entered the privy chamber with his cloak held under his arm, so that the token should be clearly seen. Essex, passing through, noticed it and asked what it was, to which Sir Fulke Greville replied that it was the Queen's favour bestowed for skill in the tilting. Essex was annoyed and made the comment: "Now I perceive every fool must have a favour."

Blount answered with a challenge. He met his critic in Marylebone Fields, disarmed him, and wounded him in the thigh. The Queen did not approve of duelling, but she was probably not displeased that young men should fight about her charms and certainly not that Essex should be discomfited. In fact, she swore by God's death that it was fit that someone or other should take him down and teach him better manners. Few men as proud and petulant as Essex were more generous or dismissed a grudge more easily. He and Blount became warm friends. And yet about this time one observer at least—though it must be admitted that he was distant from the scene—thought that Blount was the supreme favourite. Thomas Morgan, agent to Mary Queen of Scots, writing to her in prison, and in prison himself, reported on 31 March, 1586, that either Ralegh, Elizabeth's *mignon*, as he politely put it, was weary of her or she of him, since the writer had heard that she "hath now entertained one Blount, brother of the Lord Mountjoy, being a young gentleman whose grandmother she may be, for her age and his".[1]

Charles Blount may not have been in the class of the Earl of Cumberland in the tiltyard, but there exists further evidence to show that he was a stalwart at the sport and in demand on great

---

[1] Naunton, p. 52; Murdin, p. 501. "Grandmother" is of course pure spite. The Queen was just over thirty years the elder.

occasions. The poet John Ford, writing after his death, describes
him as a fine horseman and taking pleasure in various forms of
equestrian sport.

> *Now he delights to see the falcon soar*
> *About the top of heaven; then to chase*
> *The nimble buck, or hunt the bristled boar*
> *From out the sty of terror; now the race;*
> *Banners and sport of honourable grace,*
> *Not games of thriftless prodigality,*
> *But plots of fame and fame's eternity.*
>
> *For after toys of courtship he assays*
> *Which way to manage an untaméd horse;*
> *When, how, to spur and rein, to stop and raise.*
> *Close-sitting, voltage of a man-like force,*
> *When in career to meet with gallant course:*
> *As centaurs were both horse and men, so he*
> *Seemed on the horse, nor could discernéd be.*

Besides Essex, Charles Blount became the friend of Robert
Sidney, younger brother of Philip. He must also have known
Philip well, but he died in 1586, of wounds received at Zutphen,
leaving a name already clothed in glory before Charles had gone
far towards establishing his. They loved the same woman,
immortalized by Sidney and possessed by Blount. Another friend
was the Earl of Southampton, patron of Shakespere, cultivated
and popular but reckless and unbalanced: an attractive personality with some likeness to Essex himself, though in less noble
mould. Another was Charles's distant cousin, also named Charles
Blount, who has sometimes been confused with him.[1] He was
the son of Sir Michael Blount, Governor of the Tower of
London. This Charles Blount accompanied Essex to Cadiz, to
the Islands, and to Ireland, and then "in his return home upon
the sea he departed this life in his prime and flourishing years",
as his monument in Portsmouth parish church bears witness.
Others who were more particularly the henchmen of Essex and
the agents of his ambition included his secretary, Henry Cuffe,

---

[1] For example, the fact that the young cousin went on the Cadiz expedition
is the probable origin of statements that the Governor of Portsmouth did so.
The very fact that the only mention of the former is that he was knighted by
Essex proves the identification to be mistaken because the latter had by then
succeeded to the baronage and had been knighted years earlier.

the brothers Charles and Henry Danvers, and the rather sinister Gilly Meyrick, steward of the Welsh estates of Essex and his political cat's-paw in Wales.

One other member of the group needs a fuller introduction. Christopher Blount was a kinsman of Charles's, of the Blounts of Kidderminster, and some seven years his senior. Christopher's father had been in Leicester's household, yet the son grew up a Roman Catholic.[1] Moreover, he displayed a devotion to Mary Queen of Scots which was, on the face of it, highly dangerous to himself. Mention has been made of Thomas Morgan and his remarks about Charles Blount, but the correspondence concerned Christopher.

At the instance of Elizabeth, Morgan had been confined in the Bastille. He found means of talking through the window of his chamber to a messenger named Robert Poley, who brought him a letter from Blount, in which the latter declared ardently that he would serve and honour the only saint that he knew living upon the ground, as he termed the Queen of Scots. Morgan did not, perhaps, trust Poley fully, and gave him no letters to take back. On his return to England, however, Poley wrote to Blount, and that letter was taken by Walsingham's people. The suggestion has been made with some plausibility that its capture was deliberately arranged by Poley. On 20 July, 1585, Morgan wrote to Queen Mary that Christopher Blount had been visiting the country about Tutbury, where she was confined. In the letter of 31 March, 1586, which has already been quoted, Morgan suggested that Blount, by this time serving in the Low Countries, hoped to deliver an important town to the King of Spain. Morgan also remarked that, if Charles Blount were "stalled in the good grace of her of England", it would be well to endeavour to have Christopher recalled to England so that he might serve Mary's cause through his friendship with Charles. On 10 April, Charles Paget, a Roman Catholic émigré in Paris, wrote to Mary that Poley was trying to gain others to serve her by obtaining information and that he was a great friend of Christopher's. If Christopher Blount were indeed in the service of the Queen of Scots, Poley was deadly company. He was her agent, but he was also in all probability the agent of

[1] Worc. Arch Soc., Vol. XIX, N.S.

Walsingham. The correspondence was passing into the hands of the Government, which is why we can read it now. Strangely enough, Christopher must have been back in England by July— perhaps on leave, but it is an odd coincidence—because in that month Morgan, addressing letters to the Queen, recommended him to her as the bearer.[1]

Here is a curious situation. If Walsingham, and afterwards Robert Cecil, had this information about Christopher Blount in their hands—and the latter left it in his family papers—why did they not act upon it? Why was Blount not deprived of his company in the Low Countries, in view of the fact that the danger of a traitor handing over a fortress town to the Spaniards was a real one and that Deventer was handed over by Sir William Stanley? Why was Christopher Blount allowed to go as a colonel on the Cadiz expedition and as first colonel, commanding the infantry, on that originally fitted out for the Islands Voyage? If we knew that the letters reached him, there would not be much of a problem. We should conclude with little or no hesitation that he himself was in fact the Secretary's secret agent. And, though we do not know whether all the letters did reach him, that would not prevent him from being Walsingham's man.

The correspondence between them is queer. Walsingham wrote to his "dear Sir Christopher" in the friendliest way and told him not to worry about what backbiters said of him so long as he was conscious of well-doing. On 3 June, 1588, Blount wrote to Walsingham from Utrecht: "God hath altered me for my opinion in religion, and I not altered it to please any man, but to save my soul".[2] He had, then, gone over from Catholicism to Protestantism. Later on he once more changed his religion. According to Thomas Jones, Bishop of Meath, this happened in Ireland in 1599, and he was reconciled to the Church of Rome by two Irish priests. However that may be, on the scaffold he declared himself to be a Roman Catholic and refused the ministrations of an Anglican clergyman. There is one final piece of evidence, which is truly astonishing. Hundreds of historians must have read it, without, apparently, connecting it with the

[1] Murdin, pp. 447, 499, 501, 506; Salisbury, Pt. III, p. 151; Boas, pp. 119-21.
[2] C.S.P. For., Vol. XXI, Pt. IV, p. 451

correspondence about Mary Queen of Scots. When, after the Essex rising, Blount was examined by members of the Privy Council, after describing his part in the plot, he asked that a message should be carried to Queen Elizabeth.

"He doth also desire . . . that her Majesty may be particularly informed and remembered of those great services which he did in laying the way open to the Earl of Leicester and Mr. Secretary Walsingham for the discovery of all the Queen of Scots' practices".[1]

This looks plain enough: Christopher Blount must have acted as Walsingham's detective and informer. That would explain why he incurred no trouble until he plunged into the Essex plot, which had no connexion with the affairs we have been considering. It is true that the Queen forbade Essex when in Ireland to make Blount a member of his Council, but this may easily be explained by his reputation for rashness and lack of balance.

Did he then work in with Poley? That we do not know. Poley was not a safe man to walk about with. He gained the confidence and apparently the secrets of the plotter Anthony Babington. The priest Ballard was actually arrested at Poley's lodgings shortly before Babington was caught. Poley was lodged in the Tower, but soon afterwards set free, very likely on the intervention of Walsingham. He was soon back in the service of the Government, if indeed he had ever been out of it. His arrest was probably either a mistake or a blind. And to crown all, seven years later he was one of the three men who were in the room with Christopher Marlowe at Eleanor Bull's tavern in Deptford Strand when the poet was stabbed to death.[2] The tracks of the Elizabethan secret service are intricate and difficult to follow.

For the rest, Christopher was a rugged cavalryman, "a tall man and valiant". He saved the life of Sir Francis Vere at Zutphen. Not long after Leicester's death in 1588 he married his widow, as her third husband, and so became the second stepfather of Essex, to whom he was deeply devoted. He was one of a band of M.P.s elected as the nominees of Essex.[3]

[1] Corr. of James VI and Cecil, p. 109.
[2] Boas, pp. 265-73.
[3] Bagot Papers, Jan. 2nd, 1593; Neale: *The Elizabethan House of Commons*, pp. 60, 237.

The Elizabethan aristocracy was small, and the links between these young men were close. Leicester and Christopher Blount were, as has been explained, successively married to the mother of Essex. Philip and Robert Sidney were Leicester's nephews, Essex married Philip's widow, born Frances Walsingham. The young Earl of Rutland, another member of the party, married the daughter of Philip and Frances. Southampton married Essex's cousin. Charles Blount was the lover of Essex's sister, Penelope Rich, to whom Philip Sidney had poured out his heart in verse. They followed the lines of Leicester and Walsingham, which were remarkably similar, though the two men were so different. That is to say—leaving Christopher Blount aside as at some time a Roman Catholic and not a courtier—they belonged to the ultra-patriotic and Protestant, even Puritan, element. Leicester, boundlessly extravagant, makes a fantastic picture as the hope of the Low Church. Yet he was that to a large extent, as was Essex, who having first succeeded to the place held by Philip Sidney as hero of the nation, almost immediately afterwards succeeded to that of Leicester as leader of the war party and patron of the Puritans. It is almost equally odd to see Essex, wearing on campaign a cloak of orange satin covered with jewels and clothes and horse harness worth altogether 60,000 crowns, in the latter role.

They were sprigs of the Renaissance, relishing its splendour and pleasure as well as its intellectual life. None of them had anything ascetic in his composition. Puritanism was a good anti-Catholic, patriotic, and anti-Spanish drum to beat. This sounds like hypocrisy, but it is to be doubted whether they were conscious of any. And, curiously enough, Charles Blount was a first-class theologian. He studied the doctrines of the Church— mostly prior to the Reformation—for their intellectual as well as their spiritual interest, the former not being everybody's taste.

Theology was perhaps for him mainly a hobby. To make up for the deficiencies of his education, he spent all the time he could spare in the company of scholars. He read history, and made some study of philosophy, geography, and mathematics. He learnt enough French and Italian to enable him to read books in those languages, though he did not venture to speak them.[1] His other form of study was professional, undertaken to advance him along his chosen path. England was a hard-fighting country, but had fallen behind the Continent in the art of warfare. Now there was a revival. Men who had fought abroad were writing books, among them Sir Roger Williams, the military mentor of Essex, a rollicking, hard-living swordsman, something of a butt and generally accepted as the model for Fluellen, but a fine soldier, who had learnt a great deal from service in a Spanish *tercio*. Charles Blount devoted himself to this form of literature with such assiduity that people began to laugh at him. There was indeed subject for mockery in the spectacle of a strong young man, champion in the tiltyard, sitting at home reading and pondering about the art of war while others fought. It was not his fault. He wanted to be in arms abroad.

Elizabeth had long given aid to the Dutch in their effort to throw off the Spanish yoke, first in the shape of volunteers. Now it was to be more direct, both troops in her own pay and others in that of the States General. On 10 August, 1585, at a moment when they were in a serious plight, she concluded a treaty with them. First she sent over to their aid Sir John Norris with about 4,500 men. This was welcome assistance, but it came too late to save Antwerp, which had surrendered to Alessandro Farnese, Prince of Parma, before Norris sailed and was never to be recovered. At the end of the year the Queen sent the Earl of Leicester over to assume the command. He disembarked at Flushing on 10 December.[2]

It was a strange war, a fine example of that limited form of warfare which those without historical knowledge found a novelty when it appeared in Korea. England and Spain were not officially at war. The Queen even professed that she wished to see all his subjects in the Low Countries in a state of due obedience to the King of Spain. She did not care about supporting subjects against their sovereign, thinking that it created a bad precedent. Another resemblance to the Korean war is that peace negotiations began at an early stage and lasted some two years. Half Parma's troops were from what we now call Belgium, some-

[1] Moryson, Vol. II, p. 265.
[2] Leicester Correspondence, p. xi.

times fighting their own brothers. Relations between the Anglo-Dutch allies were chilly and suspicious. Dutch merchants cheerfully victualled the Spaniards by sea. Leicester said that no town was safe without an English garrison, a comment which had an unfortunate reverberation a little later when Sir William Stanley handed Deventer over to Spain—but his troops were Irish.

Roughly, the Waal divided the belligerents, but the allies held a number of strong places south of that river and the Spaniards a number to the north. The war was at this period even more a war of sieges than was then common. Actions in the open took the form of raids and attacks on convoys. Some of them, like the astonishing combat at Zutphen, were very hot, but not on a large scale. Both sides found it difficult to collect considerable field forces because they allotted so many troops to garrison duties.

On the whole the Spaniards had the better of the early campaign because they were the better commanded and the better disciplined, though in fighting quality the English soon became unsurpassed. The personality of the Spanish Governor exercised a moral as well as a material influence. Farnese—reigning Duke of Parma from 1586—had an urbanity and an air of sweet reasonableness which had already won back revolting southern provinces and now held in the cause of Philip II men who might otherwise have fought for the States. He paid charming compliments to English deeds of daring. When a representative of Walsingham's visited him to sound him about peace terms, he began the conversation by recalling pleasant days in the hunting field in England in the reign of Queen Mary, when, as a young boy, he had accompanied his kinsman Philip II to that country. Yet these graces shrouded a grim determination and the eyes of a hawk. He was inspiring, and, if not inspired, possessed of superb competence in this chess-board warfare. Generally cautious, even slow, he moved with extreme speed in emergency. Uneasy speculation about what "the Prince" would do was prevalent among the English and Dutch commanders.

Charles Blount had the wish of his heart. He got command of one of the original companies which Norris took out. This company, with three others, each 150 strong, was allotted to the fortress of Ostend. However, Charles's start was disastrous. In the modern war slang, he "walked straight into one".

In October, 1585, Norris attacked a Spanish fort on the Lower Rhine. Finding the artillery fire ineffective because the gunners were raw and the river (at Arnhem) broad, he put a party into boats to carry out an assault. Charles had hastened from his post to be present. To us this would appear an act of gross indiscipline, but it was a commonplace then. Young noblemen and gentlemen would rush into affairs of the sort when they saw a chance, even though their commands might be hundreds of miles away. A year later the real fighting at Zutphen was done by a body of horse, noblemen and gentlemen with their servants. Leicester then wrote apologetically: "There was too many indeed at this skirmish of the better sort, but I was offended when I knew it, but could not fetch them back: but since they have all so well escaped (save my dear nephew), I would not for ten thousand pounds but they had been there, since they have all won that honour they have".[1] Queen Elizabeth was derided then, and has been criticized since, for keeping young men tied to her apron-strings. It cannot be doubted that the medieval practice described was one reason. She preferred that they should fight in instalments.

Charles with his pike—volunteers fighting afoot carried the pike, still held a nobler weapon than the firearm—was ferried across. For raw troops the men behaved admirably, but the attack was repulsed and Charles was hit in the thigh by a chain-shot. Norris specially commended him for having taken part, "having no charge here", that is, not in the normal course of his duty.[2] He was probably kept in the country for a couple of months to make a partial recovery, and then sent to England. In the new year Colonel Morgan wrote to Walsingham that he hoped Captain Blount had reached home with the latest news and therefore would not give it himself. Charles was back again in the Low Countries in 1587. It may be accepted that he was the "Mr. Blunt" who came over in August with letters about peace negotiations in progress. However, by 11 October the Queen had "written a letter with her own hand to call home Sir

[1] C.S.P. For., Vol. XXI, Pt. II, p. 165.
[2] Ibid., Vol. XX, pp. 84, 87.

Charles Blount from Holland". No need to speculate whether he cursed this tug at the apron-strings. Before he left he was knighted by Leicester, himself about to return.[1]

We have to go to the gossiping Sir Robert Naunton for further light on this period and that immediately after Armada year. He states that, having returned to England, Charles "constantly" —the word is surely an exaggeration—visited his company until the Queen forbade him to do so. In early October, 1590, the Spaniards, on the invitation of the Duke of Mercoeur, leader of the forces of the Catholic League in Brittany, sent an expedition 4,500 strong which landed at Saint-Nazaire and secured the port of Blavet, later named Port-Louis. The Spaniards were commanded by a hard-fighting man whom Charles was to meet again, Don Juan de Aguila, and were not ejected until they left of their own accord after the conclusion of the Treaty of Vervins in 1598. England did, however, intervene to save the first-class harbour of Brest, sending over a force under Sir John Norris for the purpose. Charles's company was included in it, and since he appears as colonel in June, 1592, his command must by then have been raised to that of a regiment.[2] Again he "stole over" to visit his troops in the hope of action. "He was grown by reading (whereunto he was much addicted) to the theory of a soldier; so was he strongly invited by his genius to the acquaintance of the practique of the war".

Any fighting in which he took part must have been confined to sieges and minor actions. Only two great affairs occurred in Brittany. He was almost certainly absent during the first, so disastrous that evidence of his presence would surely have appeared had he been on the spot. On 10 May, 1592, Aguila and Mercoeur routed the Huguenots and English—the latter much reduced as the result of sickness and repatriation—who were besieging Craon. The Spaniards refused quarter to the English as a reprisal for the slaughter of refugees from the Armada in Ireland, while Mercoeur bade his men spare the French and strike down the English. For them it was annihilation. During the second action, a great success, Charles Blount is known to

---

[1] C.S.P. For., Vol. XX, p. 289; Vol. XXI, Pt. III, p. 263; Lodge, Vol. II, p. 354; Gawdy, p. 31.

[2] C.S.P. Dom. 1581-94, p. 64.

have been at Portsmouth. Aguila had built a fort on the north point of the Roscanvel peninsula, still known as the Pointe Espagnole, and left a garrison in it. Its guns commanded the entry to the harbour of Brest. In face of this grave threat, Norris brought out a new English army, the original force having virtually disappeared, and joined hands with the royalists under the Marshal d'Aumont. On 10 November, 1594, after a month's siege and the bloody repulse of three assaults, the attackers burst through the breaches and put the remnant of the garrison to the sword.[1] The walls were then razed.

Though Charles was absent, the action is noted because it made a deep impression on his mind. When, as Lord Deputy in Ireland, he had to decide whether to storm Kinsale, held by a Spanish garrison under Aguila, or grant highly favourable terms, he chose the latter course. He recalled the slaughter inflicted by three hundred men on an army of several thousand and concluded that it was wiser to avoid an assault on good Spanish troops behind stone walls, if they could otherwise be got rid of. It is said that the besiegers' loss amounted to 3,000, killed or died of sickness.

Whatever the nature of Charles's experience in Brittany, the Queen ended it by putting her foot down. "You will never leave it", she said, "until you are knocked on the head, as that inconsiderate fellow Sidney was. You shall go when I send you. In the meanwhile see that you lodge in the Court, where you may follow your book, read and discourse of the wars".[2]

By this time he was going on for thirty, yet here he was being alternatively scolded and laughed at as an irresponsible youngster and an arm-chair soldier. He had, it must be confessed, some compensations which do not look honourable to modern eyes but were more leniently regarded in those times. At the end of 1592 certain warrants were issued for payments to officers in the Low Countries and Ireland, notwithstanding their absence from those theatres of war. The sum of £400 was paid to Sir Charles Blount for 1590 and 1591 by special warrant of Her Majesty. And in June, 1593, the Queen wrote that Sir Charles Blount,

---

[1] Cheyney, Vol. I, pp. 299-303; Duro: *Armada Española,* Tomo III, pp. 84-9; Moreau, pp. 129-30, 157-8, 255.
[2] Naunton, p. 58.

having been kept in attendance upon her, had been forced to absent himself from his charge in Brittany. She therefore directed that he should be paid £200 (per annum), with the usual allowance for servants, from April, 1593, during her pleasure. Charles was being paid a fighting officer's wages for lodging in the Court.[1]

This situation, which cannot have failed to be humiliating to him, though far less than it would be nowadays, was not to last for ever. The Queen could be counted upon to relent in the end. After all, "the times began to be quick and active and fitter for stronger motions than those of the carpet. She loved a soldier and had a propension in her nature to regard and always to grace them."

On 26 January, 1594, Sir Charles Blount was granted by patent the office of Captain of the Town and Island of Portsmouth in succession to the Earl of Sussex.[2]

This account of Charles's service on the Continent up to that date, such as it was, has for convenience been carried to a conclusion. It is an unsatisfactory record, with elements of the ridiculous. At least it shows his willingness to fight when possible, and he bore an honourable wound, which troubled him later. Twenty years afterwards he was unable to come to Court owing to lameness in the leg in which he had received his "great hurt".[3] No mention has yet been made of his part in the Armada campaign of 1588, of his parliamentary career, or of the love affair which lasted all his adult life. Steps must be retraced to them.

[1] C.S.P. Dom., 1581-94, pp. 152, 367.
[2] Ibid., 1581-94, p. 418.
[3] Salisbury, Pt. XVII, p. 588.

III

THE SPANISH ARMADA

M OST wars are fought for more reasons than one. Several reasons can be given for the sailing of the Spanish Armada and the war between England and Spain in 1588. Formal declarations of war were not issued, and perhaps the beginning of open war may be said to date from the English attack on Cadiz in 1587. The weight to be attributed to each factor is a matter of dispute, but that is a question which need not concern us here. In the first place there was a strong religious element. This had, as has been seen, led a high-born and distinguished soldier, Sir William Stanley, to go over with his troops to the Spaniards in the Low Countries. It had led other English Roman Catholics, though relatively few, to plot against the Queen's life. It had led Charles Blount's kinsman Christopher into what appeared on its face dangerous activity, and dangerous correspondence, on behalf of the Queen of Scots.

A second reason was the challenge of English sea captains, avowedly smugglers and rated by the Spaniards as pirates pure and simple, to the exclusive commercial policy of Spain in the New World. Philip II considered the support given to men like Drake and Hawkins to be a valid reason for war. He knew that Elizabeth refused to admit the Spanish claims in America. He knew that the raiders were covered by her favour. He knew that the bulk of the loot brought home by them went into her coffers. He was faced by more than raids, by a threat to his system of maritime communications between his American and West Indian possessions and his home ports. Drake's raiding in the West Indies in 1585 and 1586 may have been among the decisive factors.

Another reason was the English aid to rebellious Spanish

subjects in the Netherlands, the background to which has already been described. Yet another was the execution of Mary Queen of Scots on 8 February, 1587. The stimulus which this event undoubtedly gave to hostilities is often attributed to Philip's anger at the deed. He was assuredly angry, and he may have been morally shocked; but he did not usually act on impulse. Another aspect of Mary's death must be taken into account. Philip was her champion. Conquest of England in her lifetime would have been conquest of the throne for her; yet in view of her background and sympathies he must have felt that this would involve turning the country virtually into a French province. That inconvenience was removed by her execution. She had left a document naming him as her successor. He might pass over her son, the young James VI, who was a heretic, because he himself, already once King of England, was descended from John of Gaunt. This descent was in his eyes a far better claim than that of Elizabeth to the English throne.[1] The Pope and the Catholic King alike considered her a bastard.

The main difficulty in the conquest of England appeared to be the distance and the transportation of sufficient troops. If shipping enough were collected to carry all the way from Spanish ports to England the whole force required to overcome English resistance, an enormous quantity would be involved. When, in 1586, the celebrated Spanish Admiral, the Marquess of Santa Cruz, was bidden to submit a project on these lines, he estimated that over 550 vessels, including 150 "great ships" of war, and 55,000 soldiers, would be needed. Philip, it would seem rightly, rejected this scheme. If such a fleet could have been assembled, it would have used up every ship Spain possessed or could lay hands upon. It would have been extremely unwieldy and wretchedly manned. The size of the convoy would have imposed an intolerable burden upon the fighting fleet and lowered its value. If, on the other hand, only enough shipping were taken up to transport half or two-thirds of the army and then sent back for the rest, it might not reappear for months. Equally rightly, the King never seems to have entertained the idea of transporting the army in two parts or "waves" successively.

The scheme which he did adopt was that the Armada should

[1] Laughton, Vol. I, p. xxvi.

carry a large number of troops, but that the main force should be provided by Parma in the Low Countries. After the English fleet had been defeated or held off in the Channel, the Armada would land its troops in Thanet; Parma would then embark his army in small ships and flat-bottomed boats and carry it across to the bridgehead. Unfortunately for Spanish prospects, Santa Cruz was not available to undertake the new plan. The sailing of the Armada was delayed for a year by the destruction wrought by Drake in his terrible raid on Cadiz, and the Admiral died during the winter. The Duke of Medina Sidonia was a poor substitute. A great naval commander had given place to a man with no knowledge of naval affairs and little of any kind of warfare.

The Spanish fleet began its move up Channel from the Lizard on Saturday, 20 July, 1588. The running fight began on Sunday. These actions favoured the English, but they were wholly indecisive and in themselves did little to diminish the danger in which England lay. The skilled naval men were confident about the result, but during that week of fighting in the Channel the shadow of Spanish might lay heavy upon England. Nearly all were anxious; not a few were terrified. In Parliament afterwards the Queen's sharp tongue scourged those who had fled inland and "left all naked and exposed" to the entry of the Spaniards. It can well be imagined that ardent young men longed to be aboard a ship to strike a first blow at the enemy.

Charles Blount was at Court, doubtless fretting. He took no part in the week's fighting which has been mentioned. He never joined the main English fleet. Yet his personal enterprise and his good fortune took him into the battle that mattered, the only one that did.

The fleet which the Spaniards had already encountered was not the only one. A secondary fleet was commanded by Lord Henry Seymour, the Admiral of the Narrow Seas, in modern parlance, of the Channel Fleet. His duty was to watch Parma's army and intercept it if it sailed. The Dutch were not prepared to undertake this task by themselves, still less to send a contingent to join Lord Howard in encountering the Armada. Seymour's fleet consisted of 13 ships, whereof only three, the *Rainbow*, the *Vanguard*, and the *Antelope*, were "good ships", each with a complement, including gunners and soldiers, of 250 men; six medium ships, and four pinnaces. Of the medium ships mention must be made of the *Tramontana* because, 15 years later, on the Irish station, she was to be so closely associated with Charles Blount. Seymour disliked his mission, but his disappointment was lifted when the Armada reached Calais and, on 27 July, he was summoned by Howard to join him off that port. He arrived about eight in the evening, to find both fleets at anchor. He was in time for the crisis after all.

Two days earlier, off Dover, he had still expected that Parma would shortly sail and that the Spanish transports would be his squadron's objective. He wrote to Walsingham on the 25th:

"Sir—I am most glad of this most happy beginning of victory obtained of her Majesty's enemies, but most sorry I am so tied I cannot be an actor in the play. But if the Duke (Parma) be as good as his threats he will now show his courage. . . . In the mean (time) we are assisted with the presence of worthy gentlemen that are of purpose come to serve her Majesty with the venture of their lives: which I thought necessary to acquaint you therewith, to the end her Majesty may give them thanks. Their names be Sir Charles Blount, Francis Carey, Richard Lee, Brute Brown".

These four volunteers served in the flagship, the *Rainbow*. She was a fine ship, built by Peter Pett of the famous Deptford family. Nominally rated as of 500 tons, more scientific measurement makes her only 364; but she embodied the new principles which were abolishing the survivals of the towering medieval form. She sailed "low and snug in the water, like a galleasse". She had been launched only in 1586 and had served in Drake's expedition to Cadiz in the following year.[1]

So Charles Blount had won an opportunity such as his spirit yearned for, an opportunity far greater than those he had hastily snatched in the land war. His biographer must bless Seymour's zeal in recording, for no personal evidence in the form of a letter has come to light. The sole facts given are that he came to Dover as a "voluntary" and that he served in the flagship. They

[1] Laughton, Vol. I, p. 310; Vol. II, pp. 324, 333; Corbett: *Drake and the Tudor Navy*, pp. 69, 145. Brown became a close friend of Drake's. He was killed as he sat with his Admiral at table in the flagship during the disastrous operations against Puerto Rico.

suffice because the part played by Seymour and the Queen's ships under his command are well known. It was the Queen's ships that did the real fighting, just as it was Philip's that bore the brunt of it on the other side. It seems reasonable to suppose, however, despite Seymour's message for the Queen, that this time Charles had not fled from her side in secret. A group of gentlemen had made for Dover, but most of them certainly did not go to sea. The reason is unknown: some of them may have been too late.

Charles may be pictured riding hard down the Dover road, over Shooter's Hill, through Sittingbourne and Canterbury, with hope in his heart but doubtless some fear also, lest he should miss the fleet. Loyalty and patriotism were with him, as with most of his contemporaries about the Court, mingled with ambition, with a passionate desire for distinction. Calm and self-contained though he was by temperament, these fires burned within him. He had been knighted for bravery in war, but was as yet no seasoned warrior. He was a needy courtier, who had stolen brief hours from that dainty life and given them to martial service. Worst of all, he was a courtier who was laughed at for his abstract study of warfare, his "theory of a soldier". "You shall go when I send you; in the mean time see that you lodge in the Court, where you may follow your book, read and discourse of the wars". Those galling words still hung in the air, and he was to hear that reproach of bookishness again when he had become a greater man. But now indeed the times were quick and active, "fitter for stronger motions than those of the carpet". And it must have been pleasant to be aware, as he could not have failed to be by now, that the Queen "loved a soldier and had a propension in her nature to regard and always to grace them". At last all doubts could be set aside. He was aboard one of the finest of the Queen's ships. He was with the Admiral, who was happy to see him. The fleet sailed.

On Sunday, 28 July, Howard held a council of war aboard the *Ark*. It was resolved to shift the Spaniards from their anchorage by the use of fireships. Eight were made ready with combustible material. At midnight wind and tide were favourable. On the firing of a signal-gun they moved in on the Armada.

The few seamen aboard set light to them and then dropped into the boats which were awaiting them.

Medina Sidonia was unhappy that night. Parma had written that his small and ill-found fleet was blocked by the Dutch, so that he could not send ammunition, of which the Armada was in need. The Spaniards were closely concentrated at anchor, as Sir William Wynter—Rear-Admiral of Seymour's squadron in the *Vanguard*—put it, "very round and near together, not far from the shore". This was a good position for defence and explains why the English preferred to launch fireships rather than attack, but an ugly situation in which to be caught by fireships on a lee shore. Medina Sidonia had taken the precaution of ordering an officer out in a pinnace with an anchor and cable, so that if a fireship came in he might tow it away; but one pinnace could be of no avail against eight of them. When the Admiral saw the fireships approaching he signalled the fleet to weigh anchor, his intention was to return to his anchorage after they had passed.[1]

In their haste the captains cut or slipped cables. As they were anchored bow and stern, this involved in most cases the loss of two anchors and made it in any case impossible to return to the roadstead. Undoubtedly also the loss contributed heavily to that of some of the many ships dashed to pieces off the coasts of Scotland and Ireland. The galleasse *San Lorenzo* had her rudder torn away by a cable and tried to make her way into the harbour, using oars and foresail only, but ran aground on the bar at half tide. Howard himself made for her, and was followed by his squadron. It was a very strange action for a Lord High Admiral, but not altogether in discord with the spirit of the times. The galleasse was boarded from small vessels and boats and taken after fierce fighting; but the French gunners opened fire and drove her captors out of her. Anyhow, she was lost to the Armada.

In their passage up Channel the Spaniards had been wearied by attack and had sustained some loss and damage, but the fireships marked the beginning of their disaster. "They dislodged us with eight vessels, an exploit which with one hundred and thirty they had not been able to do nor dared to attempt",

[1] Laughton, Vol. II, p. 364; Duro, *La Armada Invencible*, Vol. I, p. 97.

was the bitter comment of a Spanish officer. To make the irony more cruel, the fireships burnt themselves out harmlessly.

The English fleet pursued the Armada along the coast and closed in upon it at 9 a.m. on 29 July at the level of Gravelines. Now Charles Blount found himself in the thickest of the fight; in fact, Seymour in the *Rainbow* and Wynter in the *Vanguard* struck some of the deadliest blows dealt that day. The Armada had assumed the formation of a half moon, according to an English account, but the description was a favourite one often applied inaccurately. At least, the Armada had two wings. Drake attacked inshore; Howard—though his escapade with the galleasse made him late—in the centre; and Seymour on the outer flank. The Spanish wings were driven in and fouled each other. For the time being the great hostile fleet became a confused mass, pounded by the English guns. Seymour and Wynter assailed fiercely the *San Juan de Sicilia,* shooting her through and through, so that, though she managed to rejoin the fleet, she afterwards sank. Two other ships in her company, the *San Felipe* and *San Mateo,* received such a battering that they were left behind, made for the coast, were captured by the Zeelanders, and carried into Flushing. Wynter records that the fighting lasted nine hours, that the *Vanguard* fired 500 shot during that time, and that during most of it she was within the range of the Spanish harquebuses—and we know that the *Rainbow* fought in company with the *Vanguard.* It follows that no one in the English fleet saw the battle closer or was in hotter fighting than Charles Blount.[1]

Medina Sidonia wanted to turn on the English. He was a weak-minded and indecisive land-lubber, but a brave man, as he had proved throughout. The pilots, however, told him that it was impossible with a hard wind from the north-west and a high sea, setting straight on to the coast. In addition, his best ships, which had borne the main weight of the fighting since they left the Lizard, were now, as he admits, "spoiled and unable to resist longer", and in any case had expended their shot. He now enjoyed two favours of fortune which in themselves disprove the common belief that the Armada was defeated mainly by the weather: *Afflavit deus et dissipantur.* The first was a violent

[1] Clowes, p. 576; Laughton, Vol. II, p. 10.

squall, which caused the English to abandon the pursuit while they prepared to meet the danger. It was a curious episode because the squall was used by the Spaniards, though their ships were inferior as sailers, to restore their formation, while the English gave them a respite. The second was a shift of the wind which allowed the Spaniards to avoid the Zeeland banks, after the pilots had declared that the fleet was doomed.[1] Thenceforth there was no further question of a return of the Armada.

On 30 July Seymour was ordered to return and guard the mouth of the Thames in case Parma should even now attempt a crossing, though this was improbable in the extreme. The squadron entered Harwich on 1 August, and its part in the fighting was at an end. Doubtless Charles Blount was distressed when Seymour had to detach himself from the main fleet, as the Admiral himself was. Yet in fact the fighting was finished. It had now become clear that the Spaniards intended to return to Spain by rounding Scotland and passing west of Ireland. Howard talked of maintaining the pursuit as far north as the Firth of Forth, but he actually broke it off at about latitude 55. At that level, and some thirty leagues east of Newcastle-upon-Tyne, he first decided to attack, then changed his mind in view of his shortage of supplies, and turned about. He had won his victory and returned to the cautious methods he had displayed in the Channel. The Spaniards claim that twice, on 31 July and 1 August, when some of their big ships brought-to to await the English, the latter shortened sail.

It was only off Gravelines that Howard had gone all out for victory, the victory in which Charles Blount had played a part. It was no Trafalgar, no battle of annihilation, not what the country had hoped for. Yet there can be no denying its overwhelming effect. This is disguised because so few ships were actually sunk or taken on the spot. It was not easy to sink or even to cripple a ship with the armament of Elizabethan days. Yet the enormous losses suffered by the Spaniards, nearly all of which were to come, were due largely to the pounding they received in those nine hours as well as to the secondary cause

[1] Corbett: *Drake and the Tudor Navy*, Vol. II, p. 289; Duro: *La Armada Invencible*, Vol. I, p. 105.

already mentioned, the loss of the anchors at Calais. The best and most active Spanish ships had been repeatedly holed. Some of them were entirely unseaworthy. In that condition they had to make a long and difficult voyage, passing down two dangerous coasts with sick and weary crews short of water and even of food.

The losses of the Armada have been given by the Spanish historian, Captain Duro, as follows:—

Abandoned to the English	2
Lost on the French coast	3
Lost on the Dutch coast	2
Sunk in the battle (Gravelines)	2
Wrecked off Scotland and Ireland	19
Disappeared, fate unknown	35
	63

Of this huge total 26 were galleons or ships. So only nine had been accounted for even after the decisive battle off Gravelines. Yet it may be said with some confidence that, but for that battle, the subsequent losses would not have been half so great. Many ships wrecked and sunk on the Irish coast or the outer islands, many of those which foundered in the open sea, unobserved and unrecorded, must have owed their fate to those fierce hours on the coast between Calais and Dunkirk.

Charles Blount had thus fought in one of the most significant battles in English naval annals. Despite its disappointments, it was the sort of battle which participants must have recognized as making history. Those who had served in it had passed through a great experience which set a mark upon them for the rest of their lives.

IV

PARLIAMENTARIAN

CHARLES BLOUNT was elected as Member of the House of Commons for the borough of Bere Alston in the County of Devon, together with Edward Lane, in 1584 (27 Eliz.). For some unknown reason the return was not delivered and Bere Alston was represented in that Parliament by two other men. He was again elected, now with Nicholas Martyn, and sat in the Parliament of 1586. He had, it will be recalled, been wounded in October, 1585, and returned to England at the beginning of the following year. He missed the Parliament of 1588. He reached Harwich in Lord Henry Seymour's flagship after the fighting with the Spanish Armada on 1 August, so that he may have been still serving with the fleet when the election writ was issued on 18 September. He again represented Bere Alston, now as Sir Charles Blount and with Thomas Burgoyne as colleague, in the Parliament of 1593. Before the election to the Parliament of 1597 he had succeeded to his barony and now sat in the House of Lords as Lord Mountjoy. This time the Members for Bere Alston were Sir Jocelyn Blount—the significance of whose name will be indicated—and George Crooke. During the last Parliament of Elizabeth I, that of 1601, Mountjoy was in Ireland and appointed the Earl of Nottingham as his proxy. In the first Parliament of James I he sat as Earl of Devonshire. Even allowing for the long gaps between Elizabethan Parliaments and the short sessions, he thus acquired a good deal of parliamentary experience for a man who died at the age of forty-two or forty-three.[1]

He made no particular mark in the Commons. Those who

[1] *Return of Members of Parliament*, Vol. I, pp 413, 417, 423, 427, 433; Dugdale, pp. 536-8; D'Ewes, p. 598.

did were mostly officials, privy councillors, and the stout-hearted and troublesome Puritan democrats who battled for Calvinism and strove to whittle down the prerogative of the Crown. Probably, like most who did not belong to these categories, he regarded membership of the House as a feather in his cap and not much else. Though a friend and ally of Essex, he cannot be considered as belonging to the group of henchmen, in which his kinsman Sir Christopher Blount was included, for whom Essex found seats in order to form an opposition to Cecil. Charles's biography is not the place in which to descant upon Elizabethan Parliaments. It is worth while, however, to note briefly their composition, function, and character, before mentioning the part he played in them, such as it was.

A great proportion of Members, whether for shires or boroughs, were not in a true sense elected but were nominated by local grandees. Sometimes a borough returning two Members would accept one from this source but reserve to itself the right to choose the second, but even that measure of independence might bring displeasure upon it.[1] Where there was a contest, it was decided in a rough and ready way. Even the franchise was not uniform or undisputed. The predominance of a name or of two names in a "crying of names" by assembled electors might be held to make a poll unnecessary. Minds unfamiliar with Elizabethan ideas may find this a strange procedure, but the system had the merit of being virtually free from corruption. Should indignation be aroused in democratic breasts by contemplation of the picture, it may perhaps be assuaged by consideration of a result probably unexpected. Patronage led to an influx of gentry into the House of Commons as representatives of boroughs which should in theory have been represented by local men, genuine burgesses. The gentlemen brought with them a critical spirit, which may in a number of cases be described as left wing. Little men, shopkeepers and the like, supposing them to have entertained the same feelings, would not have dared to express them. They would have been overawed by the Queen's spokesmen and terrified by the Queen herself. It was the gentlemen who steadily enlarged the power and prestige of the House of Commons. The result has been labelled as

[1] Neale: *The Elizabethan House of Commons*, p. 154.

"probably unexpected", but it was obvious to contemporaries, even to a Spaniard, Mary's husband, King Philip, who had aided her in an unsuccessful attempt to prevent this intrusion of the gentry into the borough seats.[1]

Parliaments were summoned primarily to provide funds by taxation, secondly to pass laws. Queen Elizabeth I would have been prepared to dispense with much of the legislation and have summoned her Parliaments even less often than she did, had she not needed subsidies. She could not do without them. The fiction that the Crown could live by its own resources was not altogether dead, but in fact the wars rendered this an impossibility. As it was, she sold great estates, and even jewels. And in the later Parliaments the shape of things to come was indicated by a tendency on the part of the majority in the House of Commons to bargain, that is, try to get its way on certain issues such as forcing Puritan doctrine and practice upon the Church, in return for subsidies.

This subject had been well to the fore for a long time prior to Charles Blount's appearance in the Commons. A related subject, legislation against Roman Catholics, had caused struggles between Puritan fanaticism and the Queen's tolerance. Two other subjects were also linked: the Queen's marriage and the succession to the throne. The first of these had died naturally owing to the advanced age of the Queen before Charles entered the House, but the second was still very much alive. The Queen had been virtually forced to execute the Duke of Norfolk and to bring Mary Queen of Scots to trial. Mary had been sentenced but not executed when the Parliament of 1586 met, so Charles was to see the battle on that issue. The Queen's courage, adroitness, and obstinacy—but an obstinacy tempered by a sense of realities which showed her when she must yield and generally won for her renewed esteem when she did—were astonishing. Often she stood almost alone because her ablest parliamentary spokesmen, such as Burghley, Knollys, and Mildmay, had Puritan inclinations and on occasion actually opposed her policy, though Burghley came near to being her "prime minister". Whatever be the view of her struggle to maintain the power of the Crown, her stand for clemency, toleration, and

[1] Neal: *Elizabeth and her Parliaments*, 1559-81, p. 23.

moderation commands respect. She, the least fanatical of sovereigns in a fanatical age, strove to cool fanaticism in her kingdom, and in great measure succeeded.

The head of the Blount family was one of the patrons with seats in the House of Commons at their disposal, with what were later called pocket boroughs. One of these was Bere Alston, for which Charles sat. Bere Alston was enfranchised in 1584, obviously at the instance of the Marquess of Winchester and William Lord Mountjoy, Charles's elder brother.

A great deal of landed property in the West Country had passed on the death of Robert Lord Willoughby de Broke to his co-heiresses, Anne and Elizabeth. Anne married the fifth Lord Mountjoy, Charles's grandfather, and Elizabeth married John Paulet, Marquess of Winchester. The manors and other lands were held in common between the heads of the two families. One of the manors was that of Bere Ferrers, the parish in which lay the constituency of Bere Alston. It has been seen that Charles did not take his seat in 1584; but the return states that the two men who did were elected "at the request of the two chief lords", that is, Lord Winchester and Charles's elder brother. To emphasize the family connexion, in the Parliament of 1597 when Charles went to the House of Lords, the senior Member for Bere Alston was a kinsman, Sir Jocelyn Blount. The Cornish borough of St. Ives was in the same situation, but in this case the formula was slightly different and a Member was said to be returned "with the consent" of the two lords.[1] Charles thus had a seat for himself under the patronage of his brother, and on succeeding him patronage of his own. How he divided the patronage with the Marquess of Winchester is not revealed, but the inconvenience of joint ownership must have been greater than that of joint patronage.

This was evidently realized. In the year 1598, after Charles became Lord Mountjoy, measures were taken to terminate the joint ownership by resort to the Court of Chancery. They are thus recorded:

Marquess of Winchester v Mountjoy, 5 July, 1598.
Whereas divers suits have been depending between the said

---

[1] Neale: *The Elizabethan House of Commons*, pp. 143, 202; Alexander, p. 153.

parties in Her Majesty's Court of Common Pleas, for and concerning a partition to be made of divers and sundry manors, lands, tenements and hereditaments in the counties of Dorset, Wiltshire, Devon, and Cornwall, which they hold in coparcenary [joint heirship], or in common, or undivided. Now by the mediation of Sir Edmund Anderson, Knight, Chief Justice of the same Court of Common Pleas, and Thomas Walmesley and Thomas Owen, two other Justices of the same Court, and by the mutual consent of both the said parties, it is ordered that a commission shall be forthwith awarded out of Her Majesty's High Court of Chancery to Sir Thomas Dinnys, Knight, and John Crook, Recorder of London, to make a partition between them of all such manors, lands, tenements and hereditaments . . . and by both their mutual consents such partition so to be made good and effectual in the law against them and against the several heirs of Elizabeth and Anne, ancestors of the said Lords; and each party to do all reasonable further acts for the ratification and confirmation of such partition.[1]

Under the partition the manor of Bere Ferrers passed to the Blount family. When the Irish war was ending Charles looked upon it as home. Writing to the Treasurer, Sir George Carey of Cockington, on 28 January, 1603, he concluded: "Farewell, noble Mr. Treasurer, and God send you happily to Cockington and me to Bere Ferrers". He left the manor to Mountjoy Blount, his natural son by Penelope Rich.[2]

On top of this patronage in Devon and Cornwall, when he became High Steward of the borough of Portsmouth Charles enjoyed the nomination of one of its two Members. It must be emphasized that this was not party influence. There were no parties in Elizabethan Parliaments. The nearest approach to one was the Puritan group. Neither the Essex nominees nor those collected by Robert Cecil as a counterweight were parties in the modern sense.

Charles Blount did not create a ripple on the surface of the Parliament of 1586, and nothing short of a wave would have been noticed in it. It was called after the discovery of the Babington conspiracy, and the Lord Chancellor announced that it had been summoned particularly for advice about the fate of

[1] Monro, p. 717.
[2] C.S.P. Ireland, 1601-03, p. 561; Alexander, p. 153.

the Queen of Scots, not for the making of laws, "whereof her Majesty thought there were more made than were duly executed". Yet the subject brought on a fencing match. The Queen, loathing the prospect of sending Mary to the block, asked the Parliament whether any action short of exacting the extreme penalty could suitably be taken; but both Houses decided unanimously that there was none. Trouble began when the Puritan Dr. Turner declared that Mary's death would be fruitless unless means were found "to root out all Papists" and grew to a storm when the famous Peter Wentworth delivered to Mr. Speaker "articles" containing questions about the liberties of the House, so extravagant that, not for the first time, he was committed to the Tower, followed by four of his associates.[1]

Early in the session of the Parliament of 1593 Wentworth again took the familiar road to the Tower, this time for proposing a petition on the dangerous subject of the succession of the Crown. In this Parliament Sir Charles Blount was a member of a deputation sent to the House of Lords. The Lords had proposed a conference on the subject of a subsidy and the Commons had decided to refuse the invitation as against the privileges of their House. This was the spirit in which they were to establish their sole right to deal with the provision of funds, a right then indeterminate enough for the Lords to request to be shown precedents. Liberal supplies were voted, but the grant passed the House only with difficulty, after warm and prolonged debate.[2]

Mountjoy was not present in the House of Lords at the opening of the Parliament of 1597 on 24 October. He did not reach Plymouth on his return from the Islands Voyage until the following day and was detained there for some time owing to the danger from the Spanish fleet, then off the south-west coast. He was present by 24 November, and probably earlier. On that date a bill for the repeal—more properly for the alteration—of a former act for the recruitment of mariners was entrusted to a committee of which he was a member. He was likewise concerned in a private bill, giving him leave to dispose of lands of which he was tenant in tail—that is, estates limited to himself and heirs of his body—notwithstanding a private statute to the

[1] D'Ewes, pp. 377-94, 396-400, 410-12.
[2] Ibid., pp. 470, 486, 493, 507.

contrary made in the reign of Henry VIII. This suggests that he may have been still embarrassed financially, but the presumption is no certainty; he may have desired to be rid of scattered lands, on obtaining sole ownership of others previously held jointly with Lord Winchester. A bill of a similar kind, to enable Edward Molyneux to sell lands in order to pay debts, was opposed by relatives. Both parties agreed to arbitration and chose the Earl of Rutland, the Bishop of London, and Mountjoy.[1]

By far his most important role in this Parliament has been left to the last. On 8 December a bill for the relief of the poor in times of extreme dearth of corn was read a second time and handed over to a committee headed by the Archbishop of Canterbury, of which Mountjoy was a member. Though Lords and Commons alike had had the urgency of their task impressed upon them by the suffering caused by bad harvests and trade depression, they can have had no conception that they were engaged in framing one of the most important bills in the history of English social legislation. Mountjoy was one of the numerous begetters of the poor-law, which has been described as "the greatest achievement of Elizabethan society". Another historian remarks that "the spirit in which this tremendous problem for a small society with limited resources was tackled, and a solution worked out that endured through centuries, provides us with a remarkable achievement in the realm of administration".[2] It was not only a matter of humanity towards the aged, the impotent, and the infant poor, or of means to find employment for those who lacked it; society had also to protect itself against the swarm of tramps, rogues, and "lewd persons", which infested both towns and countryside.

When the first Parliament of James I met, Charles Earl of Devonshire had reached the summit. He was regarded by all as the nation's greatest soldier and was to be accorded a prestige almost as great in civil affairs. With the Lord Chancellor, Lord Ellesmere (Queen Elizabeth's Lord Keeper Egerton); the Lord Treasurer, the Earl of Dorset (the former Lord Buckhurst); the Principal Secretary of State, Lord Cecil (the former Sir Robert

[1] D'Ewes, pp. 523, 529, 532, 542, 544.
[2] Ibid., pp. 531, 577, 584; Feiling, p. 514; Rowse, p. 355.

Cecil, to become in rapid succession Viscount Cranborne and Earl of Salisbury); and the enigmatic and adroit Earl of Northampton (the former Sir Harry Howard); Charles belonged to the group of ruling spirits in the Privy Council and the House of Lords.

An epidemic of the plague caused the postponement of the calling of Parliament. It met on 19 March, 1604, still within the first year of the new reign. The first important business on which Charles was engaged was that of Wardship. Lords and Commons assembled in different spirit, the former being almost completely sympathetic to the Crown, whereas the latter were chiefly concerned with obtaining redress of grievances which had been endured so long only because of the age, sex and, one might add, political skill of the late sovereign. On Wardships, however, the two Houses were as one. The matter had become an intolerable scandal. Its necessity, real in feudal times, when a lord naturally took land into his own hands in a minority and where the heir was a female chose the husband who would lead her vassals, no longer existed. Now the King's claims were simply a means of extracting money in a most oppressive manner. Charles was a member of the Committee appointed by the Lords to confer with the Commons. The King's anxiety to lose no time in establishing the Union of his new Kingdom and his old, followed by the interruption of Gunpowder Plot, caused this matter to be postponed beyond the brief period which Charles's life had now to run.[1]

Another of Charles's activities was interrupted by his death. He was on the Lords' Committee which conferred with that of the Commons on the Union of England and Scotland. Pushed forward by the King, in face of Cecil's warning that the time was not yet ripe, and the coolness of the Lower House, this business progressed at top speed. An Act was passed naming Commissioners from both Houses to confer with a similar body appointed by the Scots. The meetings began on 29 October, 1604, and agreement was reached by 6 December. The later history of the project was disastrous. It was expected to occupy Parliament when it met in February, 1605, but signs of recur-

---

[1] *Journals of the House of Lords*, Vol. II, p. 266; Spedding, Vol. III, pp. 211-2; Gardiner, Vol. I, pp. 175-6.

rence of the plague caused a further prorogation until the autumn. Gunpowder Plot then intervened and dominated business in the next session. The Instrument of the Union had to wait until the winter of 1606, and in 1608 the whole design, to which the magnificent intellect of Francis Bacon had made so great a contribution, was abandoned.[1]

Other committees of both Houses of which Charles was a member included those on the affairs of the Church—a stormy matter in the present mood of the Commons—on a subsidy, on a Bill annexing lands to the King and his posterity, and on the attainder of participants in the "most detestable and damnable treason of Gunpowder Plot".

As his connexion in one form or other with Parliament covered most of his adult life, it has seemed worth while to preserve the few facts which can be extracted from scanty records. He lived in an age when it was of infinitely greater importance to be a Privy Councillor than a Member of Parliament. It seems probable that, in view of the swelling role of Parliament—particularly the House of Commons but the upper chamber as well—he would, had he lived, have been assiduous in its business. Normally, he would have had plenty of time before him, since if he had lived another twenty years he would still not have been an old man. As it was, he died without making a name as a parliamentarian, though he had touched some great affairs.

[1] *Journals of the House of Lords*, Vol. II, p. 307; Spedding, Vol. III, pp. 240-6; Gardiner, Vol. I, p. 356.

V

STELLA

A T AN unknown date an unknown correspondent wrote to Charles Blount, warning him to beware of women lest he should taste of their witchcraft and enchantments. He was to taste of them, but from one woman only. At least there is no serious mention of any other. He experienced the felicity of having his love returned. Yet from first to last it was surrounded by unhappy and distressing circumstances, and it ended in sorrow. He and she made heavy sacrifices for each other. Their own social world, which knew of their love, smiled upon it when it was illicit and she was the wife of another man; when Charles and Penelope were married after her divorce that world averted its favour. This is the way of the world.

It was, however, an unsuccessful rival, though one who was also a friend, who made Penelope famous. He was a poet, which Charles was not. Philip Sidney's "Astrophel and Stella" was the fount in which Penelope was made immortal. Other poets took some small part in shaping her as an historical figure. The raw material was perfect. Beauty, charm, graciousness and sweetness of disposition are constantly attributed to her. She possessed also great personality and a dangerous masculine determination. She won the hearts not only of those who knew her well but also of more distant watchers. Giordano Bruno is said to have alluded to her in the line, *E siete in terra quel ch' in ciel le stelle.*[1] An exiled Catholic, Henry Constable, was moved to write sonnets to her. A youth who was to become a distinguished dramatist, John Ford—"a mere stranger, altogether unknown unto you"—in a memorial on the death of Charles described her as:

[1] Buxton, p. 164.

His heart's delight, who was that glorious star
Which beautified the value of our land.

Walter Devereux, Earl of Essex, enjoyed the favour of
Queen Elizabeth I in the earlier part of her reign. He undertook, with her patronage, a colonization scheme in Ireland which
failed but which is in some sort the parent of the Plantation of
James I.[1] Essex died in Dublin at the age of 36 on 21 September,
1576. He left by his wife Lettice, daughter of Sir Francis
Knollys, four children. Penelope was the eldest. Dorothy, later
Countess of Northumberland, was born in 1565; Robert, the
famous Earl of Essex, in 1567; Walter, killed in Normandy, in
1569. A fifth, Francis, died in infancy.

It is needless to write of Philip Sidney's gifts and reputation.
Even as a very young man he was regarded as the paragon of
the age. He was born on 30 November, 1554, and named in
honour of Philip of Spain, at that time in England after his
marriage to Queen Mary. On learning of Sidney's death in the
Low Countries the King wrote in the margin of the despatch:
"He was my godson". When Philip Sidney first met Penelope
Devereux is unknown, but in 1575, just before his twenty-first
birthday, he was in attendance on the Queen when she visited
Lady Essex at Chartley. Penelope was then about twelve years
of age, but at once talk arose of a match between them. On
3 December of that year he wrote to his friend Hubert
Languet: "What you write in jest about a wife I take seriously".
In 1576 he was visiting his father, Sir Henry, Lord Deputy of
Ireland, when her father, the Earl of Essex, died in that country.
On 14 November Edward Waterhouse, Sir Henry Sidney's
lawyer, wrote to him in Ireland: "All these lords that wish well
to the children, and I suppose all the English lords besides, do
expect what will become of the treaty between Mr. Philip and
my Lady Penelope".[2]

Does "treaty" necessarily imply a formal contract of
marriage? Probably not, but it does imply an agreement
between the fathers of the young people, Sir Henry Sidney and
Essex, that it should take place. One difficulty was that both
were impoverished, both by their expenditure in Ireland.

[1] Falls, pp. 114-7.
[2] Fox Bourne, p. 96; Pollard, pp. ix, xi.

"Astrophel and Stella" is a long sonnet sequence, in which a number of songs are interwoven. Apart from its great, if uneven, beauty, it offers rich rewards to the student, because so much of it yields to the process of deciphering. One revelation is that it was at first thought to reveal too much. Certain indiscretions were kept back by Sidney's sister, Lady Pembroke, until the edition of 1598.

In the first place, though many phrases descriptive of Penelope's beauty are purely romantic, it provides a portrait. Her eyes were black, her forehead was white and smooth, and her hair was golden, we learn from Sonnets vii and ix: almost an unfair advantage for a woman to start with.

> *When Nature made her chief work, Stella's eyes,*
> *In colour black why wrapt she beams so bright?*

> *Queen Virtue's Court, which some call Stella's face,*
> *Prepared by Nature's choicest furniture,*
> *Hath his front built of alabaster pure:*
> *Gold is the covering of that stately place.*

Constable also speaks of her black eyes. The impression given is that she was not ethereal, certainly not pale. The poet rather insists upon the high colour of her cheeks, as in Sonnet xiii: "Rose gules are borne in silver field," and indeed he uses a stronger and far less poetic phrase elsewhere to describe those rosy cheeks—"fair claret". Her brows made Cupid better bows.

Then, the poems are written over a considerable space of time and, while the first thirty cover a period before her marriage, with the exception of the savage Sonnet xxiv, the latter are subsequent to it. Again, the poet's sentiments fluctuate. He did not love at first. Then he came to love, but his suit was coldly received. After Stella's marriage he was cast down and thrown into despair. Then he found that she loved him. His heart leapt up. He believed that she would make him happy. Then she chided him and denied him the physical fulfilment of his passion. Finally, he claimed to have driven down desire. So Sonnet ii:

> *Not at the first sight, nor with a dribbéd shot,*
> *Love gave the wound which while I breathe will bleed;*
> *But known worth did in mine of time proceed,*
> *Till by degrees it had full conquest got.*

I saw and liked; I liked but lovéd not;
I loved but straight did not what Love decreed;
At length to Love's decrees I, forced, agreed.

Sonnet viii exhibits Stella as cruel:

Love, born in Greece, of late fled from his native place—
Forced by a tedious proof that Turkish hardened heart
Is not fit mark to pierce with his fine-pointed dart—
And, pleased with our soft peace, stayed here his flying race;
But, finding these north climes too coldly him embrace,
Not used to frozen clips, he strave to find some part
Where with most ease and warmth he might employ his art.
At length he perched himself in Stella's joyful face,
Whose fair skin, beamy eyes, like morning sun on snow,
Deceived the quaking boy, who thought from so pure light
Effects of lively heat must needs in nature grow.
But she, most fair, most cold, made him thence take his flight
To my close heart, where while some firebrands he did lay,
He burnt unwares his wings, and cannot fly away.

In Sonnet xii the young soldier used an image which was a commonplace to men of his time, that of a breach effected and a town easily taken, only for the victors to find the citadel held by determined defenders.

Cupid, because thou shinst in Stella's eyes,
That from her locks, thy day-nets, none scape free,
That those lips swelled, so full of thee they be,
That her sweet breath makes oft thy flames to rise,
That in her breast thy pap well sugared lies,
That her grace gracious makes thy wrongs, that she,
What words soere she speak, persuades for thee—
That her clear voice lifts thy flame to the skies—
Thou countest Stella thine, like those whose powers
Having got up a breach by fighting well,
Cry "Victory, this fair day all is ours!"
O no, her heart is such a citadel,
So fortified with wit, stored with disdain,
That to win it is all the skill and pain.

On 10 March, 1581, the Earl of Huntingdon, Penelope's guardian, wrote to the Lord Treasurer recommending that a match should be made between her and Lord Rich, who had recently succeeded to vast estates. This must have by then been almost settled, for they were probably married in April. The first comment upon the affair is found in that interpolated Sonnet xxiv, in which occurs the punning on the name, constantly to be repeated by Sidney and other poets. The last six lines run:

> But that rich fool, who by blind Fortune's lot
> The richest gem of love and life enjoys,
> And can with foul abuse such beauties blot,
> Let him, deprived of sweet but unfelt joys,
> Exiled for aye from those high treasures which
> He knows not, grow in folly only rich.

There is no suggestion in the sequence that she was deeply in love with Sidney at the time. On the contrary, there is a suggestion from another source that she had pledged herself already to Charles Blount. The evidence, produced long afterwards, is inconclusive; in fact, it might be disregarded but for the fact that, in essence, it came from Archbishop Laud and that he had it from her lover in circumstances which must be related later. Let it be set down for what it is worth:

"This gentleman, being a younger brother of William Lord Mountjoy, and known only by the name of Sir Charles Blount while his brother lived, had bore a strong and dear affection to the Lady Penelope Rich, daughter of Walter Earl of Essex, a lady in whom lodged all attractive graces of beauty, wit, and sweetness of behaviour, which might render her absolute mistress of all eyes and hearts. And she so far reciprocated with him in the like affection (being a complete and gallant man) that some assurances past between them of a future marriage. But her friends looking upon him as a younger brother, considerable only in his depending at the Court, chose rather to dispose her in marriage to Robert Lord Rich, a man of an independent fortune and a known estate, but otherwise of an uncourtly disposition, unsociable, austere, and of no very agreeable conversation to her".[1]

Now, as has been acknowledged, the truth of this statement cannot be guaranteed. On the other hand, what the poet said is

[1] Heylin, p. 52. If Penelope was married in 1581, Charles was not knighted until six years later.

not evidence either, at any rate not hard evidence, and "Astrophel and Stella" is not a secure basis for historical fact. Some students have affected to believe that the whole sonnet sequence is highly artificial, though not of course denying that the poems are love poems. If we accept the evidence of Laud's first biographer and also that of the sonnets, Penelope was in love with Charles before her marriage to Rich and after it admitted to Philip that she loved him, though she refused to give herself to him. There is nothing impossible in such a supposition. It might be called waywardness, but then *la donna e mobile*. Whether or not this was the case, it may be accepted that she was married against her will, though again the evidence comes long after the event and from an interested party in Charles Blount, who wrote that, "being in the power of her friends, she was by them married against her will unto one against whom she did protest at the very solemnity;[1] and ever after".

In a number of sonnets Sidney poured out his grief and anger. One of the finest—barring the pun—Sonnet xxxvii, did not appear before the folio of 1598:

> *My mouth doth water and my breast doth swell,*
> *My tongue doth itch, my thoughts in labour be:*
> *Listen, then, lordings, with good ear to me,*
> *For of my life I must a riddle tell.*
> *Toward Aurora's Court a nymph doth dwell,*
> *Rich in all beauties which man's eye can see,*
> *Beauties so far from reach of words that we*
> *Abuse her praise saying she doth excel;*
> *Rich in the treasure of deserved renown,*
> *Rich in the riches of a royal heart,*
> *Rich in those gifts which give the eternal crown;*
> *Who though most rich in these and every part*
> *Which make the patents of true worldly bliss,*
> *Hath no misfortune but that Rich she is.*

Yet presently there appeared more reason for hope. Sonnet xli, one of the two or three most famous in the sequence, indeed one of the great sonnets in the language, records how Stella looked down with favour upon the poet when he had a brilliant

---

[1] That is, the solemnization of the marriage.

day in the tiltyard. The fourth line makes it likely that the incident occurred during the visit of the French Embassy which tried to negotiate a match between Queen Elizabeth and the Duke of Anjou.

> *Having this day my horse, my hand, my lance,*
> *Guided so well that I obtained the prize*
> *Both by the judgement of the English eyes*
> *And of some sent from that sweet enemy France;*
> *Horsemen my skill in horsemanship advance;*
> *Town-folks my strength; a daintier judge applies*
> *His praise to sleight which from good use doth rise;*
> *Some lucky wights impute it but to chance;*
> *Others, because of both sides I do take*
> *My blood from them who did excel in this,*
> *Think nature me a man of arms did make.*
> *How far they shot awry! The true cause is,*
> *Stella looked on, and from her heavenly face*
> *Sent forth the beams which made so fair my race.*

Sonnet lxix is a chant of triumph and happiness. It tries, says the writer, to express joy too high for his power to describe. The winter of his misery was past. Stella had given him the mastery of her high heart. It is true that she had given it under conditions, while he remained virtuous, but all monarchs made some covenants when they were crowned. It is evident that he expected to win her wholly.

At first it appeared that his hopes were to be fulfilled. Sonnets lxxiv to lxxxiii are concerned with kisses.

> *Stop you my mouth with still, still kissing me.*

But lxxxvi brings a change of looks. And soon the lovely Eighth Song tells what is in effect the end of the story. They met in a garden, amid singing birds and May flowers. They sighed and confessed their mutual love. Yet she would not yield herself. She put aside his adventurous hands, though gently.

> *In a grove most rich of shade,*
> *Where birds wanton music made,*
> *May, then young, his pied weeds showing,*
> *New-perfumed with flowers fresh growing,*

Astrophel with Stella sweet
Did for mutual comfort meet,
Both within themselves oppressèd,
But each in the other blessèd.

Him great harms had taught much care,
Her fair neck a foul yoke bare;
But her sight his cares did banish,
In his sight her yoke did vanish.

Sigh they did and now betwixt
Sighs of woe were glad sighs mixt;
With arms crost, yet testifying
Restless rest, and living dying.

There his hands, in their speech, fain
Would have made Love's language plain;
But her hands, his hands repelling,
Gave repulse all grace excelling.

Astrophel, she said, my love
Cease in these effects to prove;
Now be still, yet still believe me,
Thy grief more than death would grieve me.

Trust me, while I thee deny,
In myself the smart I try;
Tyrant honour doth thus use me,
Stella's self might not refuse thee.[1]

So the tale ends as the moralists would have it end and as poets and dramatists of that time and since have often ended such tales. It will be allowed that the moralists' ending could not have been more tender and touching.

The theory that all this was wholly fanciful or parabolic will not be discussed here because it scarcely seems to merit attention. "No doubt," writes a wise commentator, "Stella represents Virtue in many sonnets, as well as beauty; but she also represents Penelope Devereux." Yet the theory is influenced by sentiments which are worth considering. Sidney, the paragon of the reign of Elizabeth, has been somewhat distorted by the spirit of the age of Victoria. We are bidden to put aside any interpretation which does not accord with his "delicacy and sense of honour".

[1] Some stanzas are omitted from this quotation.

He possessed both in a high degree, but they differed from those of the age of Victoria. His character was complex and is not easy to understand without sound knowledge of the period. He was a child of the Renaissance, tinged with the Protestant and Puritan doctrines of his friends and of his party, but his moral earnestness was "not incompatible with an impatient rejection of all ascetic ideals".[1] The passion, and in places the remorse, in this sonnet sequence bear the stamp of reality and experience.

He bade farewell to Stella and in 1583 he married Frances Walsingham. It was an arranged marriage, as was common, and she has come off sadly at the hands of posterity as second-best. It is said she was beautiful. She hastened to him when he was wounded at Zutphen and nursed him until he died. Afterwards she married his dear friend Essex and was a second time left a widow by his execution. Then, undaunted, like her second mother-in-law, Lettice, she married a third time, and like her a man about a decade her junior, this husband being a gallant Irish loyalist who served with distinction under Charles Blount at Kinsale. It was one of the first of the Anglo-Irish marriages among the great. Only a generation back the family of Richard de Burgh, Earl of Clanrickarde, had been on the run, having exchanged English clothes for Irish, and was being chased from bush to bush by Sir Henry Sidney. In 1604 Sir John Davies found Lord and Lady Clanrickarde living at Athlone, where he was acting as President of Connaught. Frances was, says Davies, "very well contented and every way as well served as when he saw her in England".

Philip Sidney represented only a romantic episode in the life of Penelope Rich. Charles Blount was her lover. When the affair began is doubtful. "But long she had not lived in the bed of Rich", says Laud's biographer, "then the old flames of her affection unto Blount began again to kindle in her . . . certain it is that, having first had their private meetings, they afterwards convert more openly and familiarly with one another than might stand with honour unto either".[2] Their relations were at all events clear by the year 1590, though she bore her husband children afterwards.

[1] Buxton, p. 164; Wallace, pp. 237, 341.
[2] Heylin, p. 52.

The custom had been established of celebrating the Queen's accession year by year by jousting on 17 November. In the year 1590 the poet George Peele described the scene in *Polyhymnia*. It was a remarkable occasion because on that day Sir Henry Lee, who had sworn when Elizabeth came to the throne to act as her champion every year so long as health and strength remained, donned his armour for the last time and then resigned his place to the foremost tilter, the Earl of Cumberland. Twenty-four other knights took part. Among them were the members of the Essex-Sidney-Blount circle: Lord Compton; Essex himself; Fulke Greville; two of the brothers Knollys; and Charles Danvers, whose brother fought under Charles Blount in Ireland and who himself died on the scaffold for complicity in the revolt of Essex. The sixth pair who rode against each other were Charles Blount and Thomas Vavasour. Peele, like a modern journalist unable to avoid displaying his inside knowledge, returns to that wretched pun. He thus describes Charles:

> *And then, as blithe as bird of morning's light,*
> *Inflamed with honour, glistering as the sun*
> *What time he mounts the sweating lion's back,*
> *Beset with glorious sunshine of his train,*
> *Bearing the sun upon his arméd breast,*
> *That like a precious shining carbuncle,*
> *Or Phoebus' eye, in heaven itself reflects—*
> *Comes Sir Charles Blount, in or and azure dight:*
> *Rich in his colours, richer in his thoughts,*
> *Rich in his fortune, honour, arms and art.*

Clearly then it was a commonplace at Court that Charles Blount was Lady Rich's lover, though we must not conclude, just because Peele was a popular poet, that the popular world saw this pun. Her husband is a dim figure, who in a sense may be called complaisant. During the life of her brother Essex, with whom he was on good terms, he thought it best to accept the situation; only after his brother-in-law's death did he wholly separate himself from his wife, and only five years later did he decide upon divorce. Several children were born to them in the early years of their marriage. Later on they seem to have lived to a great extent apart, though not openly. Once when he was seriously ill she went to him, nursed him back to health, and then took herself off again. She is found from time to time at his country home, Leighs, near Chelmsford, the great house built by the first Lord Rich, of which only the splendid outer and inner gatehouses and a part of two sides of the outer quadrangle still stand.[1] Yet she also frequented Chartley and Wanstead, at either of which she might meet Charles. Then there was London and the Court, wherever it might be. In London he had at one time a house in Holborn, and she was accustomed to stay at Essex House. There they could meet constantly. We happen to know of one party which they both attended, the "very great supper" given by Sir Gilly Meyrick, after which they sat till the small hours of the morning watching two plays.[2] It may be surmised that they were often invited out together, as lovers in the great world have been in all times and civilizations, and often sat late over the good fare from country estates and the "sweet wines" of which Essex was the monopolist, by the light of guttering candles.

Once, it is said, she contemplated joining the Roman Catholic Church and probably at the same time cutting herself off from her lover. About 1592 the Jesuit John Gerard was living in disguise with a Catholic squire, William Wiseman, at Braddocks, between Thaxted and Saffron Walden. His host's mother reported to him that a great lady, sister of the Earl of Essex and married to the greatest lord in the county, desired to see him. The old lady stated that though Penelope had led a "life of frivolity", she now wished to talk to a priest, provided he came without anyone knowing who he was. Gerard accordingly went openly to the house—Leighs, of course—and addressed her as though he were the bearer of a message from another great lady, a relative of hers. He dined at her table with all the gentlefolk of the household and afterwards talked with her in private for three hours. First, he set at rest the doubts which she raised about her faith; then he strove to "stir her will". Before he quitted her she asked him to instruct her how to prepare for confession, and they fixed a day for making it.

"There was a nobleman in London who loved her with a deep and enduring love. To him she wrote to announce the

---

[1] R. Comm. Hist. Monuments: *Essex*, Vol. II, p. 158.
[2] De l'Isle and Dudley, Vol. II, p. 322.

step she proposed to take, intending perhaps to break with him.
But she aroused a sleeping viper. At once he rushed down to
see her and began to talk her out of her resolve for all he was
able."

Father Gerard had come up against a formidable opponent.
Charles, inveterate student of theology, met him on his own
ground. He asked his mistress for advice on certain doubts he
felt himself, begging her meanwhile to take no irrevocable step.
They discussed the subject at length, and she gradually
weakened. In the event he succeeded in persuading her to
abandon her intention.[1]

The only evidence for this story is the Jesuit's account, which
has been but recently translated from the Latin. It accords, however, closely with one side of Charles for which there is more
than one witness: the love of theological discussion, not to say
hair-splitting; the rather sophistical arguments in his apology for
his marriage, coupled with genuine knowledge of doctrine; the
cool and, some would say unscrupulous, approach and the pretence of asking for guidance where a less clever man would have
railed. The tale may have been embroidered a little by the
narrator, but it was assuredly not invented.

She sometimes visited Leighs in her husband's absence,
bringing with her ladies to keep her company. In 1593
Broughton, Essex's steward at Chartley, wrote that she had
requested his wife to go there with her and that her mother,
Lady Essex, and her sister Dorothy, "as well as many good
gossips", would accompany her.[2] Dorothy had then begun a
career as strange as, and even more stormy than, that of
Penelope. She had been married to young Thomas Perrott, son
of the famous Lord Deputy of Ireland, at Broxbourne Church,
by a strange clergyman and without the prior knowledge of the
incumbent, while men armed with swords and daggers guarded
the church door. Perrott died in 1594, and two years later she
married the Earl of Northumberland—of the restored Percy
earldom—to live with him the life of cat and dog, if not of less
domesticated animals.[3] The intense devotion of Penelope and
Dorothy to their brother Essex will appear later.

[1] Gerard, pp. 33-5.
[2] Bagot Papers, 26 May, 1593.
[3] Rawson, pp. 147-50.

It is fascinating to note how closely Charles and Penelope were linked in the society of their friends. When Lady Sidney, wife of Sir Robert, was about to give birth to a child in 1595 he wrote to her from his government of Flushing bidding her on no account to forget that the chief gossips, or god-parents, should be my Lady Rich and my Lord Mountjoy—the sex of the third depending on that of the baby. The baby was born on 1 December, a boy, afterwards the second Earl of Leicester of the Sidney peerage and the husband of Lady Dorothy Percy, daughter of Penelope's sister—how closely the comparatively small aristocracy of those times was intertwined! Rowland Whyte, Sidney's agent at Court and general factotum, had to make the arrangements. He called on Penelope at Essex House, warning her that both mother and child had measles. She answered that there was no danger after eight days and measles would not keep her from doing Sir Robert and Lady Sidney a greater kindness than this. Whyte then found Mountjoy at home and obtained his agreement also. However, the christening had to be postponed, perhaps because the disease took rather long to clear. Meanwhile Penelope went to Leighs and Charles sent a message that he had an ague and desired her to wait until he was well, since he wanted to be present in person. Lady Sidney replied that as soon as Lady Rich came back to town he should fix the day himself. No need, be it noted, to make fresh arrangements with her; he would answer for both. Once again there was a postponement, this time to New Year's Eve. Penelope declared that this was at the request of the third god-parent, Lord Compton, but Rowland Whyte, in the know like others, interpreted it differently. He thought that the cause was a "tetter" that had suddenly broken out on her fair white face. A beauty of renown would not care to be seen by her lover in such a state. The correspondence makes it clear that their attachment was accepted as a matter of course.[1] She bore her lover five children, the eldest born about 1597, and this also must have been widely known.

The background to this devotion must be imagined. No evidence of that sort extracted from "Astrophel and Stella" is to be found, and no trace of a letter. Letters would probably have been destroyed, but in any case it is likely that over long periods

[1] De l'Isle and Dudley, Vol. II, pp. 185, 194, 199, 204.

they had no need to write because they saw each other so often.
A few of her letters to others remain, some of them asking favours
for her friends. Thus, in 1595 she wrote to Sir Robert Cecil to say
that she had been asked by Mr. Tasburgh to put Cecil in mind of
him and that he had been in hopes of a knighthood.[1] If this is
Sir Thomas Tasburgh, Teller of the Exchequer, he was a knight
a few years later. Like most Elizabethans who combined influence with good nature, Penelope tried her hand at any little
piece of jobbery that was toward. In 1597 Sidney was anxious
for the appointment of Warden of the Cinque Ports, for which
he was the candidate of Essex—and Penelope. Whyte took
Sidney's letter addressed to the Queen from the Continent to
her. She kissed it, put it in her bosom, and assured him that it
should be read by the Queen that night or the next day. Then
she drew him aside and told him that lately, when the Queen
had asked for her comments on affairs of the day, she had said
she was glad to hear of the good choice of a Warden, and had
named Sidney. The Queen replied that she had not disposed
of the appointment. Alas! it went to Lord Cobham, of the
opposition.[2]

Once she was afflicted with a dreadful kind of "tetter", the
small-pox that ruined so many Elizabethan faces and went on
ruining faces until the end of the reign of Queen Victoria.
Whyte heard that she was disfigured. A few days later, however,
he had good news for Sidney, which it evidently gave him
pleasure to impart. "My Lady Rich is recovered of her small-
pox, without any blemish to her beautiful face". Even today the
reader coming on the letter sighs with relief.

Her frantic behaviour on the fall of her beloved brother
Essex must await the occasion. So too must the last acts of the
lives of Charles and Penelope. They will serve to show that this
was a love affair of no ordinary quality, unchanging and un-
assailable in difficulties and adversity.

[1] Salisbury, Pt. V, p. 236.
[2] De l'Isle and Dudley, Vol. II, p. 253.

VI

THE LADDER TO FAME

I F we would appreciate the circumstances, and even the frame of mind, in which Charles Blount went to Portsmouth as Governor, we must first get rid of cobwebs left about by more than one celebrated, or once celebrated, historian. A tradition, welcome to national pride, has been established in the minds of readers of popular history that the defeat of the Spanish Armada broke the naval power of Spain and once and for all freed England from danger from that country. Neither of these assertions bears examination. They have been rejected by more modern writers, yet the tradition survives. The significance of the famous sea fight "at Flores in the Azores" in 1591 is not so much the heroic defence and death of Sir Richard Grenville— except in so far as such heroism should always be the subject of history—as that an English fleet was forced to fly from its cruising station, on the route of the Spanish treasure fleets, by superior strength, with the loss of the *Revenge*, one of the finest ships in the Elizabethan navy. A modern historian, with little space to spare in a complete "History of England", puts the situation thus succinctly: —

> "Nothing was more disappointing than the naval war. In part this was due to rival policies, but even more to a great increase in Spanish efficiency. . . . Strong galleons of the 'Indian Guard' and swift treasure-carrying cruisers, excellent fortifications of the Islands (Azores), convoy from St. Helena for the carracks coming from India—against these Drake's method of surprise had lost its power".[1]

Feiling's words might be taken to mean that reorganization and reform started only after the defeat of the Armada and

[1] Feiling, p. 408.

embodied its lessons. This would be over-simplification. The reforms had developed gradually, but were now hastened. The galleons, the "battleships" of the time, improved, but the Spaniards did not reach the English standard. It seems clear that the two new galleons captured at Cadiz and used in the Islands Voyage were not as good sailers as their English counterparts, indifferent though some of these were. The medium ships and small craft were of improved quality. As far back as 1573 Pero Menendez de Aviles had designed a fast light galleon, long in proportion to beam, low-lying, and flush-decked, which was used in the "Flota", or Plate Fleet, not for cargo but as a treasure-carrier. Cristobal de Barros, superintendent of construction, is said to have been the inventor of the frigate type. The sons of the Marquess of Santa Cruz, Alvaro and Alonso de Bazan, were able designers as well as fighting admirals. The last invention of the period was the "felipote", of 120 to 200 tons, carrying eight to ten guns, a fast sailer and a good cruiser, effective for reconnaissance and as a despatch-boat.

Cosmography and cartography made rapid strides. Increasing attention was paid to the training of pilots, to navigation, gunnery, and hygiene, though in the second and third Spain still lagged and in the fourth all navies were so bad that one can scarcely be said to have been better than another. Slackness, incompetence, and corruption remained. The merchant fleet decayed till most of the cargoes and the supplies for armies were carried by Flemings and "Easterlings" from the Baltic. The effort brought only partial results, and these were not always maintained; but it did bring results which were felt as long as the war lasted.[1]

Another factor was the Spanish lodgement in Brittany. True, Brest had been saved by Elizabeth's well-timed intervention in aid of France, but Blavet constituted a secondary threat until it was returned to France under the treaty of Vervins. Fast Spanish ships captured small merchantmen and fishing-boats in the Channel. On 27 July, 1595, a landing party from Blavet burnt Mousehole, Newlyn, and Penzance, on the Cornish coast, with the consequence that the Queen threatened to hold up Drake and Hawkins, who were at Plymouth fitting out a large expedi-

[1] Duro: *Armada Española*, Tomo III, pp. 172-94; Monson: Appendix B.

tion to American waters.[1] At the other end of the Channel a
considerable Flemish fleet of privateers under an energetic and
ferocious Admiral, Antoine de Bourgogne, Seigneur de Wäcken,
lay in Dunkirk. The Dutch strove to keep them bottled up, but
they often enough broke the blockade and did much damage. In
1599, after Blavet had been evacuated by the Spaniards, a new
threat replaced it. The brilliant young Italian Frederico Spinola,
younger brother of the more famous general, created a scare by
working six galleys all the way from Santander to Sluys. English
and Dutch knew he was coming and strove to intercept him, but
he evaded them by a combination of nerve, seamanship, and
luck—"and so in an almost inconceivable success ended one of
the most brilliant feats of the whole war".[2]

The adventures of Spinola, some happy, some the reverse, do
not belong to our story, but his greatest feat may be mentioned.
In June, 1600, four of his galleys came out of Sluys by night and,
despite an escort, took 28 ships, heavily laden, from a Dutch
fleet with stores for an attack at Ostend. That year was also
fruitful for the "Dunkirkers" owing to Dutch and English preoccupations elsewhere. On 16 June the Mayor of Hull reported
that a single Dunkirker had taken nine coasters off Flamborough
Head in one day. In early October the Dunkirkers captured
three ships coming out of Falmouth, almost certainly bound for
Ireland with much-needed stores, and drove ashore a warship
which tried to intercept them, with the result that no skipper
would leave the harbour.[3] They also cut a vessel out of Plymouth
Sound, a galling experience for the port. Spinola met his inevitable end at the hands of the Dutch; his squadron was destroyed
and he was killed. The galleys with fore-and-aft guns—mostly
only one gun—could not live in battle against sea-going ships
with broadsides, unless the latter were very badly handled. The
Dunkirkers remained to give trouble. In the last weeks of the
Queen's life the Council on her orders sent a significant circular
to the Lord Lieutenants of shires and the principal cities.
Maritime trade, they said, had to be protected against the
depredations of ships of the King of Spain and the Archdukes,

---

[1] C.S.P. Dom., 1595-7, p. 88; Cheyney, Vol. I, p. 544.
[2] Corbett: *The Successors of Drake*, p. 287.
[3] Salisbury, Pt. X, pp. 187, 188, 343.

but the Queen's ships must be relieved of this task. A special squadron of ten or twelve ships would, therefore, be fitted out for the purpose by subscriptions. No coercion was to be used to levy them—but it hardly mattered what name was given to the process, because no one was to be allowed to plead exemption. The project was remarkably like the Ship Money levy of Charles I.[1]

All this was not of over-mastering import because Spain had not established command of the sea, but a single naval victory would have left her in a happy strategic position. And her navy was temporarily improving. By 1595 or 1596 it was better than in Armada year, 1588, and it was to cause a great deal of anxiety during the remainder of the reign of Queen Elizabeth. Spain had not only reorganized the sea routes—though less thoroughly than a few years later—but was preparing a new Armada. The last great blow she was to receive at English hands was that struck by Essex at Cadiz in 1596, and it did not prevent her from fitting out an invasion fleet.

In the passage quoted on p. 68, Feiling speaks of "rival policies". The unfortunate thing was that the less effective policy most often prevailed. Broadly, the choice was between commerce raiding—or treasure raiding—and a war of destruction against Spanish naval power. The latter was exemplified by the two great attacks on Cadiz, that of Drake and Norris in 1587 and that of Howard and Essex in 1596. Drake almost destroyed a division of the Armada and delayed its sailing for a year, during which it so happened that the ablest Spanish Admiral died. With these expeditions must be coupled that of Drake and Norris in 1589, though it failed at Lisbon.

Because a policy is not the best it does not follow that it must fail to gain important success. Critics of the younger Pitt's policy of capturing West Indian islands sometimes talk as though its returns were trifling. They were, on the contrary, very valuable. The true argument against the policy is that, on the scale on which it was carried out and in the circumstances of the war, it was not worth the cost. So of the Elizabethan raiding policy. Nor is it to be concluded that a policy of destruction could not have been combined with one of raiding. The trouble was that

[1] C.S.P. Dom., 1601-03, p. 289.

the first was subordinated to the second and that leaders sought excuses to switch over from the one to the other. Raiding brought wealth to a number of individuals and a considerable amount to the royal coffers, and it may be that Elizabeth would not have resorted to it but for her poverty. Raiding also strained and impoverished Spain. Yet it remained indecisive and it inspired the counter-measures which have been mentioned. It represented lust for gold and other spoil rather than a maritime policy. That was why it proved so attractive. The manning of the Queen's ships became more and more difficult because the best seamen preferred to sail as privateers' crews. Moreover, what our historians sometimes forget to tell us is that, while vast riches were seized in Spanish America and many ships laden with bullion and valuable merchandise were taken, the treasure fleet was never captured. The flow of bullion reached its maximum between 1590 and 1600.[1] Essex might have taken the Flota, but just failed. And not all historians make it clear that on the single occasion when an English admiral, Sir Richard Leveson, fell in with the Flota he sheered off because the odds against him were so heavy. He was, indeed, lucky to get away. There is no equally good substitute for victory. By the end of Elizabeth's reign Spain was indeed gravely exhausted and her navy, after a brief resurgence, was again falling into decay; but she remained undefeated.

In some respects the use of land forces protected by naval proved more effective than naval effort alone. The aid given to the Dutch tided them over a dangerous period. They were now growing strong, and it was becoming clear that Spain would never subdue them. Despite the errors and weaknesses which accompanied it, Elizabethan strategy had here been first-rate; from the most practical point of view, it had diminished the value of the Low Countries as a Spanish invasion base. The same may be said of the intervention in Normandy and Brittany, though Henry IV thought the aid niggardly. His position had been strengthened by his astuteness in declaring his conversion to Roman Catholicism in 1593 and winning Paris for a Mass. It was not, however, until nearly three years later that Mayenne, the leader of the League, came to terms. Even

[1] Richmond, p. 6.

then the Spaniards remained in the north and in Brittany until
the Treaty of Vervins brought peace between the two countries
—little to the liking of Queen Elizabeth—in 1598.

Charles Blount's appointment as Governor of Portsmouth
may have had some connexion with the fact that he had been for
the past four years Warden of the New Forest, a post which he
had won in competition with the Earl of Pembroke, backed at
Court by Sir Walter Ralegh.[1] His opportunity at Portsmouth
came through the death of the Earl of Sussex. He was the
younger brother of the better-known Earl who had served both
Mary and Elizabeth as Viceroy of Ireland and had led the
opposition to Leicester. In his old age the Governor had been
of no great value and had seldom set eyes on Portsmouth. He had
uttered at least one warning, but had generally let sleeping dogs
lie and ruins grow more ruinous. Money was always tight, and
the Queen and Council were probably glad that he made few
demands. He left matters in the hands of his Lieutenant, John
Munns, a man of a type found often enough in such a post,
always ready to do nothing in an orderly way and to avoid giving
trouble. Munns was the sleepiest of dogs and never barked. To
do him justice, no one in his social position could have accomplished much.

Charles Blount was directed to go to Portsmouth actually
before the death of Sussex, but in consequence of his grave sickness. The Queen's message to the Lieutenant, on 13 December,
1593, betrayed some anxiety for the safety of the place. She was
receiving, she said, daily reports of Spanish plans against the
shipping in the harbour and the pier itself. Blount was to secure
Portsmouth "against all attempts and practices". She was also
sending Sir George Carew, Lieutenant of the Ordnance, to take
an inventory of the material in the store and deliver it to
Blount.[2]

On 16 December Charles addressed to Sir Robert Cecil from
Portsmouth a somewhat excited letter. He began with fervent
protestations of determination to do his utmost to secure the
safety of the port. He would allow no one to be lodged in the
tower without an order from himself. He would keep a diligent

[1] C.S.P., Dom., 1581-94, p. 575.
[2] Salisbury, Pt. IV, p. 436.

eye on the shipping. As soon as he had thought things out he would make his proposals for the defence to the Queen. At the moment he was worried. He confessed that, full of joy at being sent to Portsmouth, he had talked about the matter to friends, but only in thankfulness for her Majesty's goodness. Now he was afraid he might have offended her by an apparent assumption that he was to be installed as Governor. He still could hardly doubt that. "Because this place", he wrote, "is a gift even according unto my own heart, because I may herein practise my honesty, the only occupation (though against the opinion of the world) I trusted to get my living by, I pray, Sir, give me leave to speak somewhat of myself and let her Majesty know it".

He could think of three possible objections to his appointment: want of honesty, want of wit or wisdom, and want of means. As for the first, he would not object to be tried by a jury of his enemies. He was not himself very sure about his wisdom, but he was quite sure that he had as much as Mr. Munns, to whose discretion the charge had been committed for the better part of twenty years. His means were not great, but a poor man was less likely to be false than a rich one; rich men were more often traitors, though poor were more often thieves. Anyhow, he was not altogether a pauper. If the Queen wanted security, he would pledge as much land as any one of half the barons of England could, namely, £400 a year. He implored Cecil to put him out of his miserable doubt as to whether the Queen had made up her mind. "By the Eternal God, if I miss this hope", he concluded, "I will leave the place safe in Sir George Carew's hands, but, as I think, I will never see her Majesty or you any more, but ever while I live pray for her and wish you well."[1]

The tone of the letter is proof of his eagerness for this position of responsibility—and profit—and also of the awe in which Queen Elizabeth held her servants. A little later Charles told Cecil that he could not quit his post even to report because he refused to leave Munns alone. He was taking things seriously indeed. All went well, and the patent was issued on 26 January, 1594.

He could not have got better support than he did from

[1] Salisbury, Pt. IV, pp. 437-8.

Carew. The latter wrote to Cecil on 21 December, 1593, that the tally at Portsmouth was finished and that he was about to take that of Southsea Castle. Like almost everyone else, he had come under the spell of Charles. "As touching the new Governor", he remarked, "I protest to your Honour without affection or flattery I do think the Queen could not have made choice of a more worthy man as well for her service as for his sweet and noble demeanour to the townsmen and garrison, who are so well pleased with the same as they think his coming amongst them to be their year of jubilee, having now some hope to grow rich, which heretofore was impossible by reason of the great dislike between them and the late Earl."[1]

In the course of 1594 William Blount, Lord Mountjoy, died, according to Camden from the effects of his intemperate youth.[2] Though the family estate had been diminished by extravagance and recklessness, Charles's succession to the title must have made him much wealthier than he had been as a younger brother. He was soon afterwards to acquire from the Devereux family the great mansion of Wanstead, and he left a large fortune. Even taking into account the facts that Wanstead may have passed into his hands by a special family arrangement and at a reduced price because he was the lover of Lady Rich, to whom a share in it had been left, and that his fortune was augmented by grants from James I, it is clear that his inheritance was considerable. He had always been magnificent in his clothes when his income was small, and it may be supposed that he now became even more splendid. His title was very valuable to his ambition. The Elizabethan nobility possessed great credit and authority, above all in military affairs. Men like John Norris, under whom Charles had served and whom he revered, might reach high command, but the case was uncommon—and Norris was the younger son of a peer. As 8th Lord Mountjoy Charles found himself with improved prospects of preferment.

His links with the town whose citizens were so well pleased with him had been strengthened by his being placed on the Burgess list on St. Stephen's Day, 1593, together with his young

---

[1] Salisbury, Pt. IV, p. 440.

[2] Camden, p. 117. The exact date is unknown, but Charles is described as "Sir Charles Blount" in May and as "Lord Mountjoy" in August.

cousin Charles, of whom mention has been made.[1] They were
further reinforced when at a court held on 3 September, 1594,
it was unanimously agreed "that the Right Ho. the Lord
Mountjoy, now Captain of this town, shall be High Steward of
this town and shall have and enjoy the same in as large and
ample manner as the Right Ho. Henry Earl of Sussex deceased
did enjoy the same, with the amenities and presents to the same
belonging: Mr. Owen Tottie being then Mayor".[2] The office of
High Steward extended his political influence because in that
capacity he was granted the nomination of one of the two
Members of Parliament returned by the borough.[3] One scrap
of evidence of his interest in the place is found in the dedication
to him, when Earl of Devonshire, of a book on the doctrine of
the Sabbath by George Widley, who held a lectureship there.
Widley, who was a favourite preacher at the parish church
between 1602 and 1606, speaks of himself as "succeeding others
in that Lecture wherein your Lordship first breathed life".

The enthusiasm of Charles on his appointment as Governor
of Portsmouth was not reflected by haste on the part of the
Queen and Council to strengthen it. Over a year later, on 12
February, 1595, he was demanding a meeting with Burghley,
Howard, and Essex to consider what should be done. He had put
in an estimate of £7,354 for work on the fortifications, but this
they reduced to £3,000. They also laid down that the money
should be paid as the work proceeded, and he had to point out
that he must provide stone and implements before the workmen
started. At the end of March, 1596, he sent in his report. He had
made the money go as far as possible, deepened the moats, used
the earth taken from them to reinforce the bulwarks of the
town, carried forward the rampart, made a covered way in the
counterscarp, and built a stone wall on the north-west side of
the town. He asked that someone on whose judgement the three
men who formed a sort of war council could rely should be sent
to inspect the progress. He did not consider that Portsmouth
was yet secure against an enterprising enemy, and would have
liked to see the work finished as he had planned it. A hint of

---

[1] Lilley and Everitt, p. 56.
[2] Murrell and East, p. 205.
[3] Neale: *The Elizabethan House of Commons*, p. 178.

the state of the troops in the maritime counties about this time is given in the order of the Privy Council to the Lord Lieutenants—including the Marquess of Winchester and Mountjoy as Lord Lieutenants of Hampshire—to supply the men with pikes in place of bills (halberds) and muskets and calivers in place of bows.[1] If the Spanish policy of seizing harbours in western France continued to be successful, Mountjoy thought it likely that Portsmouth would be the place they would choose for a landing in England. At that very moment the Spaniards were about to deliver a brilliant stroke.

In the early part of 1596 the talk was of Drake's expedition. The Queen had bidden him return by May at latest so that his ships should have a month to refit before the Spanish fleet attempted the invasion, as she confidently expected it would. The rumour spread that he had had a striking success. At the same time Essex and Lord Howard were preparing for a secret mission, which caused a great deal of speculation. In Picardy the French King had his hands full of the Spaniards. There Elizabeth would send troops only on condition that Calais were put into her charge. The stipulation was not as hard as it sounds because, having noticed a lack of determination in the French conduct of the war, she did not care about sending a force without a secure base held by English troops. The Archduke Albert, the man who had saved Lisbon from Drake and Norris in 1589, had recently become Governor of the Netherlands.

The English expedition fitting out was directed against Spain itself. Essex had the bold conception of the permanent occupation of a Spanish port. Suddenly the Archduke thrust forward a flying column which seized one of the forts defending Calais. Fear of the Spanish guns kept out English and Dutch ships with supplies. Heated arguments took place in England, and the Queen changed her mind thrice about the possibility of saving the town, as Essex frantically urged her to do. Nerves were on edge. Already the bad news had spread that Drake had been repulsed at Puerto Rico. Now details of the full disaster were arriving. Drake and Hawkins had failed, and both had been buried at sea. By 7 April the Spaniards had broken into Calais. The French still held the citadel, and while that remained the

[1] A.P.C., Vol. XXV, p. 51.

fervent Essex believed the town might yet be recovered. At last
his prayers were answered and on the 15th he got leave to sail
from Dover. But an ominous silence had fallen. Gunfire had
ceased. The citadel of Calais had in fact surrendered. Spain had
certainly scored heavily in the early part of 1596.

The usual rush of the nobility and courtiers to get a place in
the relief expedition had occurred before it was called off. It
seems possible that Mountjoy actually went aboard the fleet at
Dover; for Essex, who was anxious to avoid trouble on this score,
wrote that he had shown him a warrant.[1] This must, however,
have applied only to the attempt to relieve Calais, which was
abandoned. It was now decided to undertake the expedition to
Spain as previously arranged, and in this Mountjoy was not
allowed to sail. He thus missed one of the finest amphibious
expeditions of the reign, which resulted in the burning of Cadiz,
serious damage to Spanish shipping, and a grave set-back to
Spanish prestige, which had recently risen.

Yet the expedition had not accomplished all that it might
have. Chances had been missed, and the avarice created by the
Queen's method of waging war recoiled upon her in the shape
of personal looting and corruption. Looters had even laid hands
on captured brass guns which Mountjoy was bidden to seize if
they were landed at Portsmouth.[2] Moreover, the effect of the
raid, far from discouraging Philip II, was to light within him a
flame of revenge which aroused him from lethargy brought on
by extreme sickness. He became a new man, driving forward
preparations for a fleet to sail that year.

All this was at first unknown in England. When the fleet
returned from the Cadiz expedition in the early part of August
the Queen's ships were laid up as speedily as possible and the
troops taken from the Low Countries were ordered to return
there. Then information began to trickle in about Spanish
intentions. Once more the machinery of mobilization had to be
started, but it was not functioning properly at the moment of
greatest danger. A fleet half fitted out lay at its moorings at
Chatham, and the land forces, on whom chief reliance had now
to be placed, were unready. Considering that the Spaniards were

[1] C.S.P. Dom., 1595-7, pp. 203-5.
[2] A.P.C., Vol. XXVI, p. 141.

now installed at Calais as well as in Brittany, the situation looked very grave.[1]

A heavy responsibility fell upon Mountjoy at Portsmouth. On 2 November he wrote to Cecil that he thought the Spaniards might intend a descent upon the Isle of Wight or the capture of Portsmouth, the former hard to relieve and the latter the chief fortress in England. They might well land before he could bring in troops, in which case it was doubtful whether the small Portsmouth garrison could resist the attack. He could, he said, call upon a force nominally 2,000 strong; but it was widely dispersed, and if the call were made suddenly he doubted whether he would find 600 men well armed or any good officers. These were all-important. He rightly considered that no force of a militia character could be expected to do well without good leadership. If that were available, he was not pessimistic about the conduct of the levies, "who, believe me, sir, will not fight but by example, and, drawn out by others' valour, will do as much as any nation in the world." For the defence of the Isle of Wight he urged that the nearer parts of Dorsetshire, Wiltshire, and Hampshire should be held in a state of special readiness, and for that of Portsmouth the greater part of Hampshire and the neighbouring part of Sussex. He particularly recommended cavalry to strike a strong blow at the moment of a landing. He also said that, if he were given more arms, he would arm a number of the poor people of Portsmouth, who were good marksmen and hardy fellows. He was worried that the fortifications had not been finished in accordance with his design.[2]

His letter actually crossed an order to himself and the Marquess of Winchester to send 450 men to the Isle of Wight and a warrant to the Sheriffs and Justices of the Peace of Wiltshire for the same number of men to go to the same destination. Immediately afterwards Mountjoy went to Plymouth. The port had nothing to do with him, and it seems a little curious that he should have left his post at this moment. A possible explanation is that he expected to get at Plymouth the quickest news of the Spanish fleet; but whether his visit was by order of the Council or on his own initiative cannot be discovered.

[1] Corbett: *The Successors of Drake*, p. 141.
[2] Birch, Vol. II, p. 189.

On 7 November he wrote to Essex that there were no tidings of the Spaniards. He hoped their fleet had suffered from the recent tempest, but the English ships at Plymouth were too few to effect anything, even had they been ready, which they were not. "This country", he declared, "must be presently ordered for a war."[1]

His hopes about the effects of the gale had in fact been fulfilled. The veteran Don Martin de Padilla, Adelantado of Castile and Admiral of the Ocean Sea, was driven to sea by his King, despite his angry protests that the season was too far advanced. The Spaniards made this mistake more than once. (Yet Mountjoy, though in error in his view that they chose their time deliberately, made a good point when he remarked that, if they came late enough, they could always count on England's being unprepared, because the fleet was invariably laid up in the autumn.) The Adelantado put to sea about 24 October. His forebodings were realized; for the gale was disastrous. He was driven back with a loss of seven galleons, besides smaller ships.

A panic on the international exchanges followed. Spain was, for the time being at all events, bankrupt. Philip dishonoured the bills of the Archdukes in the Spanish Netherlands. Yet his determination remained unaltered. Again he prepared to send a fleet with an expeditionary force against the England which had so persistently balked him. And again the English Queen and her Council determined to forestall him by attack in his own waters. England's case, thanks to the Queen's much-abused care, was not as bad as Spain's, but the country was in distress. London protested when a squadron was demanded of it. A historian has suggested that, under any monarch other than Queen Elizabeth, the Ship Money controversy might have been precipitated by nearly half a century.[2]

Lord Howard, created Earl of Nottingham in 1596 and now sixty years of age, had made his last war voyage. In the programme of 1597 Lord Thomas Howard, son of the Duke of Norfolk beheaded in 1572, was to take his place, but without all his power. This time there was to be a single command, and it was

---

[1] Birch, Vol. II, p. 195. "Presently", it may be needless to say, means "immediately".

[2] Corbett: *The Successors of Drake*, pp. 152-6.

to be in the hands of Essex. On the naval side Lord Thomas Howard was to be Vice-Admiral and Sir Walter Ralegh Rear-Admiral. On the military, Mountjoy was appointed Lieutenant-General, or second in command, Sir Francis Vere Marshal, and Sir Christopher Blount First Colonel. In the expedition of 1596 no lieutenant-general had been appointed; Vere had therefore been second to Essex and what we should call Chief of Staff. Now Mountjoy had been brought in over his head. The appointment is difficult to justify. Vere was a seasoned soldier with a long record of command. Mountjoy had but little military experience. No evidence existed on which to base a forecast that he would turn out to be the greatest Elizabethan soldier. Yet the Queen herself seems to have been in no doubt about his value. She instructed Essex to add him to the council by the advice of which he was to be guided and went out of her way to describe Charles as "a noble, wise man". In a later letter she charged Essex to "forget not to salute with my great favour good Thomas [Howard] and faithful Mountjoy".[1]

Vere took it hardly. After the Cadiz expedition he had returned to his command in the Netherlands. Here he had received instructions to induce the States General to release for the expedition a thousand English troops in their pay, in addition to the fleet which they had agreed to send. This arranged, he crossed to England, arriving in the early morning to find the fleet at anchor in the Downs and Essex still asleep at Sandwich. Vere was a gruff, touchy man, and the interview in the bedroom was unpleasant.

Essex said that Mountjoy's appointment was not of his choice, but had been made on the insistence of the Queen. But, he went on, Vere would be Marshal as on the Cadiz voyage, and in English armies the man holding that office had always come second in authority to the General. The new Lieutenant-General would have a title without an office and all would be in effect as before. Vere was not placated. He replied that he had thought the matter over already. Though he was aware of no reason why he should thus be disgraced, the appointment being "my Prince's action", he would go on the voyage and would obey Mountjoy, whom he had always respected. At the same time he was con-

[1] C.S.P. Dom., 1595-7, pp. 441, 452.

81

vinced that the power of Essex was great enough to prevent
Mountjoy or any other man being foisted upon him against his
will. Vere could only conclude that he had suffered a decline in
the favour of Essex. He therefore requested the General not to
employ him under his command in future.[1] Though a good deal
of faction and bad comradeship made their appearance on this
voyage, no hint of ill will between Mountjoy and Vere can be
traced; but when Vere visited the Court later on it was reported
that Mountjoy would not speak to him.[2]

The main Spanish fleet was fitting out in the adjacent ports
of Ferrol and Coruña under command of Don Martin de Padilla.
The Queen, in her instructions to Essex, began by saying that
the Spanish preparations were the reason for the English expedition. He was to make for Ferrol and to assail the enemy by land
and sea. If the Spanish fleet had already sailed, he was to seek it
out and defeat it. That accomplished, he had permission to intercept the treasure fleet at the Azores. The weak point in these
orders was that the lure of gold was likely to act as a magnet,
dragging the fleet towards the Azores from the beginning.
Though the Cadiz venture had been successful, it had caused a
great deal of trouble. Officers, soldiers, and seamen alike had
become demoralized by loot and the desire to get home with it.
All discipline had been lost. The relations between Ralegh and
Essex had not been good, though the latter's generous spirit was
ready for a fresh start.

Essex was passing through a period of tension. As always
when on service, he was overworking himself. His political
affairs had not been going well. His worst foe, Lord Cobham,
had been appointed Warden of the Cinque Ports against his
own candidate, Sir Robert Sidney. He had wanted the two great
offices of Master of the Ordnance and Earl Marshal, and, though
he had been granted the former on 10 March, 1597, the greater
prize eluded him. He obtained it on 18 December of that year.
It was after his return from Cadiz, before he had obtained the
Ordnance, that his friend Francis Bacon addressed to him the
celebrated, subtle, and strangely sinister letter on how to fill the
role of favourite. He said that he did not like either of the offices

[1] Vere, pp. 45-7.
[2] De l'Isle and Dudley, Vol. II, p. 389.

coveted by Essex because both were related to martial greatness, and that was dangerous. The general theme of the letter was that, for the man who would rise to supreme heights, the military ladder was the more unstable. The effect of mounting that way was apt to be excessive popularity with the mob, and this was unsafe with a sovereign—the hint was that it was particularly unsafe with Elizabeth.[1]

The warning was not unjustified when addressed to a man as proud and headstrong as Essex. The Court of Queen Elizabeth did not resemble that of Henry III of France, where daggers slipped from their sheaths without sound or warning, yet it was a place of passions and dangers—dangers not only from rivals but from the Sovereign herself. The Queen was a kind and even a forbearing mistress, yet one who might at any moment strike down a too presumptuous favourite and his too devoted followers. A group about Essex, including Mountjoy, was involved in this peril. Two of those taking part in this expedition were to die with Essex on the scaffold, and it may be that only a combination of last-minute prudence and good fortune saved Charles from that fate. And after the Scottish King came in their foes, Ralegh, Cobham, and Grey, were to find themselves in a similar extremity. Too much grandeur was something to be avoided, as the astute mind of Bacon perceived. The elements of genius in Essex, together with "that kind of urbanity or innate courtesy", which won the Queen and the people, bound his political and social friends closely to him.[2] Among the closest was Mountjoy, the lover of his beloved sister. Now Essex, in a condition of over-strain even for him, and they with him, were bound upon a highly ambitious venture.

The remainder of Bacon's argument has not yet been given. The danger of greatness might be lessened by keeping away from military affairs, by acting as minister and statesman, not as warrior. The statesman could make the soldier his servant, and power was surely better than martial fame. Sound or not, the argument was not one likely to appeal to the ardent Essex. Its conclusion, however, is of interest from our point of view. Bacon advised Essex, after having raised himself above military affairs,

[1] Spedding, Vol. II, p. 41.
[2] Naunton, p. 51.

to bring in some martial man to look after them and get the Queen's assent to his being made a member of the Privy Council. He should, however, take care to choose one who would not oppose him as the result of any past grudge. "I judge", he wrote, the fittest to be my Lord Mountjoy or my Lord Willoughby".[1]

The coupling of Mountjoy with Willoughby and still more the placing of the names in that order must be accounted remarkable, even though Bacon was on terms of friendship with the former. Willoughby, though a peer, was virtually a professional soldier, who had succeeded Leicester in command in the Netherlands and had been constantly in arms. The Queen was not alone then in her high opinion of Mountjoy as a "martial man".

[1] Spedding, Vol. II, p. 44.

VII

TO THE ISLANDS

THE allied forces assembled for the expedition of 1597 were formidable. The fleet consisted of 120 sail. About half were ships of war, the Queen's Navy being represented by seventeen, including two Spanish prizes taken at Cadiz the previous year. The rest were privately owned English ships equipped for war, a Dutch squadron, transports, pinnaces and small craft, and supply ships. The troops numbered 6,000, including the trained men from the Netherlands brought over by Vere. The English rightly avoided the Spanish custom of crowding ships of war with soldiers, but on this occasion two companies were allotted to each of the prizes because their accommodation was particularly good.[1]

The venture started with a series of exasperating delays. The fleet was held up at Dover, where some of the troops were embarked. It then sailed down Channel to Weymouth, where more troops awaited it. By now, hanging about in contrary winds had resulted in heavy inroads into the provisions, none too lavishly provided to begin with. On 6 July Essex landed and held a council of war composed of Howard, Mountjoy, Christopher Blount, Ralegh, and George Carew, with Fulke Greville in attendance. It decided that Greville should ride post-haste to Court and see the Queen personally, revealing the difficulties, urging her not to let the enterprise collapse for want of support, and begging her to provide a month's supply of victuals for fleet and army. While an answer was awaited the fleet made its way to Plymouth in bad weather, which found out its deficiencies. Some of the ships were leaky and a proportion of the pressed crews were almost useless land-lubbers. The

[1] Stow, p. 783; Monson, p. 38; Corbett: *The Successors of Drake*, p. 170.

Queen and Council, far from giving up, entrusted the supply of the fleet to Marmaduke Darrell, a contractor able to handle victualling on a very big scale and who was to serve Mountjoy well in Ireland. They insisted that all provisions should be of good quality.[1]

The year was getting on and the programme, the destruction of the Spanish fleet at Ferrol and Coruña and then a cruise about the Azores, was extensive. Though the art of ship-building was improving and though ships of that age made some remarkable voyages in bad weather, few were sound and staunch enough to stand continuous heavy buffeting. It was recognized that to keep a fleet at sea for any considerable period after October was risky. Many years later Sir Clowdisley Shovell wrote that an admiral who did so ought to be shot. Time was still not pressing, but it was not now plentiful. Essex therefore put to sea without awaiting the fresh victuals, doubtless intending that Darrell's supply ships should follow him. The fleet was divided into four squadrons: the first under Essex himself, the second under Howard, the third under Ralegh, and the fourth under the Dutchman Duyvenvoord. Mountjoy and his friend Southampton were allotted to the squadron of Essex. The squadrons were to sail individually, the rendezvous being "the North Cape", Cape Ortegal, some forty miles north-east of Ferrol.

Once again Essex had no luck. On 11 July, the second day, the wind rose to gale force. Immediately the flagship sprang a leak and Essex had to struggle back into Falmouth. The big prizes *St. Matthew* and *St. Andrew*, in Ralegh's squadron, proved unmanageable. Spanish seamanship was often criticized, but, despite improvement in ship-building, this suggests that it was most of all their ships which were at fault. English captains and crews could do no more with these two than Spanish. Ralegh stood by them till they gave up. In short, ships representing roughly the squadrons of Essex, Ralegh, and Duyvenvoord all put back. Nobody knew what had happened to that of Howard. In fact he had pursued his voyage with more ships than his original squadron, Mountjoy and Southampton having accompanied him.

[1] Salisbury, Pt. VII, pp. 291, 339.

Lord Thomas Howard was of different stuff from the other English commanders. Though the son of a duke, he was a sailor by profession, a good seaman, a salt. Admirals of this type not only possess knowledge and experience but generally contrive to have smarter crews and ships in better trim than others. He had ridden out the gale, which must have been trying for Mountjoy in the *Defiance*, since she had been damaged in collision coming out of the Sound. By 20 July wind and sea had abated sufficiently for Mountjoy, Southampton, and others to come aboard the flagship for a council, which decided to sail for the rendezvous in hope of meeting the rest of the fleet there. Howard sent back the *Tramontana* to report his action. On the 25th he sighted the Spanish coast. He defiantly made boards off-shore, taking care to let the Spaniards have a good look at his squadron, but nothing came out of Ferrol or Coruña. Mountjoy was at least having some excitement on his first long cruise.[1]

Essex was now in a difficult position, through no fault of his own but because his fleet was not good enough. He made a commendably quick job of repairing the damaged ships and by 29 July was awaiting a wind to sail again. He had sent a message to Howard and Mountjoy bidding them wait for him and meanwhile avoid action, but it did not reach the Vice-Admiral, and the latter decided to return. The lost squadron entered Plymouth Sound on the 31st. Sickness was spreading, especially among the troops. The weakest point of Essex was his impatience when balked, when he was apt to propound risky schemes. Having learnt from Howard that he had affronted the Spaniards in their own ports and that they had not come out to attack him, Essex now reached the comforting but facile conclusion that this was because the fleet of the Adelantado was unfit to put to sea. In that case there seemed no need for the expedition to go to Ferrol or Coruña. Why not sail for the Cuban port of Havana with the best half of the fleet and intercept the treasure fleet there? He called another council on that question and found Vere a dissentient, on the grounds of shortage of provisions and the danger of leaving the Channel open to the Spanish fleet. Essex and Howard rode to Court to put the project before the

---

[1] Purchas, p. 1940; Corbett: *The Successors of Drake*, pp. 170-7; C.S.P. Dom., 1595-7, p. 480.

Queen, leaving Mountjoy and Ralegh in command. Elizabeth probably expressed herself forcibly, but the General and the Vice-Admiral did not tell Vere what she had said. On their return, he remarks drily, no more was heard of that voyage.[1]

Despite all accidents, Essex remained determined to effect something. While embayed by unfavourable winds he had got rid of some bad transports, bad seamen, and sick soldiers. He had sent away certain of the numerous voluntary gentlemen who were prostrated by sea-sickness, including his brother-in-law, Lord Rich, who, he said, would have died in a week if again taken to sea.[2] Now he decided on a new plan: to discharge all troops except Vere's veterans and leave behind still more ships. This plan had the advantage of making victuals go further, but, on the other hand, a thousand soldiers and such a contingent of sailors as the fleet could spare would not suffice for a landing against strong opposition. An attack on the Spanish fleet at Ferrol mainly by fireships now seemed the best that could be hoped for. The Queen gave her approval, but he does not seem to have waited for it. On 14 August the right wind came at last and he got the fleet out of the Sound. And then, luckless man, the wind shifted again and blew onshore! Infuriating as it must have been, this proved no disadvantage, since Darrell's ten supply ships arrived on the 17th. Essex sensibly gave orders that victualling should begin and should continue until there was a fair wind, after which the supply ships should follow the fleet. That night the wind went to the north and the fleet happily ran before it.[3]

One looker-on apparently did not think that the General was finished with his difficulties. During the long wait at Plymouth Sir Robert Cecil had written to him in strangely jocose vein that in the next storm it would be necessary to throw Jonah into the sea. Jonah being the captain of the *Warspite*. Now the captain of the *Warspite* was Ralegh. "I am a little saucy," wrote the Secretary, "but I love to prattle with you whilst I may". Cecil did not commonly prattle without reflection and there has been some suspicion that in this instance he was trying to increase

[1] Vere, pp. 29-50.

[2] Devereux, Vol. II, p. 447.

[3] C.S.P. Dom., 1595-7, pp. 477-8; Salisbury, Pt. VIII, pp. 352, 355; Corbett: *The Successors of Drake*, pp. 184-5.

the ill feeling between the rivals. The interpretation may be unjust, but Cecil was assuredly pessimistic about the venture. Writing on the 21st to Lord Burgh, Lord Deputy of Ireland, he informed him that the fleet had sailed victualled for ten weeks as the result of the dismissal of the land army. But, he went on, the Spanish fleet at Ferrol would not be burnt; the carracks from the East Indies were home; the Islands could not be taken; and there were only "weak, watery, hopes" to nourish the spirits of the noble Earl.[1]

This time the rendezvous was Cape Finisterre, about half-way between Coruña and Vigo, but a strong westerly wind drove the fleet towards its original destination, Cape Ortigal. The prizes again proved bad sailers. The *St. Andrew* lost her fore-mast and disappeared for three days. The *St. Matthew* was disabled off Coruña, but the determined George Carew got her into a French port, carried out the vital repairs, sailed home, laid hands on another ship, and started out again to join the fleet, though he did not succeed in doing so. Ralegh lived up to his reputation as Jonah. The *Warspite* was again disabled and could only reach southward in a wind which had turned easterly.

The moral effect was unfortunate because Essex for a time suspected that Ralegh was playing him a trick and intended to carry out an action on his own account. Material worries were more serious. Essex himself was delayed by a leak in his second flagship, the *Repulse*. The lost *St. Matthew* carried equipment for assault, certainly combustibles and probably some heavy guns. Several of the craft which were to have been used as fire-ships had followed Ralegh. On the other hand, prisoners stated that the Adelantado would not sail that year, though it was in truth unwise to rely on the evidence of the crews of coasters and fishermen in a matter of this kind. Most officers were eager to find an excuse for forgetting about Ferrol and making for the Azores, where untold riches might be met with. Essex was an honourable exception. He had a better strategic mind than any-one in the fleet, but, as on other occasions, he listened too readily to others. It must not be forgotten that he had been enjoined to act with the advice of his council. A council was

[1] C.S.P. Dom., 1595-7, p. 479; Salisbury, Pt. VII, p. 361.

called off Coruña and decided in favour of sailing straight to the Azores. A further excuse immediately reinforced the decision. Ralegh, waiting with some thirty ships off Lisbon for the main fleet, was informed at second hand that the Adelantado had already sailed from Ferrol for the Azores. This improbable tale was accepted and passed on to Essex, who sent a message to Ralegh bidding him follow the fleet to Flores. Whatever the Adelantado did or did not do provided a reason why the English fleet should make for the Islands.[1]

This time Essex made a quick passage. Passing by the island of Terceira, he looked into the most important roadstead in the Azores, that of Angra, and found it empty. Then he went on to Flores to water and take in food from his store-ships. He had more or less completed this business when, on 14 September, Ralegh arrived in the *Warspite*. According to Sir Arthur Gorges, Ralegh's friend and acting Captain, certain of the friends of Essex tried to set the General against the Rear-Admiral, alleging that he had purposely separated himself from the fleet. The extremists among the followers of Essex are known to have been Sir Christopher Blount, Sir Gilly Meyrick, and Sir Anthony Shirley. Mountjoy belonged as much as they to the Essex party, but he was better balanced and less bitter than they were. Neither then nor later is he named among those seeking to stir up trouble. Essex in fact received Ralegh in friendly fashion and told him that he had never doubted him.[2]

The Azores were of even greater strategic significance in the days of Spanish grandeur than they are today. They furnished watering-places, a supply base, and a haven of refuge to all shipping from American ports and most of that which came round the Cape. They had been until the reign of Philip II a Portuguese possession, and the inhabitants were Portuguese, with some slight Flemish mixture. The majority of the islanders disliked their new masters, but in one or two of the islands provided small garrisons of a militia type. Spain could not afford to garrison the islands fully with regular troops. Some of the troops were far from first-class: Gorges remarks that when Ralegh

---

[1] Vere, pp. 50-1; Monson, p. 53; Salisbury, Pt. VII, pp. 368-71; Corbett: *The Successors of Drake*, pp. 186-90.
[2] Purchas, p. 1942.

landed at Fayal, on which occasion the English troops hung
back, one hundred "Low Country Spaniards" might have beaten
him off, whereas some six times that number gave way before
him.

From the westernmost island of Flores—not always reckoned
in Elizabethan times as forming part of the Azores, though
under the same government as the rest—to the eastern islands
of San Miguel and Santa Maria is a distance of some three
hundred sea miles. In the centre is a group of five, Terceira,
Graciosa, San Jorge, Fayal, and Pico. Terceira, by virtue of the
harbour of Angra, was more valuable than all the other islands
put together. The aim of the Spaniards was to insure that any
ships which entered Angra should be safe from attack. Nothing
else was of prime importance, though it was inconvenient that
a hostile fleet could generally water and revictual at one of the
other islands. Two powerful forts covered the entrance to the
harbour, and the garrison consisted of about fourteen companies
of Spanish troops. The second island, from the strategic point
of view, was Fayal, also in the central group. Here also there
was a fort and a Spanish garrison.

While the ships which had come in with Ralegh were beginning to take in water and food, Essex with the remainder of the
ships of war set off to cruise, as he put it in a letter to Cecil, to
"keep the sea like a high constable to arrest all in the Queen's
name that pass by in thirty leagues space", whether it were the
Indies fleet or that of the Adelantado from Ferrol.[1] Since the
Indies fleet might pass out of sight of Flores, Essex had now
decided to fall back upon the central group, and later to San
Miguel in the eastern. Islands were parcelled out among
squadrons for supplies. Terceira was regarded as virtually
impregnable, but Fayal could be taken and, being the next
strongest, was allotted to Essex. The latter had hardly begun
his cruise when he sent a message to Ralegh, bidding him follow
to Fayal. Ralegh broke off his watering and sailed, but when he
reached Fayal found no sign of Essex and the rest of the fleet.
He waited for the General.

Two days went by, during which troops appeared to oppose
a landing. Ralegh held a council of war to decide whether to

[1] Devereux, Vol. I, p. 457.

land at once. The proposal to do so was opposed by Meyrick, but the council's advice was to wait only one day longer. The landing was carried out by seamen under covering fire from pinnaces. The resistance of the local Portuguese levies did not last long, but serious loss was suffered then, and later from fire from the fort, till the Spaniards abandoned it under pressure. Next morning, 22 September, the fleet was sighted.[1] Here was a pretty pother. Essex had earlier refused to believe that Ralegh was behaving selfishly. Now he was caught in the act. He lay open to blame from two points of view: the still surviving medieval regard for the chief as a paladin who must not be deprived of personal honour, and the more modern concern for discipline. He was called on to answer for his action before a full assembly of land and sea officers and reminded that landing without orders was forbidden on pain of death. He retorted that the veto did not apply to the principal commanders and that he as Rear-Admiral was one of them. Vere declares that some of the followers of Essex were again bitter and claims that no one showed less spleen than himself. Essex is said to have answered one who urged that he should bring Ralegh before a court-martial: "That I would do, if he were my friend". No evidence of the attitude of Mountjoy in this wretched affair is to be found. Characteristically, Lord Thomas Howard intervened to make peace. Ralegh spoke a few words of apology, which were accepted. Essex was hot-tempered as well as jealous, but he was also easily appeased.[2]

On 24 September the main body of the English fleet sailed for Graciosa. The best chance of intercepting the treasure fleet would have been to remain in the central group of islands, since, if it came, it would most probably make for Angra. Essex, however, now decided to go south-eastward to San Miguel, it is said on the advice of the master of his ship, "a dull, unlucky fellow named Gover". Meanwhile—by an error according to one account, on an order according to another—Monson in the *Rainbow* and Southampton in the *Garland* remained cruising north of Graciosa; Vere in the *Mary Rose* and Sir William Brooke in the *Dreadnought* between Graciosa and San Jorge.

[1] Purchas, pp. 1951-7.
[2] Vere, pp. 52-3; Purchas, pp. 1957-8; Wotton, p. 180.

And then, in the night, the West Indies Fleet, the fabulous
Flota, the very thought of which had year by year made the
mouths of English seamen water, arrived on the scene.

The *Rainbow*, indeed, found herself very close to it. Monson
took a boat to approach its course and hailed the nearest ship,
demanding what she was. Had the Spaniards attacked his ship,
she must have been taken, but they knew the English fleet was
in the islands and did not know how close at hand it might be.
They were determined not to dally but to get into Angra Roads.
Yet they were not scared. Mocking voices from the darkness
revealed the identity of the Flota, even shouted a boast of the
riches of its cargoes. Monson showed flares and shot off signal
guns, which were heard by Southampton and even by Vere,
though he was several miles away. Next morning Vere and
Brooke saw the Flota well ahead on its way to Terceira, and,
between them and it, the *Rainbow* and *Garland*. Monson
declares that he and Southampton made every effort to come up
with the Spaniards, but in Vere's opinion they were merely
hoping to catch a straggler and not pressing the pursuit. This
was unkind, as Vere often is, but if it were true their prudence
was not discreditable; there were some twenty-five sail in the
Spanish fleet, though most were small ships, and the best fighting power lay in the eight galleons of the Indian guard. The
English ships gained a little, but only because the Spanish
Admiral, Don Juan Guttierez de Garibay, made his leading
ships shorten sail and concentrated his fleet. That afternoon it
entered Angra Roads in good order.

Essex was lying off San Miguel when a pinnace brought him
the news. He at once sailed for Terceira with the bulk of the
fleet. On the way he came upon a big Spanish merchantman
from Havana, escorted by two frigates, and took all three. The
cargo is said to have equalled in value the cost of the whole
expedition. The wind now came from the north-west, and the
harbour was on the south side of Terceira. The fleet struggled
for two days and a half before the majority of the ships of war
contrived to weather the lofty point of Brasil to reach the
entrance.

Essex then sent in some experienced captains in a pinnace to
report upon the chances of reaching the Spanish fleet at its

anchorage. They brought back word that this was impossible. Still not satisfied, Essex tacked in in the flagship, followed by Mountjoy in the *Defiance* and some others. They found that the bottom of the bay, into which the Spanish ships had been warped, lay dead in the eye of the wind. To beat up to it would have taken all day, and on either tack the ships would have come under close fire from one of the forts. He thought it certain that some ships would have been driven aground and lost. The Spanish galleons showed so much of their white bellies that they were obviously riding high in the water after having been unladen. To go in would be to expose troops and ships to extreme risk, and all for the sake of an uncertain hope of burning empty ships. So many of his own ships had not yet watered and so much of the beer had leaked out of the casks that it was considered impossible to wait for a change of wind. He therefore decided to return to San Miguel.[1]

Here he met further trouble. On the beach in front of Punta del Gada, the chief town, the breakers were high, and 400 Spanish musketeers had entrenched to oppose a landing. Essex, therefore, left Ralegh in command of the fleet lying off the town and, accompanied by Howard, Mountjoy, and Vere, took 2,000 men in small vessels and ships' boats to seek a suitable beach. He hoped to move overland on Punta del Gada and take it with the aid of the fleet. After he had disappeared the expedition met with yet another disappointment. A small Brazilian ship came in and dropped anchor in the midst of the fleet. Following her was a huge carrack. Both captains took the English fleet to be the Spanish West Indies fleet. The carrack was warned, but had no hope of escape because she had by then reached a point between the English and the shore. Her captain promptly ran her aground and, as soon as the townsmen had taken off the crew and some of her most precious wares in their boats, set her afire. Ralegh hurried a party of men into such boats as Essex had left him, but too late. Before he could reach her she was a flaming furnace. The little ship, laden mostly with sugar, was taken, and from her crew it was learnt that the carrack carried enormous wealth. The record of her course afforded proof of the extraordinary voyages made by these

---

[1] Purchas, p. 1963; Devereux, Vol. I, p. 458.

Portuguese merchantmen, the biggest ships in the world. She had sailed from the East Indies round the Cape, watered at St. Helena, crossed to the Brazilian coast, and cruised through the West Indies, so that she was freighted with the riches of the east and the west. The fruits of what had probably been a two years' voyage went up in smoke under a regulation made by King Philip II; but that was small consolation to loot-hungry Ralegh.[1]

Essex landed at another town, Villa Franca, a few miles away. Everyone got wet in the process, but fortunately no opposition was encountered. Speaking for Ralegh, Gorges alleges that Villa Franca proved a Capua and that the old vice of English Elizabethan expeditions, loot for the sake of private gain, was rampant. On the side of Essex it is stated that the route between the two towns was too rough for guns and that the castle at Punta del Gada could not have been subdued without them. The Portuguese Governor of the island, Goncalo Vaz Continho, on the other hand, claims to have held up the English and captured a number of men from their foraging parties. At all events, Ralegh and his men waited in vain, until he was bidden to join Essex at Villa Franca. There watering was completed. Again the stories from the two sides differ greatly. The English accounts state that the withdrawal was a matter of no great difficulty. The Governor asserts that he captured seven guns, 70 boats, water-casks filled in readiness to be carried out to the fleet—this at least is an item which does not seem likely to have been invented—and that a considerable number of men were drowned in the last rush for the boats.[2]

Now October was come. The season called for immediate return; sick men and strained ships reinforced its argument. The Flota was safe under the guns of Angra, and no more ships were likely to arrive in the Islands that year. On 9 October the fleet sailed for England. The indiscipline shown on the return from Cadiz the previous year was repeated. Ships took their own course without regard to contact with the flagship. A storm blew up to increase the confusion and dispersion.

No evidence exists that any member of the expedition had given further thought to the Adelantado's fleet in Ferrol, but

[1] Purchas, p. 1964.
[2] Monson, pp. 68-70.

the wise head of the Queen had not forgotten it. She had on 16 October addressed a letter to Essex, grumbling that he had apparently missed the Flota. She had bidden him send back some of her own ships to meet the danger from the Spaniards and gone on to warn him that they would try to pick up stragglers and that he should take precautions against such an action.[1] This he had failed to do, but it must be doubted whether it was in any admiral's power to keep an Elizabethan fleet under control when it was on its way home after a long cruise. The Spanish fleet was in fact out. It was already at the mouth of the Channel.

Don Martin de Padilla had shown great energy in fitting out a fine fleet, but all his efforts had not availed to get it to sea in good time. Having moved from Ferrol to Coruña, he had been embayed there for three weeks; but even if he had got a favourable wind at once he would have been late for the expedition which he had in mind. He sailed on the very day on which Essex quitted San Miguel. The fighting section of his fleet was divided into four squadrons, one of them commanded by the best of the Spanish admirals, Pedro de Zubiaur, who in the course of a long life caused the English more loss than all the others put together. The total fleet was vast, even larger than that with which Essex had originally intended to sail and far larger than that which actually undertook the Islands Voyage. It numbered 136 ships, twenty being the King's and eleven of these of 400 tons or over, and carried some 9,000 troops, with reserves waiting in Brittany. The objective was Falmouth and the Adelantado's plan was to take it as quickly as possible, leave it held by a strong garrison, then drop back with the fighting fleet to await Essex off the Scillies, and in the event of a victory be prepared to tackle Plymouth next.[2]

There can be little or no doubt of the ability of the Spaniards to take Falmouth—which here means the bay, the ground commanding it, the fortifications, and especially Pendennis Castle. To hold it was another matter, involving sooner or later a battle with the English fleet. The English Government did not know

---

[1] Salisbury, Pt. VII, p. 433.
[2] Duro: *Armada Española*, Tomo III, pp. 162-4, 166; Salisbury, Pt. VII, pp. 455, 457; Corbett: *The Successors of Drake*, pp. 212-5.

that this was the goal, and it is doubtful whether five hundred men could have been put into the place in time to resist a landing. It was the navy which had always kept the Spaniards out, and now by far the greater part of the naval force of England was away, with the Spanish fleet between it and the English shore. Moreover, the English fleet itself was in danger. It was weaker to begin with than the Spanish and, whereas the English ships and men were worn out, the Spanish were fresh. Ralegh is known to have stowed his bigger guns in the hold because the *Warspite* was so badly strained, and he was probably not alone. Monson declares that a number of ships had lost masts, which presumably means that they were sailing under jury-masts. When the English commanders talked the matter over in council ashore, the sailors were of opinion that an English fleet meeting a Spanish on level terms would always fight with odds in its favour because English captains, ships, and gunnery were superior; in the present circumstances, however, they concluded that the odds would be on the Spaniards and they would be as likely to be victorious as the English would normally. It is curious that the naval campaign of 1597 has created so little attention. It might well be argued that the danger to England was as great as in the Armada campaign of 1588.

The matter was never put to the test, first, because the Adelantado abandoned his aim in consequence of his fleet being dispersed by the gale which Essex encountered, and, secondly, because the two fleets missed each other. The Government was taking hasty measures, commissioning the "great ships" lying at Chatham, actually recalling the land forces from France, when a letter dated 25 October arrived from Mountjoy at Plymouth. He had put in that day with four other ships, including Lord Southampton's *Garland*, and assumed command as Lieutenant-General of the expeditionary force. He had seen nothing of the Spaniards, but a pinnace had sailed into the midst of them and escaped. Sir Ferdinando Gorges had brought in 500 men to defend the town and the forts, but was short of artillery and ammunition. Mountjoy had judged it best to keep his five ships in the Hamoaze so that the wind which would bring the Spanish fleet into Plymouth Sound would allow them to put to sea.[1]

[1] Salisbury, Pt. VII, p. 443.

Essex must have come in next day or on the 27th at latest and ridden almost at once to Court, where he met with a chilly reception from the Queen. On the 29th Howard, Mountjoy, and Ralegh—who had landed at St. Ives and come overland to Plymouth—wrote to him that there was no further news of the Spanish fleet, but that Howard would put to sea with such ships as were ready and Ralegh would return to Cornwall, of which county he was Lord Lieutenant. Vere's men from the Low Countries were sent there. It soon became clear, however, that the Spaniards were gone, whereupon, in the usual way, the crews were discharged, the Queen's ships laid up, and the others returned to their owners.

The Islands Voyage had been an almost unrelieved failure. To go to the Azores at all without having looked into Ferrol was an imprudence. The port was difficult and dangerous to enter—another affair altogether from that of entering Cadiz—but Essex might at least have left some light vessels to watch it, with orders to report to him at one of the islands in the Azores, though, as matters turned out, news of the sailing of the Spanish fleet would not have reached him. That is one bad mark for his leadership. The suggestion has been made that, when he reached Terceira and found that the Adelantado was not there, his wisest course would have been to return to Ferrol. This is asking a lot of him and disregards his Queen's intense desire to capture the Flota. And, indeed, once in the Islands, he had as good a chance as any man in the course of the war of catching it. If he had got on terms with it while he had the bulk of his fleet with him he would have taken the better part of it. Richard Hawkins, who was a prisoner of war aboard one of the Spanish ships, wrote, in a letter to Essex which was smuggled away from Terceira, that the bulk of it consisted of small ships heavily laden and that the escort was altogether insufficient to withstand an English attack. Essex changed his mind too often on this voyage, but his fatal error was that of going to San Miguel. This verdict is not reached on the basis of wisdom after the event. Let it be admitted that Essex had heard from islanders some gossip to the effect that the Flota would not put into Angra Roads on this voyage. Even if that report had been worthy of credence, it would have been mere common sense to remain in the central group of islands. No harm could have come of doing so, whereas no good was likely to come of cruising, in a region of generally south-westerly winds, off the south-easternmost of the islands. The Flota reached Lisbon safely, but not until February, 1598.

It would be interesting to have Mountjoy's views on his friends' conduct of the enterprise, but he was too cautious to leave any record of them. Others made their comments, and the surly but loyal Vere defended Essex hotly to the Queen herself, actually shouting down arguments of the triumphant Ralegh faction in the garden at Whitehall. Essex, who had retired in dudgeon to Wanstead, was presently restored to favour, as indeed was just. He was a man in whose spirit the spark of genius always burned but was only at intervals blown to a white flame. Of the men of action in a reign rich in them he was the greatest personality after Drake and Philip Sidney. Yet a man of less inspiration but dowered with a little more calm, a little more patience, would have caught the Flota in the Islands, solved the Irish problem, and left a name as glorious as that of Drake. Mountjoy had food for reflection about the Islands Voyage, just as he was to have about the viceroyalty of Essex in Ireland, which left him with a Sisyphean labour. He would not fail for lack of calm or patience.

The result of the disbandment of the greater part of the military force before the expedition sailed had been that he had been given no opportunity of exercising the functions of Lieutenant-General in any real sense, except for the brief moment during which he assumed command of the defence of the West Country on his return. Queen Elizabeth certainly did not associate him with the failure of the voyage. Shortly after his arrival in England he was created a Knight of the Garter.

VIII

SHADOWS FROM IRELAND

THE Queen's last years were troubled by revolt in Ireland. Irish convulsions were nothing new; three rebellions of note had already occurred since she ascended the throne, besides many lesser broils. This was of another character altogether. Though Ulster had never been subdued, yet when, early in the reign, her Viceroy Sussex, and later Sir Henry Sidney, had advanced into the province to attack Shane O'Neill, about one thousand men had sufficed them, and part of this force had been of poor quality, the levies of the Pale known as "the rising out". Sussex and Sidney had marched with no fear of defeat. Their one foreboding, and it was well justified, was that they would fail to catch Shane. Now a far greater power confronted their successors.

The change was due to several causes, but, first and foremost, to one man. Hugh O'Neill, Earl of Tyrone, had been brought up —partly for his own safety after his youthful father had been killed by Shane O'Neill's men, partly in the hope of making him "a good subject"—at Penshurst. Robert Sidney as a boy had known him well. He spoke English, of course, and he wore English clothes; he had been anglicized enough to make it difficult for him to establish himself on his return. Then his own people, the purest Irish stock, the least touched by English influence, received him into their midst. They gave him unquestioning loyalty and obedience, but at the same time they encompassed him. He planned for them, mustered and trained them, led them to war; but they remoulded him, urged him forward, in a sense controlled him. An element of emotion—he and they alike were highly emotional—appears in their relationship. But for their influence he might have made his peace early. He was curiously hesitant at moments of crisis, when he sometimes let slip through his hands the reward of patient endeavour. English officers compared him to Hannibal after the victory of Cannae and quoted the Roman verdict: "Thou knowest how to overcome; but thou knowest not how to use victory".[1]

Tyrone's power had been increased because the English principle of *divide et impera* had broken down in Ulster. The O'Donnells of Tyrconnell or Donegal had provided some counter-balance to the strength of the O'Neills of Tyrone; had been at times allies of the English against them. Now the feud between the families had been healed, largely as the result of the ill-treatment of the young Hugh Roe O'Donnell, overlord of Donegal, at English hands. Hugh Roe lacked Tyrone's acumen and military genius, but he was the more ardent spirit, a goad to action when the cautious partner was inclined to temporize.

O'Neill was an organizer, a type not common in Ulster. The pith of his fighting force was constituted by his "bonaghts", professional soldiers billeted on the countryside when not under arms. He trained pikemen to fight in the European style from his own experience as a former ally of the English and with some aid from Spanish drill sergeants. He trained musketeers, and bought them muskets and calivers, powder and match, from Scotland. He made an army in place of the horde that had followed Shane. Yet it retained most—not quite all—the early virtues of mobility and invisibility. Tyrone fought by preference in defiles, in woods, in bogs. He rarely attacked by push of pike unless he had first weakened and worn out the enemy and if possible caused the opposing musketeers to expend all their ammunition.

The bigger and superior forces which he put into the field made it necessary to employ larger forces against him. Under the primitive Elizabethan system of recruitment that in itself handicapped the English. Troops were raised only when need was pressing and often long after it had become so. They were commonly sent on campaign before they had been trained or seasoned. Wastage from sickness was high. Thus most English armies during the Tyrone rebellion were raw.

[1] Moryson, Vol. II, p. 274.

Another factor in the strength of the Ulstermen was the increased use of firearms and the replacement of the harquebus by the musket and its lighter type, the caliver. At first sight this looks strange, but British soldiers on the North-west Frontier of India would have had no difficulty in understanding that the long-range weapon, provided it was one carried and fired by a single man, favoured the irregular. The caliver proved an ideal weapon for the Irish skirmisher, and it was fortunate for the English that Tyrone could not obtain all the firearms he wanted. The Irish often became better marksmen than the English. A battle or combat on the march, upon ground chosen by the Irish, was now attended with heavy risks. From about 1595 letters from Ireland are full of dolorous reports of the growing efficiency of the rebel troops and in some instances statements that they were superior to the English. The most celebrated English soldier of his day, Sir John Norris, was sent over, but he obtained no appreciable success.

A third factor had as yet scarcely made itself felt, except as a new menace. Spain had, a little surprisingly, refused to take much interest in Ireland, though offering a refuge to men who fled the country and expressing sympathy with them. Here a change was appearing. A policy of intervention had been adopted by Philip II, though not yet carried out, and not to be in his lifetime. Yet in 1596 the first cargo of arms was landed at Killybegs in Donegal, probably better firearms than those from Scotland, and free of charge, whereas nothing for nothing was to be got from the Scots. The King's envoy also brought the promise of a Spanish expeditionary force, and Tyrone professed himself eager to accept from Philip a Spanish Governor of Ireland.

It is difficult to give a date for the start of Tyrone's rebellion because it opened with a period of half war, and that was broken by truces and pardons. In August, 1598, when, to the Government's discredit, there had been no viceroy since the death of Lord Deputy Burgh in the previous autumn, the English suffered a crushing disaster. The Anglo-Irish Earl of Ormonde was military Lieutenant-General of the kingdom, but he delegated to the Marshal, Sir Henry Bagenal, the task of relieving and revictualling the Blackwater fort, besieged by Tyrone.

Calling O'Donnell to his aid, Tyrone attacked the English on the march between Armagh and the Blackwater and inflicted upon them the heaviest defeat ever suffered by English arms from Irish in Ireland. Bagenal was killed and the remnant of his force was driven back in flight into Armagh, in such a state as to be useless. It was a grievous blow both materially and morally. The main body of the Irish garrison had been virtually destroyed. Yet it had been over three thousand strong and a fairly good army by the standard of the time in Ireland, including what remained of the troops from the Netherlands who had sailed with Essex and Mountjoy on the Islands Voyage. The battle was followed by rebellion all over the country. Armagh was abandoned. Tyrone and O'Donnell sent forces into Munster, and with their aid the natives wiped out the English colony on the escheated Desmond estates. The settlement in Leix and Offaly met with much the same fate. The veteran Ormonde, used to Irish warfare since the reign of Mary, did his best. The walled towns were the framework of the English power, and he preserved them by running in arms and munitions to those that could not be reached by sea. He could accomplish little more, but that much counted.[1]

Since the stirring days that followed his return from the Islands, Mountjoy had been living a relatively quiet life. The fortifications of Portsmouth were complete, and peers who were governors of naval ports did not sit in them unless there was urgent need for their presence; not always even then. He bore a fair amount of responsibility for the district because, besides being Governor and High Steward of Portsmouth, he was also joint Lord Lieutenant of Hampshire with the Marquess of Winchester, and Warden of the New Forest. When, however, he took part in the Islands Voyage and the sole charge of the county of Southampton fell upon Winchester, a kinsman of the latter's, Hampden Paulett, was appointed Lieutenant-Governor of Portsmouth, in which post he would command any forces of the county assigned to the relief or defence of the town. On the death of Winchester, it was considered advisable in March, 1599,

---

[1] A full account of events in Ireland at this period, of the recruitment, organization, supply, and tactics of English forces and of Tyrone's new army, is given in the writer's book, *Elizabeth's Irish Wars*. Only the barest sketch can find room here.

to appoint two Deputy Lieutenants of the county, Sir Thomas West and Hampden Paulett.[1]

Excitement and apprehension flared up momentarily in February, 1598. Sir Robert Cecil was about to set off to France as Ambassador Extraordinary. The Queen of England had been invited by the King of France to take part in the negotiations between his country and Spain. In point of fact, Cecil's mission was to deter Henry IV from making peace. The prospects were not good to begin with, but, such as they were, they were ruined by the action of the Spaniards, their second brilliant *coup* concerned with Calais. A Spanish fleet passed up Channel unmolested and landed 4,000 troops there. At once there occurred the usual bustle, inevitable in days when navies and armies had to be mobilized in every emergency. Mountjoy hurried to his post at Portsmouth, Lord Cobham to Dover, Ralegh on a tour of the coast to collect naval stores. Cecil was ordered not to put to sea. He disregarded or failed to receive the letter, showing considerable nerve, and announced his arrival at Dieppe on 19 February. He mentioned that he had had a rough passage in the *Vanguard* and that, among other members of his suite, young Charles Blount, Mountjoy's kinsman, had been very sick. Then the anxiety was forgotten, but Henry's determination to make peace had been strengthened.[2]

Otherwise the year 1598 was not active, except in Ireland, where it was disastrous. At sea the chief event was the Earl of Cumberland's capture of Puerto Rico, where Drake had failed. On the Continent, Spain, finding her hands too full, abandoned her Channel holdings, Calais and Blavet, as the price for peace with France, signed at Vervins in April. An age seemed to be out when Burghley died, just before Tyrone's victory at the Yellow Ford. Philip II lived to hear the Irish news, which brought him comfort, and that of Cumberland's great privateering expedition, which brought him none. Then he too passed away.

The indecision and procrastination of Tyrone, who may have believed that he could gain his ends without a death-

[1] A.P.C., Vol. XXVII, p. 200; Vol. XXIX, p. 281.
[2] C.S.P. Dom., 1598-1601, pp. 26, 29; Corbett: *The Successors of Drake*, pp. 228-32.

struggle, afforded the Queen and her Council more respite than they deserved. As often happened, long discussions and negotiations preceded the despatch of a new Viceroy—they had, of course, begun after the death of Lord Burgh in September, 1597. Here was one office at least for which there was no strong competition, and even less after than before the Battle of the Yellow Ford. A reputation and a career might be sunk in an Irish bog more quickly than anywhere else. Before the disaster several names had been mentioned. One was Sir William Russell, Burgh's predecessor; but he had had enough of Ireland. Another was Sir Walter Ralegh; but this proposal by Essex was too clearly due to desire to see a rival removed from Court. That was a weighty consideration and one of the causes of delay in reaching a choice. Either faction would have been pleased to send a stalwart of the other into the exile of Dublin; neither wanted to let its stalwarts go. So the Cecil party submitted Sir William Knollys, Essex's uncle, and Essex used his power to veto that proposal. Essex put forward the name of Sir George Carew, a friend of both Robert Cecil and Ralegh, though apparently not particularly hostile to himself. At this stage, about midsummer, 1598, he lost his temper in the Queen's presence and she boxed his ears. Off he went, as usual when out of favour, to Wanstead. The Yellow Ford stirred him out of his sulks, and in September he was allowed to return to Court.

By now the appointment of a Viceroy had become more urgent and his high quality more important. An ingredient of quality was prestige. So the signs pointed to Essex, whose prestige had suffered but a slight check on the Islands Voyage and who was regarded as unquestionably the greatest English general —no other, said Francis Bacon, could "ascend near him in competition".[1] Yet the wretched political issue created further delay because it scared those who had to make a decision. They can be compared to a group of betting men watching the bookmakers' market in Tattersalls before venturing to put their money on. The Council feared to put Essex forward lest he should believe they wanted to get rid of him and undermine him when he was gone. He probably hesitated to put himself forward lest he should be accused of excessive military ambition, and he

[1] Spedding, Vol. II, p. 43.

certainly suspected that if he went his foes would destroy him and his friends.[1]

What of the Queen herself? She had always been a believer in that "noble, wise man", Mountjoy. Little had occurred to confirm her intuition that he was exceptionally able since she had written those words because he had had little opportunity to prove it on the Islands Voyage. Yet she was prepared to put him to this severe test. She prophesied that it would fall to him to extinguish the rebellion and bring her in peace to the grave. "The Queen and most of her Council cast their eyes upon Charles Blount, Lord Mountjoy". Again Essex objected, and this time indicated that he was a candidate. "But Essex closely gave them to know that he (Mountjoy) was of no experience that way, only but that he had been a captain in Holland and Brittany; that he had not means enough, nor clients good store, and that he was too much given to studies". So the old reproach of knowing war only from books was revived. Essex concluded that the new Viceroy should be a man of great honour, great wealth, beloved of soldiers, and with previous experience as a general. These qualifications were desirable, but no one had them to the same degree as himself.[2]

We move now amid evidence that is uncertain and may be tainted, a state of affairs which continues to the end of the Essex drama and Mountjoy's connexion with it. No necessity exists, however, to analyse the conduct of Cecil and Bacon or to decide whether or not they desired to send Essex to his doom. What is clear is that, having taken the decision to go, he afterwards doubted its wisdom, though at first his words had been brave: "I have beaten Knollys and Mountjoy in the Council, and by God I will beat Tyrone in the field; for nothing worthy her Majesty's honour hath yet been achieved".[3] Ireland represented the supreme task. Whether he liked it or not, he could not afford, now that he had reached the summit, to let another man undertake it. Mountjoy's views at this time are not known. Later, when Essex returned, he was to do his best to avoid being sent to Ireland.

---

[1] Abbott, p. 106.
[2] Camden, p. 237.
[3] *Nugae Antiquae*, Vol. II, p. 29.

The dangerous delays continued into the spring. At last, however, all was arranged. On 27 March, 1599, Essex rode out of London, accompanied by a gallant band of noblemen and gentlemen. The streets were crowded, and for four miles from the outskirts of the city the people thronged the fields and jostled to lay eyes upon him, crying out: "God bless your Lordship! God preserve your Honour!". Some of them followed him until the evening. He was the most popular man in England, the hero of the nation.[1]

The stream of his popularity flowed warmly beneath the sun, but it had chilly under-currents. In instructed minds foreboding was present. Suspicion that all was not what it appeared to outward view haunted acute observers. This uneasiness appears in sinister form in the letter from Robert Markham to Sir John Harington, commissioned to take a company or squadron of cavalry to Ireland. Harington was enjoined to be careful in the extreme, to obey the Lord Lieutenant in everything but keep his opinions to himself, lest they should be heard in England. If Essex performed in the field what he had promised in the Council all would be well, but, though the Queen seemed to have placed her confidence in him, Markham knew not what to think. When a man had so many open friends and so many secret enemies, who could prophesy what his end would be?

"Observe the man who commandeth, and yet is commanded himself; he goeth not forth to serve the Queen's realm but to humour his own revenge. Be heedful of your bearings; speak not your mind to all you meet. I tell I have ground for my caution. Essex hath enemies; he hath friends too. Now there are two or three of Mountjoy's kindred sent out in your army; they are to report all your conduct to us at home".[2]

Both sides had their reporters in the army, and to be ill reported on by either might be dangerous. The suggestion in the last sentence is that Mountjoy had appointed his kinsmen, Sir Christopher and the young Sir Charles, to watch elements hostile to Essex.

The sequel, though one of the most celebrated episodes in Elizabethan history, is often misunderstood. Essex did not, as is

[1] Stow, p. 788.
[2] *Nugae Antiquae*, Vol. I, p. 288.

asserted, suddenly prove that everyone had been mistaken in him by revealing himself to be completely incompetent. Nor did he rush blindly into action without advice from the experienced. He took advice from the Irish Council when it would have been better to follow his own instincts. Though capable of fine strategic conceptions, he had never been an organizer and he failed in organization now. He had always had an eye for tactics, and one cannot quarrel with his tactics in Ireland. The task before him was stiffer than that which confronted English generals in the Netherlands. The only tactical defeats suffered while he was in Ireland were those incurred by subordinates fighting independently. Yet his viceroyalty was the most disastrous of the Queen's reign.

He began with every advantage. He was appointed Lord Lieutenant, being the first to bear that title since the Earl of Sussex, Elizabeth's first Viceroy, instead of the humbler title of Lord Deputy. He was given by far the biggest army ever sent to Ireland, nominally 16,000 foot and 1,500 horse, an establishment later increased, though, as always, the real strength was a good deal lower than the strength by the list. Most of these troops had been hastily levied, but about one-eighth consisted of well-trained men from the Continent.

The Irish cause depended on Tyrone, who lay in the north with the bulk of his forces, apparently undecided what to do next or inclined to caution till the Spaniards arrived. The obvious course seemed to be to move straight against him. The timid Irish Council urged Essex to clean up Leinster first and then march north in June or July, when he would find ample grazing for his cavalry and train. He agreed. He decided on "a present prosecution in Leinster, being the heart of the whole kingdom", and left Dublin on 10 May to join his army in Kildare. If he had kept to his programme all might have been well, but he discarded or forgot it. Accompanied by Ormonde after they had joined hands at Athy, he went on down into Munster, and even there no enemy met him. The only fighting was the capture of Caher Castle, where a rebel force disputed his passage of the Suir, and a combat in a defile. Both affairs he managed well, and indeed showed himself competent whenever the enemy appeared.

Afterwards he carried out a progress rather than a campaign. The towns—Kilkenny, Clonmel, Limerick, and Waterford— with their English blood and tradition of allegiance, welcomed and flattered him. Rushes were strewn in his path. Mayors greeted him with high-flown addresses of loyalty, in bad Latin or indifferent English. It was delightful to find everyone as enthusiastic as at home.[1]

Then he was awakened by ill news. A force which he had left to subdue the O'Byrnes in the wild Wicklow glens had been defeated and chased out with slaughter and in shameful panic. He decided that he must return. He did not follow his original route, "through the tribes", perhaps because he was not sure of getting through that way, but moved up the Wicklow coast. He had to face serious fighting now, and he showed great energy. Yet he and his army were both sick and dispirited. Moving up and down the south, he had marched his men off their feet. The weather was wetter than usual, as many have since declared it always is. Disease was rife. While his strength was diminished by sickness—and by a small reinforcement which he had left in the south—he was accompanied and cumbered by a horde of Irish horse-boys and women more numerous than the soldiers.

Back in Dublin, he had to face reproaches from the Queen, who divined that his expedition, save for the revictualling of a few garrisons, had been without military value. Next came news of a defeat heavier than that in the Wicklow glens. Sir Conyers Clifford, Governor of Connaught, set out in early August with the immediate object of relieving an Irish loyalist, O'Connor Sligo, in his castle of Collooney, and also to make easier an invasion of Ulster by Essex. In the Curlieu Hills Clifford was routed and killed—and O'Connor went over to the enemy. Essex had not gone against Tyrone in the spring on the ground that it was too early; now it was getting late. His garrisons needed many troops and, together with his losses, reduced his striking force to about four thousand. Yet he had to do something to appease the Queen and public opinion. The oft-quoted lines of Chorus, describing the return of Henry V to London from France, suggests how eagerly a victory was looked for.

[1] *Nugae Antiquae*, Vol. II, pp. 31-59.

The mayor and all his brethren in best sort,
Like to the senators of the antique Rome,
With the plebeians swarming at their heels,
Go forth and fetch their conquering Caesar in:
As, by a lower but loving likelihood,
Were now the general of our gracious empress—
As in good time he may—from Ireland coming,
Bringing rebellion broachéd on his sword,
How many would the peaceful city quit
To welcome him!

William Shakespere probably put these lines in to please his friend Southampton, serving in Ireland. One commentator professes to see in them a trace or two of uneasiness; at least we do not discern complete confidence.[1]

A letter written as he put foot in stirrup does not suggest that Essex looked for a victory. The troops were murmuring, and for the first time in his career he was not served by that spell which is so great a gift of leadership. He marched on 28 August. At Ardee, in Louth, Tyrone appeared in superior strength, but did not attack. Indeed, he sent a flag of truce to propose a parley. The two commanders agreed to talk in private across a ford over the Lagan; but, the stream proving too wide, Tyrone, always well-mannered, rode into it. For half an hour they talked, Essex on dry land, the Irishman in the water up to his horse's belly. In that age, and especially in the situation of Essex, only a man grievously overstrained—or a traitor—would have conversed thus with a rebel leader without witnesses. After some days of negotiation a truce was signed, with arrangements for renewal and the proviso that it should be terminable by fourteen days' notice.

This was bad enough, but worse was to follow. Essex had been forbidden to return without leave; now he disobeyed the order. His motives appear to have been mixed. He desired to report by word of mouth the proposals of Tyrone which he alone had heard and which had not been recorded at the time—but permission for a visit to England for that purpose could have been given or refused within a fortnight. He was physically ill and psychologically sick of the country. He was inspired by an

[1] Strachey, p. 204.

impulse to reassert himself, win back the Queen's favour, and defeat his enemies at home. According to the evidence of Sir Christopher Blount at his trial, Essex had contemplated a more desperate course. He had proposed taking with him two or three thousand men to cover him at his landing until he had raised enough adherents in England to allow him to go further, but had been dissuaded by Blount.[1] He sailed on 24 September, rode hard to London and on to the Court at Nonsuch, where he went straight to the Queen's bedchamber. She was at her toilet, with her hair about her face. Shock tactics indeed! At first they succeeded, but the success did not outlast the day. She had often been enraged with him, but never before had he frightened her. She was rather frightened now in her ignorance of how deep his designs went. He was ordered to keep his chamber. On 1 October he was placed in the charge of the Lord Keeper, Sir Thomas Egerton, at York House.

The opposing factions were clearly defined. On 29 September Cecil went to dinner with the Earls of Shrewsbury and Nottingham (the former Lord Howard of Effingham), Lord Thomas Howard, Sir George Carew, and the three extreme foes of Essex: Lords Cobham and Grey and Sir Walter Ralegh. On the other side the Earls of Worcester and Rutland, the Lords Rich and Mountjoy, Lord Harry Howard—though he was thought to be more or less neutral—Sir William Knollys, Sir Edward Dyer, and Lord Lumley did not hide their sympathies for Essex. Lord Effingham, Nottingham's son, was seen in this company. Rich's name is somewhat surprising, not because any doubt existed that he was a supporter of his brother-in-law but because he was not a bold man. After Essex had been sent into confinement men became tautened by excitement. Courtiers were watching each other, probing each other's minds. There seems to have been little substance in the story that Essex had brought a large body of adherents with him, but within a few days a number of his knights and officers, some of them wild and reckless, arrived in London. Rowland Whyte, reporting to Sir Robert Sidney, who was in the Essex circle but not near its centre, was glad his patron was at his post in the Netherlands.[2]

[1] Spedding, Vol. II, p. 356.
[2] De l'Isle and Dudley, Vol. II, pp. 395-8.

Once more names for Ireland were bandied about. Whyte thought that if Sidney had been at home he might have been sent. This time, however, Mountjoy was indicated more clearly than before. "He laboureth the contrary", wrote an observer in December, 1599, though by then the matter was settled.[1] He said that he would not be able to stand the climate, and may have been serious because from now onwards he was worried about his health. He may, on the other hand, have taken this line in the hope that Essex would be sent back. His credit was still high with the rebels. Tyrone liked him and might not preserve the truce unless he returned. The Queen and her Council had been angered by the truce, which appeared to them ignominious; but, since it had been signed, they did not want it broken in a hurry. Again according to the well-informed Whyte, Mountjoy was at the end of October told to prepare himself for the mission, but privately informed by Cecil that there was no hurry. The most obvious explanation is that the Secretary thought Essex might go again. Another factor in Mountjoy's objection to the appointment may have been his attachment to Penelope Rich. Ireland might represent a long task—it was to be one of nearly three and a half years—and, in the Queen's present mood, a task from which there would be no leave.

A graver consideration lay upon his mind. The subject now to be approached is shrouded in fog, and we find it hard to decide to what extent the glimpses caught amidst its eddies represent realities, chimeras, or inventions. The basis was the succession to the throne. It was a topic which the Queen would not discuss. She had, when pressed, declared to her second Parliament: "I stay it for your benefit, for if you should have liberty to treat of it there be so many competitors . . . some would speak for their master, some for their mistress, and every man for his friend, that it would be an occasion of a greater charge than a subsidy"—in other words, it would provoke bloodshed.[2] That was over thirty years ago, but she had not changed her view, more insistent though the question had become.

The task of unravelling the knotty problem of the succession need not here be attempted. In brief, the best legal title may

[1] Gawdy, p. 108.
[2] Rowse, p. 298.

have been that of the Suffolk line, but the most obvious successor was James VI of Scotland.[1] Were he to be rejected as an alien, next could come the Lady Arabella Stuart, like him descended from Henry VII, but born and domiciled in England. A formidable pretender was the Infanta Isabella, wife of the Archduke Albert. A dozen names or more were talked of, but few seriously, and the common sense of the majority of those who counted pointed to James VI. Essex and his adherents professed to believe that the men in the highest offices favoured the Spanish Infanta. This was a fantastic theory, which may have bubbled out of the conflict between the peace party of Cecil and the war party of Essex and the negotiations which led to the abortive conference between representatives of England, Spain, and the Archdukes at Boulogne, in May, 1600. Setting aside the possibility that Essex and the others believed Cecil to be the champion of the Infanta—which is virtually incredible—if they could prove to James that they were *his* champions, they would make sure of his favour in the event of his succession and might derive present benefit from his support against Cecil.

According to the confession of Lord Southampton, Mountjoy came to him on the confinement of Essex and said that he had always foreseen his ruin; he had therefore sent a message to the King of Scots desiring him to take some action to prevent England from being wholly given over to his enemies. Sir Charles Danvers said of this incident that Mountjoy had protested he was acting out of a sense of duty to Queen and country and did not consider the country would be safe unless it were strengthened against the assaults of its potent enemies (the Spaniards), who claimed the right of succession to its throne. This is the evidence of men in direst peril of their lives and relying upon memory. Yet the story may be accepted as true in substance.[2]

Towards the end of October Mountjoy is alleged to have taken a more reprehensible step. He was now under orders for Ireland. He was leaving behind him a friend who was not only under confinement but gravely ill and distracted in mind. Again according to the declaration of Sir Charles Danvers, one

[1] Gardiner, Vol. I, p. 78. Here the question is fully discussed.
[2] Spedding, Vol. II, pp. 336, 358.

of the best of the young men about Essex, Mountjoy was urged by Essex to devise some means of aiding him. First swearing an oath to defend with his life the Queen's person and rule and then exacting the like oaths from Southampton and Danvers, he resolved to send his former messenger to Scotland again, offering to act as Essex had proposed, that is, bring over to England from Ireland four or five thousand troops, who, with the adherents of Essex, would suffice to overthrow the men in power.[1] He left before the messenger returned, and James's answer seems to have been cautious and inconclusive. Taking into account all differences between the sentiments and ideas of that age and its present judges, this action, if it occurred, is inexcusable. Once more, it must be assumed that the account is generally true.

Another anxiety which Charles had to bear with him on his journey was the conduct of his mistress. Penelope's love and zeal for her brother were rashly expressed. The impression that she had been a dangerous adviser to him, and was later even more unfortunate in the role, is hardly to be avoided. (She had in all probability been a bad influence on her lover also in this affair.) Early in December she and her sister Lady Northumberland appeared at Court, a pair of handsome, reproachful sybils, clad aggressively all in black. Their immediate objects were to have Essex moved to better and more airy quarters, the Lord Keeper's house being somewhat confined, and permission to visit him. They failed in their plea, yet the Queen's refusal was gentle. She was not stony-hearted and she was distressed by reports of the sickness of their brother. At least once, just before Christmas, she spoke graciously to Penelope. An undated letter from Penelope to Sir Robert Cecil must belong to this period. She wrote that she had been an importunate suitor to the Queen and that, though she had not granted the request, she had been so kindly in her reply that she might grant it if Cecil would second it. Yet the request remained unavailing, though the practical Queen kept the jewels sent in support of it.[2]

There was no great harm in this, and Penelope's anxiety

[1] Spedding, Vol. II, p. 336.
[2] De l'Isle and Dudley, Vol. II, p. 422; Salisbury, Pt. IX, p. 428; Sidney, Vol. II, pp. 153, 158.

was natural because the doctors thought that Essex was likely to die. Yet she went further. She wrote what Bacon calls a "piquant" (sharp) letter to the Queen. Copies of it were printed about the time Charles set out for Ireland, and a few were sold in the streets before they could be seized. Penelope was sent for by Lord Treasurer Buckhurst to be reprimanded.[1] This letter must have been the following, a good specimen of a florid and tortuous style popular at the time and to which the Queen herself was no stranger:

"Early did I hope this morning to have mine eyes blessed with your Majesty's beauty. But seeing the sun depart into a cloud, and meeting with some spirits that did presage by the wheels of their chariot some thunder in the air, I must complain and express my fears to the high majesty and divine oracle from whence I received a doubtful answer; unto whose power I must sacrifice again the tears and prayers of the afflicted, that must despair in time, if it be too soon to importune heaven when we feel the misery of hell, or that words directed to the sacred wisdom should be out of season, delivered for my unfortunate brother, whom all men have liberty to defame, as if his offence was capital and he so base dejected a creature that his life, his love, and service to your beauties and the state had deserved no absolution after so hard punishment, or so much as to answer in your fair presence, who would vouchsafe more justice and favour than he can expect of partial judges or those combined enemies that labour on false grounds to build his ruin, urging faults as criminal to your divine honour, thinking it a heaven to blaspheme heaven; whereas by their own particular malice and council they have practised to glut themselves in their own private revenge, not regarding your service and loss so much as their ambition, and to rise by his overthrow. And I have reason to apprehend that if your fair hands do not check the courses of their unbridled hate, their last courses will be his last breath . . . But at least, if he may not return to the happiness of his former service, to live at the feet of his admired mistress, yet may he sit down to a private life, without the imputation of infamy . . ."[2]

And more of the same sort. It was a considerable effort, including a sentence of nearer two hundred and fifty than two

[1] Spedding, Vol. II, p. 199; Chamberlain, pp. 65, 76; De l'Isle and Dudley, Vol. II, p. 435.
[2] Birch, Vol. II, p. 442.

hundred words, and its manner may have made a certain appeal to a virtuoso like Elizabeth. The matter, however, made of the Queen's servants malignant and treacherous ruffians and, what was far worse, imputed weakness to the Queen herself. Penelope expressed to Buckhurst her penitence and sent by him a humble message in which she acknowledged her faults to the Queen.[1]

While Essex was in Ireland, it had appeared for a short time that Mountjoy might find very different employment from that of succeeding him there. The year 1599 was that of the so-called "Invisible Armada", the Spanish fleet which, without ever approaching the English shore, caused a panic in the country. Early in the year a certain anxiety had been felt about Spanish preparations, but these were allayed when news arrived that on 1 June a powerful Dutch fleet was off Coruña. However, the Dutch Admiral did not relish what he saw of the strength of the batteries and of the fleet in the harbour, and, after a brief exchange of fire, passed on down the coast. Late in July the English Government got news which ended its complacency; the Dutch fleet had quitted the Spanish coast and had taken Grand Canary. That left the Spanish fleet at Coruña free. Immediately all the naval and military forces of the realm were mobilized in haste. This time Mountjoy's service was to be with the land forces. The Lord Admiral, the Earl of Nottingham, was to be General, presumably because he was too old to go to sea and therefore of a suitable age to command an army, with Mountjoy as Lieutenant-General. He must have gone to his post; otherwise at this critical moment he would have been at Portsmouth, whereas the letters from the port to the Privy Council in August were sent by a subordinate. The scare came to nothing because the Dutch went on to the Azores and the Spanish fleet under the Adelantado followed them there, instead of sailing for England. The first great naval expedition of the Dutch proved a failure, with enormous losses from disease, but they took the Spanish fleet off English hands, as the Queen graciously acknowledged. Some of the scenes while its arrival was expected did no credit to the England of Elizabeth.

"Upon Monday", wrote John Chamberlain to Dudley Carleton, "toward evening, came news (yet false) that the

[1] C.S.P. Ireland, 1600-1, p. 346.

Spaniards were landed in the Isle of Wight, which bred such a fear and consternation in this town as I would little have looked for, with such a cry of women, chaining of streets, and shutting of the gates, as though the enemy had been at Blackwall. I am sorry and ashamed that this weakness and nakedness of ours on all sides should show itself so apparently as to be carried far and near, to our disgrace both with friends and foes".[1]

At last the matter of the Irish deputyship was settled; the bargains about men, money, and supplies of food clinched; the valuable captaincies allotted; the strategy adumbrated; the directives of Queen and Council issued. Charles rode out from London on 7 February, 1600, "being in all points very honourably accompanied and attended, though not in such magnificence as was the Earl of Essex". He could not attract as many young grandees as had followed Essex, which was just as well. Probably Sir George Carew rode by his side, since he crossed by the same ship. He was to be President of Munster. No Lord Deputy could have hoped for an abler second, but he was the friend of Ralegh and the protégé and confidant of Cecil, so that according to the Elizabethan custom, his correspondence with the Secretary was certain to be more confidential than that of his superior. The chronicler recording Mountjoy's departure pauses to mention that he was "of a mild disposition and very gracious with the peers and common people".[2] Doubtless he had a friendly smile for the folk in the streets who wished him good fortune, but he had a great deal on his mind, little of it pleasant in rumination, and by no means all of it concerned with Tyrone, who in himself provided ample cause for thought.

The Lord Deputy reached Chester on 14 February. His suite appeared to the Mayor, who entertained him and it to a banquet on the 17th, to be a "great train". The halt in the town lasted five days, doubtless employed in the inspection of troops to be shipped there. Then Mountjoy went on into Wales, to embark in all probability at Holyhead.[3]

[1] Corbett: *The Successors of Drake*, ch. XI; Chamberlain, p. 58.
[2] Stow, p. 789.
[3] Hemingway, p. 154.

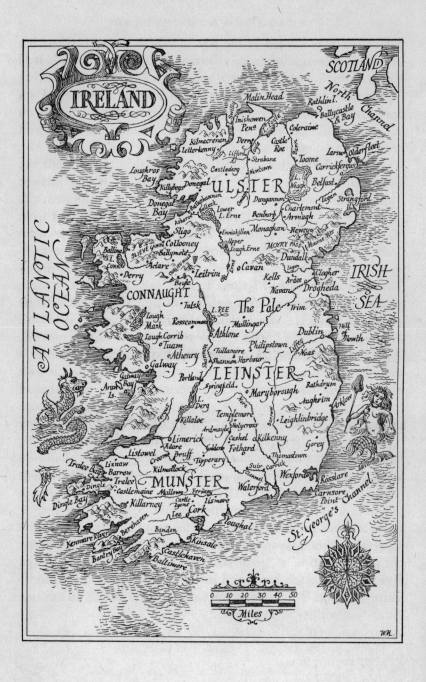

IX

PORTRAIT OF THE LORD DEPUTY

CHARLES BLOUNT, LORD MOUNTJOY, was thirty-six years of age when he left London to take up his office in Ireland.[1] He was a blend of types: soldier, courtier, dandy, scholar and bookman, and latterly something of a valetudinarian. He had matured, but his characteristics had altered little. He was still ardent, to the point of rashness in political affairs, as has been revealed; but calm, self-controlled, and self-contained in action. His ambition was as lofty and insistent as in youth. Perhaps it possessed him at this moment more completely than ever. Now was the testing-time. Of all the Queen's Irish viceroys only Sir Henry Sidney and just possibly Sir John Perrott had returned with enhanced reputations. The task was now greater than it had ever been. Yet for that very reason success would be the more glorious, the rewards the richer. He was as eager for glory and rich rewards as when he first went to Court.

His ideal had now become a retired life in a fine house, where he could entertain his friends in beautiful rooms full of beautiful things, enjoy his garden, take the air on a well-paced hack, go fishing, play cards and shovelboard at night, and devote the rest of his time to his library, especially to the play-books in which he now took most pleasure. The Bodleian Library contains some works in Latin which were his property: P. Massonus: *Vitae trium Hetruriae procerum Dantis, Petrarchae, Boccacii,* 1587, inscribed "Charles Mount-" (the rest cut away); *Sexti Philosophi Pyrrhoniarum hypotypwsewn libri III,* 1562, in-

[1] We do not know the month of his birth in 1563. Supposing him to have been born between 1 January and 7 February inclusive, he would have been thirty-seven when he quitted London. The odds in favour of his being still short of his thirty-seventh birthday are therefore ten to one.

scribed "Carolus Blounte Felicitas sine inuidia";[1] Antonius Thylesius: *Opuscula aliquot*, 1545, inscribed "C. Blount"; Petrus Plateanus: *Opusucla*, 1587, inscribed "Charles Blount"; *Tractatus universi juris*, 18 vols. in 25, and Index, 3 vols., 1584-6, inscribed "Charles Mountioye" on each title-page; Egidius: *De regimine principum*, 1498, inscribed "C. Mountioye".

Hope of advancement by means of the war, as the road to such a retired life, reconciled him to the political risks of the Irish venture. The occupations mentioned above bear a surprising appearance of the tastes of middle or indeed old age. He established at Wanstead a country home, within an easy ride of Whitehall, where all these occupations were available. Yet he can seldom have had much time for them. Typically, inevitably, unquenched ambition carried him on and after the war led him to give his life to the affairs of state, though he had little real relish for them.

Pursuit of glory may be noble. Pursuit of station and of wealth to support it does not necessarily corrupt, but it is more likely than the other to leave a stain or two. Mountjoy's chief secretary, Fynes Moryson, who was his warm admirer, is severe on this point. Charles had become "frugal in gathering and saving, which in his latter days declined to vice"; this was shown, not so much in cutting down his former free spending as in "greedy gathering". Yet, though his expenses in Ireland were enormous—and he was often chidden about them— Moryson goes on to admit that he was more parsimonious in spending the Queen's treasure than his own revenue.[2] The Irish accounts were audited very carefully during his viceroyalty without involving accusations affecting his handling of funds, as in the case of others. Yet he would seem to have made money out of the war and the evidence that he had become grasping must in a measure detract from his virtues.

---

[1] This inscription is not in his hand and may have been written by a donor. The top of the title-page, where he had in all probability put his signature, has been cut off. Samuel Daniel speaks of Mountjoy's habit of marking books in his library at Wanstead. This work, like the Egidius, is liberally marked. There are also a few annotations.

[2] Moryson, Vol. II, p. 264. This portrait is very largely drawn after his. Moryson is the chief authority on Mountjoy as a man in later years, as Naunton is for earlier. Both are vivid writers. The secretary, who lived with his master for two and a half years, is the more reliable, though even he has to be used with caution.

Says the poet Samuel Daniel:

> *His tongue and heart did not turn backs, but went*
> *One way, and kept one course with what he meant.*
> *He us'd no mask at all, but ever ware*
> *His honest inclination open fac'd;*
> *The friendships that he vow'd most constant were,*
> *And with great judgement and discretion plac'd.*

Kindly and charming as ever, he was more reserved than in old days; good-tempered and slow to anger, but speaking straight and to the point when annoyed. The over-talkative and indiscreet did not remain long in his entourage. He realized at once what some men who had spent many years in the Irish service overlooked, that careless talk was reported to Tyrone, who knew full well how to make use of it. He would converse freely about the past and, being a gallant man, often did so with the Anglo-Irish ladies.

He knew that, whatever precautions he might take, some risk existed of plans when once discussed reaching hostile ears. So he reduced discussion to a minimum. Sometimes he kept his designs locked in his own breast, so that even senior officers did not know them till they were put into effect. Daniel, whose comments in *A Funeral Ode upon the Death of the late noble Earl of Devonshire* show him to have been exceptionally well informed about his patron's methods—so well indeed that he must have learnt of them from the mouth of Charles himself—describes the speed and secrecy of his actions in a passage which may have been intended to fit particularly the campaign against the O'Byrnes in December, 1600:

> *Here is no room to tell with what strange speed*
> *And secrecy he uséd to prevent*
> *The enemies' designs, nor with what heed*
> *He marched before report, where what he meant*
> *Fame never knew herself till it was done.*

With Essex, Charles's best friends were Southampton, Robert Sidney, and in Ireland three of his officers: Sir William Godolphin, a Cornishman whose family must have been long known to him; Sir Richard Moryson, brother of his secretary, Fynes Moryson; and Sir Henry Danvers, younger brother of Sir Charles, who was one of the most devoted of the followers of Essex and Southampton. When reproached by the Queen with being too much influenced by these young men, he retorted that they were all older than Alexander the Great when he conquered the world. The Queen's real complaint was that they were all friends of Essex. Yet even in his friendships Mountjoy was inclined to be reserved. To his servants he was mild, seldom reproving them, and then only with a look of displeasure; in fact, those who came to know him best obeyed his looks almost as much as his words. Here again, however, he was not as prodigal of gifts as many others in high places.

He was deeply religious, at least in his intense interest in theology and in his exactitude in religious observances. Like many of the Blounts, he had experienced a tenderness for the Roman Catholic faith in youth and remained tolerant towards it. He considered that the weakening in the spirit of the troops had been due in part to disregard of religion and set himself to remedy this fault. In the "Laws and Orders of War" which he established for the Irish service he laid down that sermons and morning and evening prayers were to be frequented and that men who wilfully and often absented themselves should be punished. No man was to speak impiously or maliciously against the Holy and Blessed Trinity on pain of death. The blaspheming of God's name was to be punished by loss of pay, imprisonment, and perhaps further punishment. Adultery and fornication were to be punished.[1] He could perhaps dictate the word "adultery" without a blush or a smile because he did not hold Penelope's forced marriage to have been sanctified.

If he was a little aloof from most of his officers, he came as close as he could to the rank and file. With them he was gay, friendly, ready to make or listen to a joke and to laugh over it. His attractive manners served him well. He was popular, and his popularity brought with it good service. He could not check desertion—virtually always with the object of returning home, not of going over to the enemy—because that was the inevitable result of the pressing of recruits for a detested war, but he inspired the troops to feats of arms such as had not of late been seen in Ireland. Yet he tried them very highly. His project was to campaign all the year round, but in winter even more than

[1] Carew C., 1589-1600, 502.

in summer. Since he now had an improved administration behind him, he considered that his troops could stand the strain better than the Irish, even though the latter were the hardier. Driving the enemy's cattle to and fro in bad weather, when there was no grazing, would waste them. The stored grain in the barns could be destroyed more easily than the standing corn. The woodlands in which the Irish sought refuge from attack would be bare of leaves, wet, and cold. Again Daniel showed understanding of the strategy.

> *Nor will this place conveniency afford*
> *To show how he, when dismal winter storms*
> *Keeps peace and makes Mars sheath his sword,*
> *Toils him abroad and noble act performs;*
> *Nor how by mast'ring difficulties so*
> *In times unusual and by passage hard*
> *He bravely came to disappoint his foe*
> *And many times surpris'd him unprepared.*

Charles had no doubt about the improvement of the spirit of his men. Six months after his arrival he wrote confidently to Cecil: "And now that, with being a nurse to this army as well as a general, I have given it more health and strength, you must hereafter look to hear of deeper blows that we shall either give or receive."[1]

No one swayed him. He always took the advice of his Council in Ireland; in fact, on his major expeditions he commonly split the Council and took the more military and more active members with him, so that letters from Dublin were addressed by the Lord Chancellor "and part of the Council" to the Lord Deputy "and the rest of the Council." This measure, however, was due to the fact that the Lord Deputy was enjoined to consult his Council, and taking part of it with him was at least a partial means of covering himself in case of an accident and of avoiding reproof. All his military operations depended on his judgement alone, not only in conception but even in detail. Except to Carew, Docwra, Chichester, and the Governor of Connaught, all of whom had necessarily to act independently, he delegated little, perhaps too little to build initiative in officers. He listened to what men about him had to say, and, if it contained accusa-

[1] Falls, pp. 255, 263.

tions against others, took note of them. If, however, they gave him food for thought, they did not lead to condemnation of the accused unless supported by other evidence. His subordinates "seconded" or helped to work out his plans. No one but himself formed them. He complained indeed that even the knowledgeable and experienced men were without originality and unpractical. "Some of them that have gone long round in this Kingdom like mill horses", he wrote to Robert Cecil, "may tell me the form of the circle they have trod in; but I protest I think no men are more deceived touching the true estate of this Kingdom and nature of the war than they are. And I could never yet receive so much benefit by any of their experiences as to receive the true nature of any ground or passage to fight on until with my own eyes I had seen it".[1]

On campaign he saw with his own eyes all that he could. He made frequent reconnaissances in person, often to within easy musket shot of the enemy. His courage in these affairs left a good impression upon an army in which the common soldiers and even officers were depressed by earlier defeats. The Irish being so nimble and fighting as a rule only in wooded or boggy defiles, the war was of a kind which exposed the commander to heavier risks than any other. Charles came through without a scratch, but he was not safe company. His favourite horse was killed under him. The greyhound that used to trot at his stirrup was shot through the body. His helmet, carried by an attendant of one of the Scottish gallowglass families, was dented in the man's hand. One of his chaplains, Doctor Richard Latewar, was killed —he was commemorated by his Oxford College, St. John's, by a memorial in the chapel. Another chaplain had his horse shot under him. Cranmer, his chief secretary, was killed, Fynes Moryson getting his place; Fynes himself had his leg bruised by a spent bullet. One gentlemen of his chamber was killed near him, another wounded.

He took pains to praise active spirits. The troops in general he broke in gradually, leading them warily at first and setting them relatively easy tasks to restore their confidence. It was more important that the soldiers should not be foiled than that the enemy should be assailed with boldness. Later on he

[1] C.S.P. Ireland, 1600-01, p. 516.

demanded heavy sacrifices and incredible exertions from his men.

He was still splendid in his attire. In Dublin he wore white or black taffetas or satins, and two, "yea, sometimes three", pairs of silk stockings, black silk grogram cloaks, fine ruffs, black beaver hats, bright waistcoats, and the Garter below his knee. In the field he wore jerkins and round hose, cloth cloaks lined with velvet, and in winter as many as three waistcoats and a scarf round his neck. Over his silk stockings he then wore another pair of wool, over that high linen boot-hose, and over all riding-boots. He replaced the Garter with a ribbon above the knee hanging over his boot. "I never observed any of his age and strength to keep his body so warm", says his secretary.

Though he breakfasted on a crust and a cup of ale, into which he sometimes put sugar and nutmeg in winter, he fared well at dinner and supper, eating the best meats and drinking plentifully, though never to excess, the best wines. After the war, when his means allowed him to, he kept the best table of any lord in England. He slept in the afternoons whenever he could, even when it was in his tent on campaign. He smoked the finest tobacco, which of course all came from Spanish territory and the most prized types of which entered England by way of Dutch ports. This, he thought, preserved him from the notorious "Irish ague". It also eased the migraine which troubled him for a spell of three days about once every three months.

In fact, the warm clothes, the afternoon nap, the nutmeg cordial, the good fare, and the tobacco were all at least part of a careful plan to keep himself fit and enable him to endure the strain to which he subjected himself. His anxiety about his health was apparently justified, but his precautions were successful. He was never seriously sick in Ireland except when he temporarily collapsed with virulent influenza aggravated by fatigue after the surrender of Kinsale.

In all things he was fastidious, mentally and physically. This is illustrated by his love of beautiful things, and his patronage of poets, of whom a number, including Daniel, Markham, Peele, Ford, Lok, and Bastard, addressed English or Latin verses to him or wrote elegiacs on his death. It is shown in a trifle such as his hatred of swearing. He never used bad language himself and flashed a furious look upon anyone in his company who did. It is shown in his care of his person and his liking for clean linen. Fastidiousness does not necessarily go with mercy to foes. Wars were cruel in those days, and very cruel in Ireland. He was not merciful, and he could be Machiavellian. He suggested, for example, that Arthur O'Neill, Tyrone's kinsman, might be set up against him in Ulster; if this brought Tyrone down, the Government could then "clip Arthur O'Neill's wings as we list".[1] That was held to be fair enough against rebels. On the other hand, if he gave a safe-conduct or a pledge of any sort to an Irishman, it was sacred. The only known instance to the contrary, his treatment of Neill Garve O'Donnell, does not look pretty, but may be excused by the man's own conduct. He never failed to give his attention to pleas or complaints made by the Irish, so long as they avoided rebellion or aid to rebels.

In appearance Mountjoy was still handsome, but his hair had receded from his forehead and was becoming thin above. He wore a beard in Ireland—it was then held to be the mark of a soldier, and Essex had grown the beard with which he is depicted in the National Portrait Gallery after he had won his spurs as a general at Cadiz. In the last few years of his life Charles reduced his beard to a little "pikedevant" or tuft beneath his lower lip, such as that worn half a century later by Turenne. In Ireland his cheeks retained their fullness and good colour, but sorrows just before his death thinned and made them swarthy, and then his air was dejected. Otherwise his countenance was young, amiable, and cheerful though somewhat marred by a blunt nose. He caught the eye however he was clad, but in his Garter robes looked magnificent.

When Tyrone heard of his coming, he made merry about the new Lord Deputy, who would always miss occasions for good service in the field because his people would not be able to get him dressed and given his breakfast in time. The reality proved different.

---

[1] C.S.P. Ireland, 1600-01, p. 300.

X

INTO THE IRISH WAR

MOUNTJOY landed at the Head of Howth, seven miles east of Dublin, on 26 February, 1600, and spent the night at Lord Howth's castle. On the 28th he formally assumed his appointment, taking the great sword which was the symbol of his office and which would be borne before him on all ceremonial occasions while he remained the Queen's Lord Deputy in Ireland.

The situation was gloomy and confused. Tyrone had denounced the truce in January and marched south. He was now in the County Cork, where most of the Irish nobility and gentry swore to adhere to his cause. The principle on which the military affairs of the kingdom were normally administered was that the Lord Deputy, head of the Government and supreme commander of the forces, took Leinster directly under his charge and was immediately responsible for all expeditions into Ulster; Munster's affairs he delegated to the Lord President and his Council established at Cork, and those of Connaught to the Governor at Athlone, on the Shannon, both of whom acted on his general instructions. Now, however, nearly all the field army was in the south under the orders of the Lieutenant-General, the Earl of Ormonde, and there was no President of Munster, the province having been in the hands of Commissioners since the death of Sir Thomas Norris. Mountjoy could not even send the new President to his province, unless by sea, because the way was barred by Tyrone's army and the Commissioners for Munster were virtually shut up in Cork. He was, in fact, glad to keep Sir George Carew for the moment by his side. He himself was a stranger both to high command and to the country. There were those who could provide information—the

Secretary of State, Sir Geffrey Fenton, had a good intelligence service, which even included an Irish priest—but none whose judgement he valued. Carew knew Ireland and was a level-headed, capable man.

Mountjoy had brought with him or shortly received various orders and instructions. These were generally to the point, but for the most part political and administrative. They included the modern-sounding arrangement that the captains of companies should keep war diaries in duplicate and send one copy to the Lord Deputy. This intelligent provision was that of the Lord Treasurer, Lord Buckhurst. Among those made by the Queen was the seemingly obvious one that captains who left their posts without the Lord Deputy's leave must be discharged. It was in fact practical because in all armies of those times officers, captains and upwards, paid visits to their homes in the most casual way. Churches in Dublin and Meath were to be repaired and the clergy reassembled; the Clerk of the Council was to attend in person and not to be represented by a deputy; waste of powder was to be stopped; the victualling accounts were to be better kept, so that the Queen should not be defrauded.[1]

By an ironical twist, the best appreciation of the situation before the eyes of Mountjoy was one drawn up by his predecessor, who had failed and fallen into disgrace. Essex had addressed it to the Queen on 25 June, 1599, during his southern expedition. It began by pointing out the advantages on the side of the Irish.

They were skilful in tactics and the use of arms, mobile, and extraordinarily hardy. Emboldened by their military successes, they had lost the respect for English arms which had earlier in the reign denied them self-confidence and made them unwilling to press home an attack on forces much inferior to their own. The Anglo-Irish nobility, who might have been a great source of strength, were divided from the English by religion and disgusted because they were prevented from exercising the absolute power of Irish chiefs. The towns, though still an asset, could not resist the gains to be made by trading with the enemy. The rebels expected aid from Spain. In these circumstances, he said prophetically, the war was bound to be long and costly.

[1] C.S.P. Ireland, March-Oct., 1600, pp. 272-8.

MOVNTIOY · HONORAT. D̊.

CO: DEVON BAR

CAROL: BLVNT

The
Right honourable CHARLES BLVNt
Earle of Deuon; Baron Mountioy
and Knight of the Garter.

Left: Robert Devereux, Second Earl of Essex. Portrait by an unknown artist which is now in the National Portrait Gallery.

Right: Robert Cecil First Earl of Salisbury. Portrait attributed to John de Critz which is now in the National Portrait Gallery.

SERO SED SERIO

He recommended that the towns should be kept well garrisoned to provide firm bases for operations, and that it should be made a capital offence for any merchant to have dealings with an enemy. He also advised that magazines should be established in the home ports of the west and north-west and ships kept ready to transport supplies to Ireland. Perishable goods, if not required, could be turned over by sale and restocking.

Then he turned to the Government's resources, a formidable list. First, the rebels could not storm a walled town or a strong castle. Therefore the Queen could remain mistress of what she held and her troops could be well lodged in winter and readily supplied. Second, her cavalry was so incomparably superior to that of the Irish that it could make her mistress of all the cavalry country, or champaign—and after all, despite the hills and the vast bogs and forests, there was plenty of that. Third, if the army were fed from England and the country were spoiled, the rebels could be starved. Fourth, if ships and pinnaces were kept on the coasts, the Irish would be unable to obtain muskets and powder, which could come only from Scotland or Spain. Fifth, the English service was rich in gallant colonels, captains, and gentlemen of quality, whose example and bravery in the field was "of more use than all the rest of your troops". Here he spoke of more than what is counted as leadership today: the officer, superbly mounted and wearing the finest armour, could turn the issue in his neighbourhood by his individual prowess; he might almost be likened to a modern armoured car. "So that," said Essex, "although their common soldiers are too hard for our new men, yet they are not able to stand before such gallant men as will charge them." Sixth, in a pitched battle the English ought always to win; where they had not won the fault had lain with their leadership.

Comparing advantages and disadvantages, though the rebels were more numerous, superior in physique, and better versed in the use of arms than the raw recruits sent over from England, yet, with the towns, the castles, and the open country always at the Government's disposal, with a brave nobility and gentry, better discipline, superior organization, and the means of withholding from the Irish the necessities of life, the campaign should in the long run be successful, though it would cost dear.[1]

The paper was masterly. Mountjoy assuredly profited by it and, so far as it was in his power to translate it into action, did so throughout his viceroyalty.

The number of rebels in arms had been estimated at 2,300 horse and 18,00 foot before Essex left Ireland and was believed to have swollen by a few thousand since. Some guesswork must have entered into these figures, and they obviously did not stand for that number of trained soldiers. The men in the Irish ranks shaded off from first-class musketeers and pikemen trained and drilled on English or Spanish lines to wild kerne as primitive as those who had fled before Sussex and Sir Henry Sidney. Yet a useful soldier in guerrilla warfare is a man who can wage it, and they could all do that more or less. Fairly well-equipped and trained "bonaghts" or hired soldiers may have numbered as much as one-third of the foot. The royal army numbered nominally 1,200 horse and 14,440 foot; but it had suffered serious wastage, the extent of which the Lord Deputy was to begin with unable to discover because he was out of touch with his forces. Moreover, the Queen in Council had decided to reduce the establishment of the infantry to 12,000. Mountjoy protested vigorously, and the Queen relented. The former establishment was maintained and eventually reinforcements were sent to bring the strength up to it.[2]

In the instructions which the new Lord Deputy had carried with him the only important strategic provision was the establishment of a strong force in Lough Foyle. Ulster was a forbidding, almost trackless region. From the Blackwater to the Erne its inner fastness was defended by the hardiest and most determined of the Irish. The prospect of subduing it entirely by land might well daunt the boldest. Lough Foyle, however, carved a deep cut into its northern coast at about the dividing line between the power of the two great chiefs, Tyrone and Hugh O'Donnell. It could be reached and supplied by sea. A few miles up the River Foyle, which flowed into the lough from the south, was the site of a little settlement, now ruined, named Derry, which would afford a suitable base. On either side lay granaries

---

[1] Birch, Vol. II, pp. 415-7.
[2] C.S.P. Ireland, March-Oct., 1600, pp. 66, 81, 87; Moryson, Vol. II, p. 283.

on which the Ulster chiefs greatly depended. It was proposed to work up the river, establishing a line of forts and spreading out east and west as occasion offered. Thus a force might be planted in the heart of Ulster not dependent on a long and ever-menaced land supply route. The prospects were the better because a number of local magnates, including some of their own kinsmen, were discontented with Tyrone's and O'Donnell's autocratic methods and might be detached.

With the Lough Foyle scheme went one for Ballyshannon, at the mouth of the Erne. Probably from Lough Foyle, a force was to be sent round to the west coast, to take and fortify this place, not long lost to the English. From Ballyshannon detachments would move out to fortify and garrison half-a-dozen fords over the River Erne and control the cattle-boats known as cotts, of which there were said to be some four hundred, on the loughs. It was also proposed that the English should establish on them seven or eight boats, each carrying a small piece of ordnance. These would be based on Belleek because there was no water communication between the loughs and the sea owing to water-falls on the River Erne. Such action would put a barrier between Tyrconnell (Donegal) O'Donnell's country, and Connaught, on which he continually preyed and which he kept in turmoil. If it did not succeed in locking him into Tyrconnell, it afforded a good chance of locking him out when he was trying to return, laden with spoil.[1]

The force for Lough Foyle was to number a round 4,000, three-quarters of it coming directly from England and the rest from Dublin. The plan was admirable. However, the only contribution which the Lord Deputy could for the moment make to it was to take up shipping at Dublin for the thousand men to go from the capital.

Meanwhile Tyrone, encamped in the Lee Valley west of Cork, had heard not only of Mountjoy's arrival but also of the Lough Foyle scheme, which made it desirable that he should return to Ulster. Now for the first time Ormonde had assembled a force strong enough to face him, some five thousand men by the list, three thousand of them English. He expected Tyrone to cross the Shannon and return north through Connaught, but was also

[1] C.S.P. Ireland, March-Oct., 1600, pp. 279-90.

prepared for him if he marched by the way he had come, through Tipperary, Westmeath, and Cavan. The precautions were of no avail. Marching as only the Irish could, Tyrone slipped by through the Tipperary hills.

Mountjoy for his part had been able to scrape together only some 1,500 horse and foot, which he stationed at Trim and Athboy in Meath. On 13 March he went to Trim himself to lead a dash into Westmeath across the path of Tyrone. He was too late; the messenger with Ormonde's warning letter had taken five days to reach him.[1] This was a miserable start. He hid his anger with himself behind anger with Ormonde. What a country to campaign in! What a people to fight, these ghosts who flitted at twenty-seven miles a day through mountain, bog, and wood!

At least the way was clearer for action. Tyrone had left some two thousand Ulster and Connaught bonaghts in Munster, but it was now safe to order Ormonde to bring the bulk of the army into the Pale. With his elaborate courtesy Charles informed him of the Queen's desire that he should continue to act as Lieutenant-General of the army and, writing to an earl and a man a generation older than himself, added that, when he had divested himself of his present office, he would be happy to serve under Ormonde's command. The letters patent issued just afterwards to Ormonde stated that the Queen had acted on the advice of Charles Lord Mountjoy.[2]

It was now also possible to send Sir George Carew to his Munster post; in fact, an escort of a hundred horse was considered enough to accompany him to Ormonde's home, Kilkenny Castle, where he would be in touch with the troops of the province. Seven hundred foot followed him. He set off on 7 April. With him rode the Earl of Thomond, an O'Brien of pure Irish blood, not "English-Irish" like most of the aristocracy, and a man of ability and determination.

Calamity followed on calamity. Nothing, it seemed, would go right in Ireland. Carew and Thomond, reaching Kilkenny, were invited by Ormonde to come with him next morning to a parley with one of the outstanding rebel leaders, the young

---

[1] C.S.P. Ireland, March-Oct., 1600, pp. 41, 43; Moryson, Vol. II, p. 287.
[2] C. Ormonde Deeds, Vol. VI, p. 111.

Owen (Owny) MacRory O'Moore, of Leix, or Queen's County, and agreed to do so. At the parley Ormonde was treacherously seized and carried off. Carew and Thomond barely broke away, Thomond being stabbed in the back with a pike.

"Black Tom" of Ormonde was a part of the history of the English in Ireland since the reign of Queen Mary, and his house for many generations. Well might the Deputy write "Haste, haste, for thy life!" on the message to Cecil on receiving the alarming news. Ormonde's prestige with the Irish was immense, and on it depended the attitude of a number of the Butler family, some of whom had been out in revolt as recently as the viceroyalty of Essex. Moreover, the succession to the earldom was disputed. Ormonde had no legitimate son, and his brother's blood was attainted. His daughter was the greatest heiress in Ireland, and other members of the family might seize her person and force her into a marriage. Tyrone would try to get the prisoner into his hands—he did try, but, fortunately, the O'Moores were too jealous of him to let the prize go. He might try to kidnap the girl and marry her to one of his sons.[1]

Rescue was out of the question because Owny MacRory had sworn to kill the Earl with his own hands if it were attempted. All the Deputy could do was to provide for the safety of the Countess and the Lady Elizabeth. He bade Carew and Thomond halt at Kilkenny till the five hundred troops which he was sending to hold the place had arrived. This affair was shortly followed by the arrival of Spanish ships at Killybegs in Tyrconnell, bringing 2,000 calivers, with powder, lead and match, 2,000 pikes, and an almost equally valuable passenger, the Franciscan Mathias de Oviedo, titular Archbishop of Dublin, who promised a Spanish army of liberation. The two events raised the spirits of the rebels. It could not be denied that the viceroyalty had opened with one setback after another.

However, the Deputy now had a force under his hand, including reinforcements from England. He considered that after making provision for Munster and Connaught and providing garrisons for Lough Foyle, Ballyshannon, Carrickfergus, and the small places in Leinster, he would eventually have a field army of 400 horse and 4,600 foot at his disposal. He intended to

[1] *Pacata Hibernia*, Vol. I, pp. 41-9.

move north in order to take pressure off the Lough Foyle force when it was about to land. While awaiting it, he had to revictual the fort of Philipstown in Offaly and in the process strike the rebels in that region as smart a blow as he could deliver before turning his back on them by heading north. He sent Sir Oliver Lambart, whom he knew well as having been his colonel in Hampshire in 1596. Lambart did his job after ferocious fighting. Mountjoy was pleased with the troops, who had "turned kerne" and stripped themselves naked to pass through a bog to the assault, and with the leadership. He annotated Lambart's report of 24 April thus drily: "It was a principal good service . . . and by this you may see that our men begin to forget to run away".[1]

The fleet from England for Lough Foyle reached Carrick-fergus on 27 April. The Dublin fleet was delayed, but Mountjoy began his march on 5 May. He halted at Drogheda to await victuals which were reaching Ireland by sea only gradually, and to give Lambart time to follow him. On the 11th, without await-ing Lambart, he passed through Dundalk. The usual road into Ulster ran through a defile known as the Moyry, favourable to resistance, between Dundalk and Newry. On this occasion, how-ever, the Irish did not hold it, and the army passed through without fighting; but Mountjoy had the satisfaction of learning that Tyrone, with a considerable force, was in County Armagh, so that the diversion in favour of the Lough Foyle expedition had succeeded in its object. The landing took place on 15 May, though, of course, Mountjoy did not get the news for some days. On the 16th he advanced northward from Newry and found himself in the presence of the enemy.

Next day, in the course of some manoeuvring, an Irish scout called to one of the English to ask when Lord Southampton and Lambart were expected. Charles at once divined what was in the wind. Southampton must be at Dundalk; his force numbered only the two companies led by Lambart and forty mounted gentlemen volunteers; and Tyrone was evidently planning to slip round and fall upon him in the Moyry. Mountjoy sent a force of 550 men to meet him and convoy him through the defile. It was well that he took this precaution. Hot fighting broke out,

[1] C.S.P. Ireland, March-Oct., 1600, p. 120; A.P.C., Vol. XXVI, p. 308.

in which Southampton performed deeds of valour in his usual style; but Tyrone did not commit the bulk of his force and the Irish were driven out after Mountjoy had intervened in person.[1]

Southampton had only just arrived in Ireland, from which he had been absent since following Essex home seven months earlier. The conversation must have been very grave when the two men found themselves alone in the Deputy's tent that night. Southampton had come to propose the revival of the desperate and treasonable project already mentioned, that Mountjoy should bring over to England a force strong enough to overthrow the Government and drive out the enemies of Essex. Charles was being reminded of his former sin; for this had been his own proposal. If he now debated with himself whether he should carry it out, that evening marked the most critical moment of his career.

We must incline to the belief that he answered without hesitation. The evidence that follows was not published with the Government's "declaration" of the treason of Essex because it would have implicated Mountjoy. "He [Mountjoy] utterly rejected it as a thing which he could no way think honest", said Southampton in his suppressed confession. Charles persuaded his friend to put the idea from his mind. The business looked different over here, away from the angry, intriguing atmosphere of the Court. He had realized the magnitude of his task and his fitness for it. In any case, Essex was no longer a prisoner at York House. He had been allowed to return to his own roof, though still with a guard. The attitude of the Queen held out promise of complete freedom, which indeed soon followed. Essex was in no danger, unless the story leaked out. To commit treason—and wreck his own career in the process—would be mad as well as wicked in Mountjoy. Was this decision a betrayal of his friend? It is reasonable, not merely charitable, to ascribe it to a return to a sense of duty.[2]

The expedition had served its purpose. Mountjoy was not ready to invade Ulster deeply. He would first have to muster greater strength, train and season his troops, and give the Lough Foyle force time to prepare the way. On 28 May he set off for

[1] C.S.P. Ireland, March-Oct., 1600, pp. 190, 227.
[2] Spedding, Vol. II, p. 359; Corr. of James VI and Cecil, p. xxii.

Dublin, moving by Carlingford instead of through the Moyry. He returned to meet more trouble. In his absence bands of rebels had broken into the Pale to burn villages, particularly in Meath and Westmeath, and carry off cattle. The Anglo-Irish lords and gentry had remained quiescent in their castles. Shortly afterwards they sent over a deputation to lay their grievances before Cecil, without first approaching the Deputy. The Queen roundly scolded them for this, but did not refuse to hear them. Their chief complaint was that forces which should have been stationed on the borders of the Pale were quartered on them and despoiled the country, without ever incurring punishment. The Queen bade the Palesmen apply to Mountjoy, but she let him know that the complaints must be redressed.[1]

This incident probably influenced his bold demand for greater strength. After threatening to cut down the establishment of the infantry from 14,000 to 12,000, the Queen had consented to let it stand at the higher figure. He had now decided that he needed still more troops and requested that the establishment should be raised to 16,000. By mid-July this increase was sanctioned. The Queen was not stinting her Deputy.[2]

This is not a history of the war, and events can be related in relative detail only where they touch Mountjoy directly. As regards those of Munster, Ulster, and Connaught it must suffice to record the general progress of the efforts to subdue the rebellion.[3]

In Munster the President, Sir George Carew, had made a more successful start than Mountjoy himself. Carew was an excellent soldier and in particular an expert artilleryman, a specialist in battering castles; but he was at least as much politician as soldier. The feature of the war in Munster was that the bulk of its gentry were inclined to look on the fight as Tyrone's quarrel with the Government and therefore to take only a lukewarm interest in it. Tyrone's action in taking hostages of the chief men before returning north showed how he regarded them.

[1] C.S.P. Ireland, March-Oct., 1600, p. 236; Moryson, Vol. II, p. 333.
[2] C.S.P. Ireland, March-Oct., 1600, pp. 217, 314; C.S.P. Dom., 1598-1601, pp. 382, 443.
[3] They are much more fully described in *Elizabeth's Irish Wars*. For Neill Garve O'Donnell see also my article, "Neill Garve: English Ally and Victim", *The Irish Sword*, Vol. I, No. 1.

The astute Carew thought that by a mixture of blows, bluff, and play upon their rivalries he could get submission and perhaps service from most of them. The two most important Irish leaders in the province were James Fitzthomas Fitzgerald, a pretender to the title of Earl of Desmond, known as "the Sugane (Straw-rope) Earl", and Florence McCarthy, who had been appointed by Tyrone McCarthy More, or senior chief of this great family. However, James Fitzthomas was not of particular ability and Florence McCarthy, a clever man, was timid and temporizing, avoiding open rebellion. The real strength of the rebellion lay in the Ulster and Connaught bonaghts and their principal leader, Dermot O'Connor, a man who had risen from nothing to become a successful and sought-after mercenary captain and married the sister of the real Earl of Desmond, now a prisoner in the Tower.

Carew and his captains—notably Richard Graeme, whom the President described as "the best horse captain in the kingdom" —so handled Fitzthomas that he was presently reduced to hiding in the woods with a handful of followers. He made Munster so lean a place for O'Connor that the Irish *condottiere* departed into Connaught with most of his troops, eventually to be murdered. He kept McCarthy the right side of rebellion, though hovering on the edge. He stormed or seized or had handed over to him a number of important castles south of the Shannon, which he repaired and garrisoned to prevent incursions from Connaught.

Sir Henry Docwra, Governor of Lough Foyle, achieved nothing so striking, but then he had entered a region where the people were harder and less given to compromise than those of Munster. From the first he found his commitments bigger than he had expected, and was pleased when the Ballyshannon expedition was postponed for lack of troops, though this was unfortunate for the general cause. However, he, like Carew, found some useful allies. To begin with he did not tie down Hugh Roe O'Donnell, for the latter made in June a great raid into Connaught, reaching the Shannon estuary virtually unopposed. Docwra's most effective work was to be done in the following year, but already sickness, the bane of this force, was making it clear that without strong Irish allies little would be effected.

The men went sick in hundreds and died in scores, probably from drinking water which they themselves had contaminated. Docwra was hoping for the aid of an almost legendary figure, Hugh Roe O'Donnell's cousin and brother-in-law, Neill Garve, a restless, truculent, and ambitious man, with a high reputation as a warrior; but he did not come in until late in the year. The other principal holding in Ulster was Carrickfergus, where the extremely able and ruthless Sir Arthur Chichester was in command. Chichester's greatest exploits also belong to a later period.

Connaught was the least satisfactory of the four provinces. Mountjoy could afford it no troops except the garrison of Athlone, though another walled town, Galway, was held for the Crown by its own levy. The matter of the governorship of the province had been bungled, though not by the Deputy's fault. Mountjoy's original instructions had been to appoint the Earl of Thomond and Viscount Dunkellin, son of the Earl of Clanrickarde, to the joint command—a bad arrangement in itself—with a Justice and Council for the management of civil affairs. Thomond, however, preferred to serve with Carew, with whom he had struck up a friendship, unless his own county of Thomond (later named Clare) called for his presence. His influence was so great that he did not need to visit it, except for a brief period during O'Donnell's raid, already mentioned.[1]

Dunkellin, like Thomond, was an Irishman, whose father possessed vast and stony territories in Connaught, though, unlike Thomond, he descended on the male side from an Anglo-Norman. He was an enthusiastic royalist who had been to Court; but the family had a relatively recent record of revolt, and in any case the Queen did not care about employing a great lord in his own country. Within three weeks of Mountjoy's assumption of office, Dunkellin wrote to him to complain that in England he had been promised command in Connaught, but now found that this did not include Athlone and Galway, without which strongholds he could not effectively exercise it. He did nothing to oppose O'Donnell's raid, and probably lacked the means. Then he proferred his resignation. Mountjoy was

---

[1] Carew C., 1589-1600, p. 360; C.S.P. Ireland, March-Oct., 1600, pp. 34, 143, 265. Clare at this time was included in Connaught. It was by the influence of this Lord Thomond, afterwards known as "the great Earl", that it was transferred to Munster.

bidden to accept it, but in the most gracious terms, and to invite the young Irishman to serve directly under his orders. Dunkellin succeeded his father as Earl of Clanrickarde in May, 1601. Immediately after the death of Queen Elizabeth he married, as already stated, the widow of Essex as her third husband, the first having been Sir Philip Sidney.[1]

Mountjoy was ordered to appoint Sir Arthur Savage, hitherto in command of Athlone, provisional Governor. On 8 June he put forward an alternative suggestion. He considered that the Governor should be "of greatness and reputation". Here was the factor on which stress has previously been laid, the value of a title of nobility. Mountjoy had a nobleman ready. "Out of my affection I can name no man that I love better than the Earl of Southampton, neither out of my judgement any on whom I think the Queen should bestow the government thereof to more purpose to the service". He was recommending a man who was in the Queen's bad books. She had been infuriated by his marriage to one of her maids of honour, Essex's cousin, the more so because the wedding had had to be celebrated in unseemly haste, and a daughter, significantly named Penelope, had been born within three months. Elizabeth had countermanded Essex's appointment of him as Master of the Horse in Ireland, but he had none the less proved himself a dashing cavalryman both under Essex and on the single occasion when he had fought under Mountjoy. "In the Moyry I protest he saved our honour", wrote Charles, and concluded by assuring Cecil that he would take great joy in the assistance and company of so dear a friend and so noble a gentleman.[2]

Without doubt he meant every word of his eulogy. Southampton was a brilliant, if erratic, figure. Yet it is possible that Charles was anxious to keep his friend out of harm's way, that is, to find him work which would prevent him from returning to England and being involved in trouble by Essex. Charles was in irritable mood. He had come under sharp criticism which he felt to be unjust and against which, even when it came from the Queen herself, he defended himself boldly. At the end of August, 1600, he went so far as to ask to be relieved. In

---

[1] *Four Masters,* Vol. VI, pp. 2, 237; Manningham, p. 165.
[2] C.S.P. Ireland, March-Oct., 1600, p. 223; Moryson, Vol. II, p. 325.

September he told Cecil flatly that the troubles were due to the Secretary's habit of listening to every man against the chief Governor. The custom of the time was for anyone in an official position, civil or military, to write to the Secretary, and it was one whch Cecil encouraged. Charles divined that the fault-finding which he had to endure was fed by the tittle-tattle of the correspondents. He suspected that some of the adherents of Essex, were prominent among them. Away from the influence of Essex, he was by no means as ardent a partisan of his cause as he had been; at all events he had no intention of marching into folly behind him.[1]

The application for Southampton to be appointed Governor of Connaught failed, and Savage got the provisional title. The young Earl, protesting that he felt in no way disappointed or hurt, but that he could not afford to remain in Ireland as a volunteer with a train of gentlemen, stayed only for Mountjoy's next operations in Leinster and then departed on his way to the Low Countries. However, the lure of Essex drew him back to London in the winter, with consequences all but fatal.[2]

One stroke of good fortune was the liberation of Ormonde in mid-June. The O'Moores, after the Irish custom, took a number of hostages, to execute if he proceeded against them; but he contrived almost immediately to buy back some of these, and Mountjoy afterwards rescued others. The importance of Ormonde was illustrated by the Lord Deputy's immediate visit to him at Kilkenny, since the veteran was too ill and shaken to come to Dublin. Mountjoy judged it essential to discover personally what Ormonde's attitude was. The parley with the rebels and the ease with which the most experienced soldier in Ireland had been kidnapped by a young wood-kerne had aroused suspicion in Mountjoy's mind and he had expressed highly unfavourable views about the episode to Cecil. He was reassured by his interview. Ormonde would, he believed, serve as energetically against the rebels as his health allowed. Charles retracted some of his unkind words. "I cannot but bear a kind of reverence to so ancient a servant of her Majesty, and a compassion to the miserable fortune he was in", he wrote to Cecil.[3]

[1] C.S.P. Ireland, March-Oct., 1600, pp. 272-8, 308, 349-52, 397, 431.
[2] Ibid., 1600, p. 328.
[3] Ibid., 1600, p. 299.

Ormonde in fact served again with vigour, though that winter he was once more prostrated, this time by the death of his wife. Some of the English thought his loss would kill him. They little knew this most robust of the Anglo-Irish. He married a third wife and survived Mountjoy, over thirty years his junior, by eight years.

The Lord Deputy's activity did not slacken. In mid-July he marched through Meath, almost up to the border of Cavan. There Connor Roe Maguire, one of the rival chiefs of Fermanagh, came in and made his peace, but could not yet be established in his country. Mountjoy was now minded to move again in full force into Armagh, against his chief enemy, Tyrone. For the moment, however, pacification of Leinster was more urgent. Owny MacRory of Leix, that "bloody and bold young man", had increased his stature by the affront he had put upon Ormonde. He and his O'Moores, with the Kavanaghs of Offaly, were still strong and defiant. Mountjoy left the northern borders well held against Tyrone and ordered preparations for the northern expedition, including the building up of a depot of stores at Newry. He had arranged for Lambart, then in Kildare, to come to a rendezvous in Offaly, Savage to move east from Athlone, and Ormonde to meet him later at Cullenagh, in southern Leix.

His method of campaigning is of interest. The forces holding the northern borders were largely those which he would at the last moment concentrate for the big expedition to Armagh. If he advanced concentrated, Tyrone would have to concentrate too, so the northern borders could be largely denuded of regular troops and handed over to the Pale levy. If he hit the O'Moores and Kavanaghs hard, Savage need leave only a skeleton garrison in Athlone. The advances from the four points of the compass would bewilder the O'Moores and Kavanaghs. He was always trying to make the Queen and Council understand that his garrisons, which they considered were idle and too numerous, did not sit still but were used whenever possible on expeditions. The timing of these manoeuvres was difficult and even risky, but Ormonde, Lambart, and Savage were reliable

This time, however, it was necessary that the blow should be hard. He did not want during his absence in the north any more burnings in the Pale, followed by loud appeals to the Queen from its nobility and gentry. His first objective was the standing corn because, if the harvest were spoiled, the enemy could not maintain his forces in the field; but he hoped that the rebels would be compelled to defend both their crops and their live-stock, and thus be brought to battle.[1]

There was no question of the enemy not fighting; in fact, Savage was fought so hard that he did not get through to join the Deputy. Mountjoy moved by Philipstown, and then had to pass a great bog, all the men, including the Deputy himself, going afoot, and the cavalry horses and baggage being led on a pathway of hurdles. A great spoil was taken, including seven or eight hundred horses. On 26 July, the day appointed for the meeting, Lambart duly appeared, having had heavy fighting. They had to do not only with the local men but with an able captain of mer-cenaries named Richard Tyrrell, who had been in the Queen's service and commanded a body of trained troops. This captain rated Mountjoy high. He laid an ambush of a hundred muske-teers to wait for him at a ford, let the cavalry pass, and then attacked the Deputy, who was accompanied only by a few gentle-men and his servants. The English foot came up too slowly, and Charles went through an ugly moment. This was the occa-sion of his losing his horse Gray Davies. He was rash to ride a grey.

Now he was on his objective. Fields of corn, well grown and well fenced, lay before him. He had brought with him scythes and sickles, and according to Irish evidence used long-toothed harrows, found on the spot, to tear out the crop; but most of it had to be cut by swords, the officers setting the men an example of hard work. Our own age has little right to complain of lack of humanity in such matters, but in any case this method has con-stantly been used in fighting rebellion and was a commonplace of Irish warfare.[2]

The most important result of the enterprise was, however, the death of Owny MacRory. The flames of burning houses brought him down from the hills to the rescue, and he was killed

---

[1] Moryson, Vol. II, 329. (Moryson has got the date wrong). C.S.P. Ireland, March-Oct., 1600, pp. 337, 394.
[2] *Four Masters*, Vol. VI, pp. 2, 187.

in the skirmish that followed. The loss of their vigorous chief appalled the O'Moores, and they dispersed in all directions.[1]

Still the burden of Essex rested on Mountjoy's shoulders. At some time during August, after the departure of Southampton, another messenger arrived in Dublin. After being freed from his keeper, Essex had summoned Sir Charles Danvers, whose devotion to him was intense, and asked him to visit Mountjoy. He had indeed begun by talking once more about the project of bringing over troops to England, but Danvers had begged him not to give further thought to the scheme, to which he was convinced Mountjoy would never consent. Essex then sent him by the hand of Henry Cuffe a curious proposal, that Mountjoy should write a letter complaining of the misgovernment of the State and a summons to Essex to redress it. So Danvers came over. Mountjoy did not approve of the plan. He desired Essex to have patience and recover the Queen's favour by "ordinary" measures—the best possible advice. He might, he said, send a letter, but if he did it would be one that he could justify. If he ever did send a letter it was certainly not the sort of document Essex wanted, which was Mountjoy's endorsement of his policy and commitment to his conspiracy. The real friends of Essex, like Mountjoy, Southampton, even the rash Charles Danvers and his brother Henry, were now trying to save Essex from himself; but Southampton and Charles Danvers were too closely bound to him to resist his pleading when he called them.[2]

Now came the northern expedition. The two thousand troops to increase the establishment had arrived, so that Mountjoy was able to muster 375 horse and 3,500 foot and to leave 157 horse and 2,700 foot with Ormonde, in and about the Pale. He was, however, still awaiting victuals from England and so short of money that he had to pledge his personal credit. He did not start until 15 September, rather late in the season. Meanwhile Tyrone was fortifying the Moyry. "God willing," wrote the Lord Deputy, "we will march over him; for by him we cannot". He knew he could not garrison Armagh unless the victuals arrived.[3]

---

[1] Carew C., 1589-1600, p. 439.
[2] Spedding, Vol. II, pp. 338-341.
[3] C.S.P. Ireland, March-Oct., 1600, pp. 421, 423, 425, 430, 445.

The Irish September played its part. He was held up at Dundalk and again at Faughart Hill, south of the Moyry, by rain which made the streams impassable. Tyrone's men were in the pass, and his three lines of trenches were covered by great ramparts of earth and stone and barbed with thorn bushes. On 2 October Mountjoy drove the Irish out of their first trenches, largely through the gallantry of an Irishman. The trenches spanned a gully between two steep hills, from which the cross-fire of musketeers covered the approach. The men of the company of Sir Thomas Burke, Dunkellin's brother, wavered and fell to their knees in face of the enemy's volleys, whereupon he dashed forward with a handful, carrying the colours, threw them over the rampart, and was the first to leap over after them. The English suffered 152 casualties. After some further warm fighting another pause followed; it was of no avail to push Tyrone out while the wet prevented his being followed. Tyrone had, in fact, had enough. He drew back to Armagh, and Mountjoy razed his defences and cut down the trees in the Moyry.

However, the delay had been too long. Mountjoy decided not to go on to Armagh. Instead he built or dug an earth fort eight miles north of Newry, placed in it a garrison four hundred strong, and named it Mountnorris in memory of his old master in war, Sir John Norris. This could more easily be revictualled from Newry than Armagh could have been. Then he returned by way of Carlingford, having a sharp fight on the way. The troops behaved well and returned in good heart to the Pale, though the weather had been atrocious, their stomachs had been none too well lined, the enemy had fought with great resolution behind his entrenchments, and the losses amounted to about fifty killed and two hundred wounded

The Irish annalists naturally describe the result as a defeat for the Lord Deputy because he did not advance to Armagh, much less to the Blackwater. It was assuredly not a full success. Yet there is no evidence to suggest that Mountjoy was daunted by the resistance. It was the victuallers who had let him down. They had not shipped the food when the winds were favourable, and when they did the winds turned against them. The sickness in the Lough Foyle force denied him its aid. It looks as though

Mountjoy regarded the fighting in the Moyry as in great part a trial of strength.[1]

The Lord Deputy cannot have disguised from himself the fact that Carew in the south was so far effecting more than he himself was able to, but had no doubt that it was he who bore the heavier burdens. One ingenious political scheme set on foot by Carew failed. He induced the Queen and Council to release the real Earl of Desmond from the Tower and send him over to create enthusiasm in Munster. The luckless young "James of the Tower" reached Youghal on 14 August. He was received with delight, even adulation, but his first Sunday ruined all. As soon as he entered the Protestant church at Kilmallock he was finished as an influence. In the end he returned to England, where he died soon afterwards. The astute Carew had made a serious miscalculation. Otherwise he was successful. By the end of the year 1600 he had so well mastered his province that he was prepared to lend the Lord Deputy a regiment for Leinster. Not a castle remained in rebel hands. Cattle could be left out by night as well as day.[2]

Though Docwra had not been strong enough to lend a hand to Mountjoy on his last northern expedition, he also had some achievement to his credit, largely due to Irish allies. Early in October the long-awaited paladin, Neill Garve O'Donnell, came in, during the absence of his cousin Hugh Roe, again raiding in Connaught. With an Anglo-Irish force Neill Garve at once seized Lifford, a valuable strategic point at the confluence of the Finn and the Foyle, and held it against Hugh Roe on his return.[3]

On 3 December the Queen wrote to her Lord Deputy a friendly and gracious letter, all in her own hand. In reply to her scolding he had bitterly described his role as that of a scullion, and she began with a jocular allusion to this.

"Mistress Kitchenmaid—Comfort yourself therefore in this, that neither your careful endeavour, nor dangerous travels, nor heedful regard to our service, could ever have been disposed upon a prince that more esteems them, considers, and regards them, than she for whom chiefly, I know, all this hath been done,

[1] C.S.P. Ireland, March-Oct., 1600, pp. 483, 513, 522, 524; *Four Masters*, Vol. VI, p. 2, 223.

[2] *Pacata Hibernia*, Vol. I, pp. 154-65, 191; Falls, p. 286.

[3] C.S.P. Ireland, 1600-01, p. 7; *Four Masters*, Vol. VI, pp. 2, 217.

and who keeps this verdict ever in store for you: that no vainglory nor popular fawning can ever advance you forward, but true vow of duty and reverence of prince, which, too, after your life, I see you do prefer . . . I would have you know for certain that, as there is no man can rule so great a charge without some errors, yet you may assure yourself I have never heard of any that had fewer". She subscribed herself: "Your Sovereign that dearly regards you".[1]

In the words "no vainglory nor popular fawning" lay a hint, typical of Elizabeth's subtlety, of the conduct of Essex and a warning to avoid such courses. Yet the letter as a whole made pleasant reading and balm for much fault-finding. Charles could carry on his task with the certainty that, if he was, as he felt, unjustly criticized, his service was appreciated.

[1] Carew C., 1589-1600, p. 481.

XI

SWEET ENGLAND'S PRIDE IS GONE!

M OUNTJOY believed in campaigning in winter. He did not rest long in Dublin after his return from the northern expedition in November, 1600. He gave out—even to Cecil— that he would keep Christmas at the castle of Monasterevin in Kildare, and sent tapestries there to confirm the story, He would, he said, take some further action against the O'Moores and O'Connors. In fact, these people had been cowed, at least for the time being, and he was looking elsewhere, closer at hand. Marching in the direction of Monasterevin, he suddenly turned left-handed and made a dash towards Wicklow. This was the country of the O'Byrnes, who often raided up to the gates of Dublin and who had ignominiously defeated a force which entered the fastness of their glens in the time of Essex. Mountjoy's first object was to catch their chief, Phelim McFeagh O'Byrne, in his fortress of Ballinacor, in Glenmalure. He marched from noon on 23 December, 1600, to nightfall on the 24th with a halt of only three hours. Approaching Ballinacor, he detached six hundred horse and foot to come in upon it from another direction. He surprised the O'Byrnes—a feat in itself—but narrowly missed Phelim McFeagh, who jumped naked from a window and fled into the winter night. But for the snow which clogged the feet of the troops he might have been caught. However, his son was taken, his Christmas dinner eaten, his drink drunk, and his land despoiled.

Mountjoy then marched towards Monasterevin, but within six miles of it turned back towards Wicklow again, again surprised the O'Byrnes, and took a great number of cattle. Some sharp fighting followed, and it came to push of pike before the enemy was driven off. Phelim McFeagh made his submission in March.

"I never saw any L. Deputy take the like pains in my life", Captain Nicholas Dawtrey wrote to Cecil, "for he gives his body no rest, and although he were a very sickly gentleman in England yet he keepeth health here the best of any man, besides that he is endued with notable virtues befitting a general in such a country as this is; for he hath excellent temperament in all things to discern between man and man, as matter and matter, that cometh before him. He hath secrecy in so excellent a measure that his intent cannot be discovered before it be done; also he hath affability to please all men of service and severity to make the wicked live in fear of him, valour to do as beseemeth his place when he entereth into any action against open rebels, judgement to drive any rebel or rebels to draw good blood of the rebellion he cometh from before he will take him to mercy. As for pledges and hostages, he regardeth them not. These virtues God hath endued him plentifully [with] and withal hath given him a great blessing, that all things that he himself, or any man by his direction, taketh in hand, prospereth and goeth forward, insomuch as his Lp. hath cast the coward out of her Mas. army, that sometime troubled it very much, and driven him amongst the rebels, where I hope he shall continue unto the end of this rebellion."[1]

The phrase "to draw good blood of the rebellion he cometh from" is an allusion to the custom of requiring all men who had fought in the ranks of the rebels to perform some useful service against their former allies before being received into submission. This served as an insurance against their subsequent relapse, though not a complete one.

Mountjoy put garrisons into Wicklow town and Tullagh, on either flank of the O'Byrnes' country, to hold them down. Then he did indeed visit Monasterevin, but not for a long stay. Most men in his position would have returned to Dublin after such exertions in such weather. He remained absent from the capital for nearly four months in all, though he kept close touch with his Council by messenger, to deal with a stream of letters from England, mostly concerned, as was customary, with recommendations for the filling of jobs or with Irish complaints. He moved next into Kildare, halted at Maynooth, and passed on to Trim in

[1] S.P. Ireland, Vol. CCVII, Pt. I, 25; Moryson, Vol. II, p. 350.

Meath, where he remained some time. Then, hearing that Tyrone was about to send reinforcements into Munster down the centre of Ireland, he entered Westmeath on 11 February, 1601. He himself rode as far as Athlone to visit Sir John Berkeley, then deputizing as Governor of Connaught for Sir Arthur Savage, who was in England. Mountjoy valued meetings with subordinates and undertook several long journeys to achieve them. His march into Westmeath was effective. Tyrone's men appeared in force in Cavan, but were drawn back by their master when he learnt that the Deputy lay across their road to the south. On 19 February Mountjoy moved to the castle of Donore.[1]

He was resting in that solitude when dreadful and bewildering news came to him in a packet from England. Essex had put himself at the head of a revolt, had failed, and was now in the Tower.

The date of the outbreak was 8 February, 1601, but the report did not reach Donore until the 22nd. Mountjoy had left his friend in the hands of the Lord Keeper. About 20 March, 1600, Essex had been removed to his London house, still under confinement. Yet mercy was now in the air, and this had been the reason put forward by Mountjoy for refusing to entertain the project of Southampton in May. On 5 June Essex had been brought before a commission and censured. Early in July his guard had been removed. On 26 August he had been given leave to go where he would, save that he might not come to Court. After a visit to the country to restore his health, he had returned to Essex House, where at first he had lived quietly. Continued denial of access to the Court, the Queen's refusal to renew his monopoly of the sweet wines, and the mad advice of certain of his intimates—especially his secretary, Henry Cuffe—inflamed his mind and led him to take the last fatal step.[2]

He formed a council which met commonly at Drury House, but sometimes at Mountjoy's house in Holborn. This finally decided that the conspirators should seize the Palace and force the Queen to dismiss Cecil, Ralegh, and Cobham. He gathered about him all his available associates and spread his net for

[1] C.S.P. Ireland, 1600-01, p. 195; Moryson, Vol. II, pp. 351-4.
[2] Birch, Vol. II, pp. 443-462; *Reliquiae Wottonianae*, p. 180.

other fish. Roman Catholics were given half-promises of toleration, and more than one young man who joined him was later to be implicated in the Gunpowder Plot. His antecedents made appeal to restless Puritans easier. He collected a large following, it is said three hundred gentlemen; but to most of them he imparted only generalities and kept his object for his small circle, of which the chief figures were Southampton, Sir Charles Danvers—and his sister Penelope. There is no room for two opinions about this object. It was stark revolution, that is, overthrow of the Queen's rule. The real issue was whether it was to be the Queen or Essex who was to exercise sovereign power in the realm. On 7 February he got evidence that the Court was nervous about the size of the gathering at Essex House. The Second Secretary of State, John Herbert, was sent to request his attendance at the Privy Council. He refused to go, alleging that his person was in danger. It has been said that the summons was a ruse on the part of Sir Robert Cecil to push Essex into revolt; but this is speculation, probably over-subtle. Since, however, the Court was presumably on the alert—which in fact it scarcely was as yet—Essex had no hope of surprising it and securing the Queen's person. He must raise the City to begin with. There he was popular, and depended on one of the Sheriffs, Thomas Smith, to bring out his trained band in his favour.

The squib proved damp. Babble about a Spanish plot made no appeal. No one would join him; rather did his followers fall out. The Sheriff would perhaps have supported him if he had been stronger, but as it was preferred to slip away. Trying to return down Ludgate Hill, the conspirators were stopped by pikemen and, being themselves armed only with rapiers, failed to break through in a skirmish in which Sir Christopher Blount was wounded and taken. With some fifty followers Essex got back to Essex House by water. The place was then invested by forces of the Crown. Their commander, Lord Nottingham, threatened to blow up the house, "which he might have done sooner, but that the Lady Essex and the Lady Rich were within it." That night the defenders of Essex House surrendered unconditionally.[1]

[1] Spedding, Vol. II, chs. vii and viii; Birch, Vol. II, pp. 463-9; C.S.P. Dom., 1598-1601, p. 565.

To the Queen's Lord Deputy, reading the despatch in the Westmeath plain, the words signified the possibility of ruin. This was treason, to be punished by death, and, though he was not involved in the outbreak, he was involved in the dealings which had preceded it, and they were treason too. The prisoners would talk under examination. He could cherish no illusion that his part in the affair would be concealed. He might be doomed. Yet there was a fair amount of hope. If they found out all, they would discover that he had backed out when Southampton called on him to act. He thought the matter over. His first precaution was to remove his secret papers from the hands of his secretary. Poor Fynes Moryson was hurt, and probably annoyed at losing valuable historical material—verbal as well as written, because his master became uncommunicative. He was grim instead of gay now. Nearly two years later the keeper of a journal noted: "The Lord Mountjoy in Ireland will never discourse at table; eats in silence."[1]

It was not until the second day after receiving the despatch that he sat down to write a careful note to Robert Cecil, in his own hand, not Moryson's copperplate. The interval had been employed in anxious consideration. The statement that he was prepared to die if the Queen should consider that he no longer deserved the trust she had reposed in him almost amounted to a confession of past unwisdom, though he represented his conscience as untroubled. It must have been hardy if so.

"Sir, I am and ever shall be glad that any man's life, though it were mine own, may give any safety to the estate of my dear sovereign, unto whom, above all private affections, I do owe a love and duty. And although my long and inward familiarity with the principal actors of this miserable tragedy may give just reason to a provident estate to look upon me in this matter with some jealousy, yet I am confident in my own conscience and in my prince's favour and justice, and doubt not but my proceedings hitherto, and hereafter, shall show themselves to be fruits that proceed from a root without all corruption. And for the present I dare assure you the army is free from the infection of this conspiracy and doubt not but to contain it firm and obedient to resist or suppress anything that shall grow in this kingdom, if therein

[1] Moryson, Vol. II, p. 354; Manningham, p. 104.

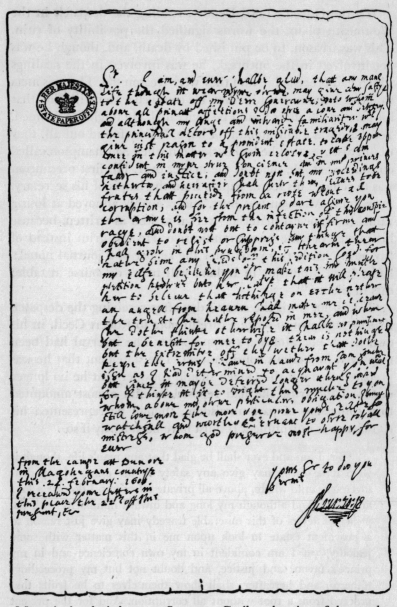

Mountjoy's adroit letter to Secretary Cecil on hearing of the revolt
of the Earl of Essex. The text is printed on the facing page.

there hath been any seeds of this sedition sowed. For myself, I beseech you, Sir, make this my humble petition known unto Her Matye, that it will please her to believe that nothing on earth, neither an angel from Heaven, shall make me deceive the trust she hath reposed in me, and when she doth think otherwise it shall be no punishment, but a benefit, for me to die. There is nothing but the extremity of the weather that doth keep the service I have in hand from some such issue as I have determined to acquaint you withal, but since it may be deferred longer than I looked for I think it fit to write thus much to you whom, above my own particular obligation, I must still love more, the more you prove yourself so watchful and worthy a servant to our royal mistress, whom God preserve most happy for ever.

from the camp at Donore   Yours, Sir, to do you Service,
in MacGeoghan's country
this 24 February 1600 [1].   Mountioye"
I received your letters in
this place the 22nd of this
present.

The composition of the letter was adroit, even masterly, without an inexpedient word. It had to bear the scrutiny of two pairs of exceedingly sharp eyes.[1]

He had not been mistaken about the confessions. Everyone confessed, one might say lavishly, from Essex downwards. Everything came out, including the missions of Southampton and Danvers to Ireland. Essex, though he was to die nobly, passed through a weak and shameful hour after his condemnation, breaking down in a passion of penitence in the presence of members of the Privy Council and charging one after another of his associates with having pushed him into revolt. Mountjoy heard of this some time later, when, in a friendly personal letter of 31 May, Lord Nottingham described the embarrassing scene. He disclosed the worst infamy: Essex had involved Penelope and had linked her name with that of Charles. "And now," Nottingham reported him as saying, "I must accuse one who is most nearest to me, my sister, who did continually urge me on with telling me how all my friends and followers thought me a coward, and that I had lost all my valour". Penelope's lover could not fail to realize that the story was true—this was

---

[1] S.P. Ireland, Vol. CCVIII, Pt. I, 54. (Reproduced opposite).

Penelope to the life. But Essex had said more. "And spared not," went on Nottingham, "to say something of her affection to you. Would your Lordship have thought this weakness and this unnaturalness in this man?"[1]

Ugly as the business was, there had been a respite, and Nottingham's letter indicated that the Government did not mean to proceed against Mountjoy. Yet for several weeks this had not been certain. In fact, the Queen proved merciful. Southampton, in the plot up to the neck, was saved by his youth, his penitence, Elizabeth's moderation, and the unremitting efforts on his behalf of the much-abused Robert Cecil. Only four besides Essex suffered the extreme penalty. Sir Christopher Blount and Sir Charles Danvers—him Cecil could not save— were beheaded on Tower Hill; Sir Gilly Meyrick and Henry Cuffe were hanged at Tyburn. One other was executed in different circumstances. Captain Thomas Lee, a rash veteran of the Irish wars, had formed a wild plan to seize the Queen and compel her to sign a warrant to liberate Essex and Southampton from the Tower. He was caught watching the door of the privy chamber, awaiting his opportunity, and was immediately tried, condemned, and hanged. This was before the Earls had been brought to trial, and indeed Lee's plot contributed to making the fate of Essex certain. Some noblemen and gentlemen, headed by the Earls of Bedford and Rutland, were heavily fined, though by no means all the fines were actually paid.

The Government had been startled, if not scared. In most countries the result would have been a bath of blood, but not in Elizabethan England. As regards Mountjoy, the policy was that suggested by Nottingham's letter. Every scrap of evidence which pointed to him was suppressed—this was not difficult, as the evidence had been given in confessions behind the scenes. In one of those made by Southampton he mentioned that he had been forbidden to speak of a certain matter which he had previously disclosed. This was surely the evidence implicating the Lord Deputy. The Queen knew that Mountjoy was personally devoted to her. He was succeeding where others had failed; but the final test would probably come in the shape of a Spanish expeditionary force. Mountjoy was irreplaceable.

[1] Tanner, p. 36.

It may have been long before he learnt what had been revealed about his activities, perhaps not until he met Southampton, liberated by James I on his accession. News about Penelope is, however, likely to have reached Ireland. In September, 1600, she had acted in a manner typical of her best side, the side that brought her universal popularity, by going down to Leighs to nurse Lord Rich, who was gravely ill. That duty accomplished, she had returned to London and thrown herself with gusto into the plotting. She had been one of the inner circle connected with the rising. On the previous night she had made one of the little party which supped with Essex and his lady after the visit of Secretary Herbert, the others being Southampton, Sir Christopher Blount, Sir Charles Danvers, and Sir Robert Vernon, Essex's cousin and Southampton's brother-in-law. Later that night, still restlessly plotting, she had sent a messenger to a friend, Sir Henry Bromley, had him roused from his bed and brought to her, told him of Herbert's message, assured him that her brother's life was in danger, and besought him to act in the City next day. On the fatal morning itself she had driven out from Essex House to call on the Earl of Bedford and about 11 a.m. carried him back in her coach without the knowledge of his family. But "the poor, toiling, Penelope might have spared her pains." Bedford took fright, escaped her, collected a party of horse, and rode to the Court to put himself at the service of the Queen.

As the result of her brother's accusations Penelope was confined in the custody of Henry Sackford, Keeper of the Privy Purse. The thoughtful Privy Council, however, allowed her to send for her own male cook and directed—not merely permitted—her highly-tried husband to supply her with all the bedding and hangings she required. Nottingham and Cecil interrogated her and were delighted to be able to report to the Queen that she had behaved modestly and humbly. Elizabeth was probably equally relieved to be able to order her release.[1]

By a coincidence, on 4 February, four days before the outbreak, Mountjoy had written to ask leave to come home and report. He remarked, with justification, that it was desirable for

[1] C.S.P. Dom., 1598-1601, pp. 456, 572; 1601-03, p. 4; A.P.C., Vol. XXXI, pp. 166, 176; Sidney (Collins), Vol. II, p. 215; Tanner, p. 37; Rawson, p. 244.

governors to give the Queen personal accounts of affairs from time to time. This had indeed been the custom in Ireland in the easier days of the Earl of Sussex and Sir Henry Sidney, both of whom had visited England during their viceroyalties. He wrote: "If she will have it so, (I will) lie in the porch of her doors and not see my wife till my return to her army, as Uriah did." This was a curious sentence. "Not see my wife" might of course be considered symbolical, but there could be little doubt of the writer's intention to make it clear that he did not want to come for the sake of seeing Penelope and would not see her if the Queen objected. Even before the rising the subject was delicate by reason of her rash behaviour.

Nottingham, in the letter already quoted, commented on Mountjoy's application. "I think her Majesty could be most glad to see and look upon your black eyes here, so she were sure you would not look with too much respect of other black eyes." Nottingham was in astonishingly jocose mood on the subject. "But for that," he wrote, "if the Admiral were but thirty years old, I think he would not differ in opinion from the Lord Mountjoy." The Admiral was indeed gallant, since Penelope was nearer forty than thirty. He also ventured to forward a letter from Penelope to himself, trusting that there had been no impropriety in his receiving it: Mountjoy knew, he wrote gaily, what a youth he was, but he would never betray a friend. The letter is Penelope at her best, noble in her reference to her brother and fine in her anxiety for her lover:

> "For my deserts towards him that is gone, it is known that I have been more like a slave than a sister; which proceeded out of my exceeding love rather than his authority. . . . Your lordship's noble disposition forceth me to deliver my griefs unto you, hearing a report that some of those malicious tongues have sought to wrong a worthy friend of yours. I know the most of them did hate him for his zealous following the service of her Majesty, and beseech you to pardon my presuming thus much, though I hope his enemies can have no power to harm him".[1]

Mountjoy's request to visit England was refused, but graciously, with a promise that it would be reconsidered when the Spanish threat had ceased to overhang Ireland. Fynes

[1] C.S.P. Ireland, 1600-01, p. 173; Tanner, p. 37; Rawson, p. 250.

Moryson asserts that if his application had been granted
Mountjoy would have fled to France, rather than "put his neck
under the file of the Queen's Attorney's tongue." The reference
is to the brutal methods of Sir Edward Coke in the trial of Essex
and Southampton. The story cannot be disproved, but it has a
doubtful ring. Is it not likely that, had Mountjoy been as
alarmed as all that, he would have returned to Dublin or moved
to the neighbourhood of some other port and kept a ship ready
there? In fact he stayed in the inland parts until mid-April. At
the end of February he dispersed Tyrrell's troops in Offaly and
left the mercenary captain wandering in woods and bogs with a
few kerne. In March he was in Meath. From Ardbraccan he
carried out one of his typical enterprises. He marched all night
and entered Ferney, the southern barony of Monaghan, which
had belonged nominally to Essex, but was now in the hands of a
chief of the MacMahons, Ever MacCooley, a strong adherent of
Tyrone's. Simultaneously Sir Richard Moryson and Captain
Thomas Williams converged upon the barony, the one from
Dundalk, the other from Ardee, in Louth. The speed and force
of the invasion rendered resistance out of the question. Three
thousand cattle were swept in, besides horses, sheep, and swine.
Ever MacCooley made humble submission. In Cavan, some of
the O'Reillys were seeking to be received to mercy. In Tyrone
itself one of the great chiefs, Tirlagh MacHenry O'Neill, had
come over. The Lough Foyle force was in possession of
O'Dogherty's country, the rich peninsula of Inishowen, and the
redoubtable Neill Garve O'Donnell had established himself west
of Lough Swilly. Ulster was not subdued, but Tyrone's power
was seriously diminished.[1]

Meanwhile Mountjoy had received an encouraging letter
from the Queen, confirming her trust in him. He had expressed
his confidence to her and his prophetic belief that a long peace
would follow his viceroyalty. There is no evidence that his
anxiety continued. What the crazy conduct of Essex seems to
have done for him was to establish in his mind a policy which
had perhaps already entered it half formed. He would in future
follow the orthodox path. This involved good relations with Sir
Robert Cecil. Cecil was the man of the present and probably still

[1] C.S.P. Ireland, 1600-01, pp. 126, 144; Moryson, Vol. II, p. 355.

more of the future. If James VI came peaceably to the English throne, Cecil might well be the first power in the land. On the other hand, the Essex party had stood for the Scottish succession, so that its survivors might expect the favour of the King of Scots. Were Mountjoy's Cecil's ally, he would be armed doubly.

Mountjoy drew closer to Cecil, though he disliked some of his associates, including Ralegh. A bridge existed in the person of Cecil's dear friend, Sir George Carew, the only man in Ireland in whose judgement Mountjoy placed full reliance—as he had even when they were not on the best of terms. Henceforth Carew took every opportunity to foster friendship and confidence between the two men. Mountjoy knew that there was an element of the fox in Carew, that he was jealous, and that he carried on small intrigues with the Secretary over his, Mountjoy's, head. He could put up with that, knowing that neither of them would ever fail him. Once, believing that he had found out Carew in an outrageous piece of backstairs work, he let his temper break loose in a letter of fierce reproach; but, deciding that the offence was much less serious than he had thought, he made a handsome apology. He was too politic to indulge in a needless feud with so valuable a second.

Carew could be used as a channel for comments on Cecil's treatment of Mountjoy which the latter could not so easily make directly to the man himself. "I am so much in my heart a servant to the worthiness he hath showed in his kindness to me, that if he should desire me to trail a pike under a far meaner friend unto him than you, by God I would do it willingly!" Nor were these words written, he asserted, in base obsequience to the Secretary's power. "Upon my Christianity I do acknowledge him to have deserved more of me than all the world beside." Of course these words were passed on to Cecil, who wrote in reply: "My heart dearly loves him."[1]

Was this pure self-interest on the part of Mountjoy? Clearly a measure of self-interest entered into it. Yet the message is more deeply imbued with gratitude. It would appear certain that Mountjoy attributed the generous manner in which he had been treated, the sponge passed over past faults, in large part to the influence of Cecil He may have possessed positive evidence of

[1] Carew C., 1601-03, pp. 143, 151.

this—not all correspondence remains in our records, and, unfortunately, it is often in the most secret and fascinating business that they fail us. The relations of the two men after the war suggest genuine friendship.

At all events, from now onwards Mountjoy and Cecil began to understand each other. They could work together, in the war or after it was over. If one all-important danger did not materialize, it would be over soon—and then Mountjoy promised Carew a happy meeting "in the land of good meat and clean linen". The danger was Spanish aid to the rebellion.

So, while at home folk still lamented their dazzling lord and in the taverns sang mournfully,

> Sweet England's pride is gone!
> Welladay! Welladay!

Mountjoy had put that episode behind him. The people would presently forget their sorrow for Essex. They did after a time, all but—at first sight paradoxically, but not untypically—the Irish.

XII

SPANISH INTERVENTION

PHILIP II OF SPAIN had, as recorded, promised his Irish friends the aid of a Spanish army in 1596, but had failed them. His death in 1598 put back the project into the melting-pot. Whether, cautious man as he was, he would have revived it in face of the growing strength of the Dutch States General is a question that cannot be answered. The new King, Philip III, was not averse to trying his strength in a venture which his father had cherished but postponed, and his powerful minister, the Duke of Lerma, was in favour of the plan.

From the beginning of the year 1601 both the English and Irish Governments had information that a Spanish expeditionary force was likely to arrive. Agents' reports, intercepted letters, and examination of Irish skippers who had visited Spanish ports or picked up news at French, all told the same story. On 30 April the prudent Cecil made a note that he must provide for the transport of another 4,000 men to Ireland. Mountjoy resolved not to commit himself too deeply to Ulster. Carew thought the Spaniards would come to Cork or Limerick, and Cork rather than Limerick. He did not believe they would venture as far east as Waterford, as too close to English ports. Everyone realized that a Spanish landing force would be most dangerous in Ulster, where the rebellion was still strong, but few thought the enemy would extend the length of the voyage by 250 miles, if to Killybegs, or 300, if to Lough Swilly. When the decision to land in the south is criticized, as it was criticized then by the Adelantado of Castile, it is well to recall that the Spaniards did what appeared reasonable to Carew. The objections to carrying on to an Ulster harbour lay in the rough and broken nature of Donegal, the extra length of the voyage for the

SIR GEORGE CAREW

Depicted in his later years as Earl of Totnes.

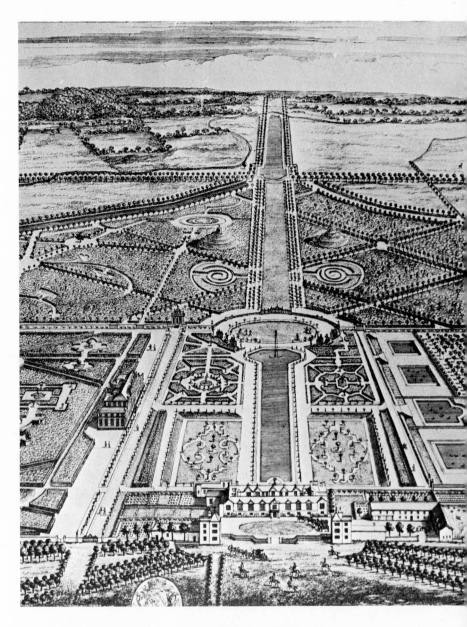

WANSTEAD HOUSE

This print dates from about a century after Mountjoy's time when the gardens had been extravagantly elaborated.

original force, and the extra time which would be required if the same ships had to make a second voyage with reinforcements and supplies. And the Spaniards were very short of shipping.

The Spanish Council of State sent an officer to Tyrone and O'Donnell to find out their views on the subject. When he arrived Tyrone was not available, being, as will appear, heavily engaged with Mountjoy. O'Donnell wrote from Sligo that he would prefer the fleet to make for the Shannon estuary or Galway, but it is not known whether his letter written in August reached Spain before it sailed. What has been made clear is that a decision to put into Kinsale was made aboard the Spanish flagship, probably against the opinion of the land commander, though he acquiesced in it.[1]

Mountjoy was not going to let his troops stand idle while he awaited the Spaniards. He meant to keep up the pressure, because, if it appeared that they were not coming after all—if, for example, their preparations proved to be concerned with the Low Countries instead of Ireland—a prospect existed of virtually extinguishing the revolt before the end of 1601. He had determined on a third expedition to Ulster and one which was likely to be more fruitful than those of the previous year. The way had been prepared by Docwra and his Lough Foyle force and by Chichester and his Carrickfergus garrison, while the Deputy himself had pacified the barony of Ferney and established a force in Cavan.

Chichester, with small resources, had done valuable work. He had driven Tyrone's nephew, Brian MacArt O'Neill, out of Upper Clandeboye, the country west of Strangford Lough, and, since there were no English troops to hold the area, garrisoned it with Irish bonaghts. He had opened negotiations with the Scottish settlement on the Antrim coast, though the Macdonalds were for the time too nervous and suspicious to come in. He had raided across Lough Neagh from a boat-station on the eastern side and carried fire and sword almost to Dungannon, forty miles from his headquarters at Carrickfergus. This was a measure of success worth supporting.[2]

[1] C.S.P. Spain, 1583-1603, pp. 676, 690; Jones: *The Irish Sword*, Vol. II, No. 5.
[2] C.S.P. Ireland, 1600-01, pp. 303, 332.

On 8 June Mountjoy reached the Moyry, which he knew the look of by now. It was not held, but, as on the last occasion, his supplies from England were delayed. He had with them a force of a nominal strength of 2,750 foot and 300 horse, not counting 500 foot and 50 horse under Sir Richard Moryson at Dundalk, which he intended to establish in Lecale, south of Strangford Lough. Already established on his line of advance were the Newry garrison of 200 men, that at the fort of Mountnorris of 150, and under Chichester at Carrickfergus 750 foot and 125 horse. Docwra had 3,000 in list, though only 1,675 for the field, in Tyrone and Tyrconnell. On 14 June Mountjoy wrote to Docwra that he had to wait for the general hosting in the Pale to supply him with transport animals, but that meanwhile he could plant garrisons at Armagh and on the Blackwater. After that he hoped to put pressure enough on Tyrone to give Docwra a chance of seizing Ballyshannon, if he could do it with his own resources; if not, Mountjoy would try to break into Tyrone and meet Docwra there. With extraordinary daring, when the danger of a Spanish landing in Munster is considered, he bade Carew send a thousand foot into Connaught, adding the doubtful consolation that if the Spaniards did come the most that could be done in any case with the forces in the province would be to hold Cork and Limerick and that further defence must depend on reinforcements from England.[1]

The project of the Lord Deputy was marred because Docwra had not enough fit troops for Ballyshannon and also because at the last moment he discovered that he had no match in his store for his musketeers and therefore could not come to a rendezvous. Docwra, Mountjoy was learning, was inclined to be casual and careless. Still, useful work was carried out. The garrison for Lecale was established. Sir Henry Danvers was placed in Armagh, where the half-ruined cathedral furnished a fort of some strength. Mountjoy met Chichester in Lecale and reinforced him with two hundred men whom he could be relied on to make good use of. The march to the Blackwater followed the track taken by the English force routed in the Battle of the Yellow Ford in 1598. Viewing the ground with an eye now expert in the tactics of Irish warfare, Mountjoy felt himself at a loss to explain the

[1] C.S.P. Ireland, 1600-01, pp. 381, 394; Moryson, Vol. II, p. 398.

defeat. He himself would, he declared, be glad to meet the Irish here. They did not oblige him now, and he had to return to Newry to await more stores, cattle on the hoof, and transport horses. He returned to the Blackwater on 16 July and found it held in strength by Tyrone.

Mountjoy had thought it worth while to drag with him a couple of small guns. These he loaded with musket bullets. After a few rounds the Irish began to vacate their trenches on the far bank, so that he effected a crossing without difficulty. On 16 June he reached Benburb. There he fought a long and sharp action, time after time feigning retreat and punishing Tyrone's men severely when they followed up. The brunt of the fighting fell on his Irish troops, who suffered about one hundred casualties, whereas the only Englishman killed was his chaplain, Dr. Latewarr. Mountjoy's secretary observes philosophically on the losses: "And these Irish being such as had been rebels, and were like upon the least discontent to turn rebels, and such as were kept in pay rather to keep them from taking part with the rebels than any service they could do us, the death of those unpeaceful swordsmen, though falling on our side, yet was rather gain than loss to the commonwealth". Moryson believed that over two hundred of Tyrone's men were killed. The great advantage on the side of the royal army was that it had unlimited powder, whereas Tyrone had to husband his.[1]

In former actions the Ulster forces had generally been well provided with powder. It therefore seems possible that the supply from Scotland was at last being checked. During the viceroyalty of Essex the navy had kept several ships on the Irish coast. At the time of Mountjoy's appointment two "crompsters", or 200-ton cruisers, and a 60-ton pinnace had been fitted out for this purpose. This was not a very formidable force for the work because there was need to patrol the west coast also. Two Connaught septs, the O'Malleys and O'Flaherties, were owners of galleys and had been more or less longshore-pirates for many a year. In war they could combine patriotism and gain by preying on small merchantmen and fishing-craft from Galway and by transporting rebel troops. In April Carew learnt of their inten-

[1] C.S.P. Ireland, 1600-01, p. 401; Moryson, Vol. II, pp. 399-410.

tion to land 600 men in Kerry, but he scared them off by keeping at sea an armed merchantman and some small craft. These Irish galleys must not be thought of in terms of the fine craft commanded by Spinola. They carried no guns. Yet they did carry musketeers. Though they could not face the smallest ship which carried a gun, they could bring havoc to an unprotected coast, and any unarmed ship which they encountered when becalmed was doomed. In July the *Tramontana* ran a galley of the O'Malleys, with a hundred shot, ashore between Teelin and Killybegs, on the Donegal coast.[1]

If Docwra had been on his toes at the right moment Mountjoy would have risked a deeper penetration into Tyrone. As things were, he did not want to be tied down, as he might have been without aid from Docwra. He withdrew to Newry on 24 August, leaving all his northern garrisons well established. In the Moyry itself he had built a small fort, which stands to this day. On the 25th he moved to Trim, in Meath, a convenient station from which he could move quickly back into Ulster if the Spaniards did not come or march to Carew's aid if they appeared in Munster. On 12 August Cecil learnt that English pinnaces had sighted some fifty Spanish sail at sea. His message took over three weeks to reach Carew at Cork, but fortunately the gale which delayed it also forced the Spanish fleet back. Mountjoy meanwhile rode south with a small escort, met Carew, and accompanied him to Kilkenny Castle. There on 22 September they sat in council with Ormonde, Sir Richard Wingfield (the Marshal), and Sir Robert Gardiner (the Chief Justice). News was brought to their board that a Spanish fleet had been seen off the Old Head of Kinsale. Next day, in the midst of another council meeting, a messenger came in from Sir Charles Wilmot, left by Carew in command at Cork, that the Spanish fleet had entered Kinsale harbour. The test which had been under discussion for years was now at hand.

All the council but one advised Mountjoy to return to Dublin to assemble his troops. The one was Carew. He declared that if the Lord Deputy were seen to turn his back on the enemy the effect on the country people would be calamitous; he ought

[1] C.S.P. Ireland, 1600-01, p. 436; Carew C., 1601-03, p. 53; C.S.P. Dom., 1598-1601, pp. 349, 376, 382.

to go forward even if he had no follower but his page. Mountjoy was ready to adopt this suggestion, but was worried because he had little in the way of victuals in Dublin. Carew answered that during the past six months he had been issuing the Munster garrison with a cash allowance in lieu of rations and so had a good store. Mountjoy jumped up from his chair and embraced him. If their friendship wanted sealing it was sealed then.[1]

It is notable that the tone of Mountjoy's letters displays a new calm from the moment that the danger became a reality. Grievances were forgotten. The burden of guilt had been lifted from his shoulders. Yet he did not make light of the difficulties. He was disappointed about the north, where some of his work must now be undone. He had hoped to leave there all the garrisons which he had established, but, owing to an unfavourable wind which had held up his reinforcements, he would now have to use every man whom he could venture to withdraw—for example, Sir Henry Danvers was to bring down the force, 750 strong, recently posted at Armagh. Nor would it be possible to secure the Pale against Tyrone. Yet he bade the Privy Council not to worry about what the Irish did or indeed about any happenings except those at Kinsale. The Spaniards represented the objective. All stood or fell by them.

"If we beat them, let it not trouble you though you hear all Ireland doth revolt, for (by the grace of God) you shall have them all return presently with halters about their necks: if we do not, all providence bestowed on any other place is vain. . . . I apprehend a world of difficulties with as much comfort as ever poor man did, because I have now a fair occasion to show how prodigal I will be of my life in every adventure that I shall find to be for the service of my dear Mistress, unto whom I am confident God hath given me life to do acceptable service, which when I have done I will sing *Nunc dimittis*."

Again, having informed Cecil that the Spanish commander was one of the best generals in the service, with veteran captains and good, well-armed, troops, and having sketched the darkest possibilities, a Spanish success followed by the organization of a Spanish-Irish army for the invasion of England, he summed up:

[1] Carew C., 1601-03, pp. 122, 179; *Pacata Hibernia*, p. 196.

"And now, Sir, that you know (as I hope) the worst, I cannot dissemble how confident I am to beat these Spanish Dons as well as ever I did our Irish Macs and Os."

The confidence of the Queen and Council matched his own. Elizabeth declared more than once that she could not wish her army and the safety of her kingdom in better hands. She directed that Mountjoy's first private letter to Cecil on the arrival of the Spaniards should be read aloud to the Council, "as being written in a style wherein she discerned both the strong powers of your own mind in promising to yourself all happy success (against such an enemy) and the lively affection you bear to her person". The Lord Deputy was promised all he required in men, munitions, victuals and money. Of the 4,000 men Cecil had made up his mind five months earlier to hold ready, about half had already landed. The rest would be sent with a fleet of ten ships of war. Another 2,000 would arrive towards the end of October. The Queen's last Parliament, which met that month, was left in no doubt of the financial effort involved. Ralegh told the Commons of the sale of the Crown lands and jewels— actually, in the course of her reign Elizabeth sold lands to the value of £876,332, the major fruits of the dissolution of the monasteries which had come into the hands of the Crown. Sir Edward Hoby revealed that since Essex went to Ireland she had spent £300,000 and that, since the subsidy, double "fifteenths and tenths", and a special subsidy from the clergy, came to £160,000, her Majesty was down by £140,000. A big effort was made by a country weary of the burden of war because such an effort was vital. On 5 December the loyal Commons sent up to the Lords a bill granting four subsidies and eight fifteenths and tenths.[1]

Carew had advised Mountjoy to go forward even if he had none but his page to accompany him. He rode to Cork with no bigger escort than a hundred horse. This was a bold action, though there proved to be no danger. The Munster Irish had remained quiet and the Spaniards had shut themselves up in Kinsale. They had no cavalry, though they had brought saddles for the horses which they hoped their Irish allies would provide.

---

[1] Moryson, Vol. II, pp. 454-61; A.P.C., Vol. XXXII, pp. 243-5; D'Ewes, pp. 630, 668; Rowse, pp. 334-9.

Far from being able to intercept Mountjoy, they could not even prevent him from reconnoitring Kinsale on 29 September. He found the Spaniards hard at work on their defences. Most of their fleet had sailed for home and the few ships still in the harbour were about to do so.

The first of the English troops summoned reached Cork on 3 October. On the 8th and 10th more arrived, including those of Danvers, who must have made a fine march from Armagh. Mountjoy decided that the best way to hide his weakness was to take the field. On the 17th he encamped on Knockrobin Hill, close to Kinsale. On the 26th he moved to Spittle Hill, just north of the town, and began to open parallels, the first act of the siege.

The Spanish Admiral, Don Diego Brochero, had, as was the custom, sailed from Lisbon rather late in the year, on or about 1 September, and had met with the usual Spanish luck in the way of weather. His fleet consisted of thirty-three ships, carrying 4,464 foot, six pieces of artillery for use ashore, large quantities of food, and arms for the Irish. When he was not far from the Irish coast nine ships became detached and put back into Coruña. This was unfortunate for the expedition. The nine ships, one of which was that of the highly competent Vice-Admiral, Pedro de Zubiaur, were carrying 650 troops and, a still more serious matter, a considerable proportion of the stores.[1]

The land commander was Don Juan de Aguila, a veteran of many campaigns, against whom Mountjoy had served as a junior officer in Brittany. Since he landed with only 3,814 men, some already sick, and a certain shortage of stores, he knew he would be heavily out-numbered in Munster. As has been stated, the Spaniards were well aware that the main strength of their friends lay in Ulster, but it was not until Aguila came ashore that he realized how indifferent the situation in Munster was. During the summer Carew had disposed of the only two men who were seriously troubling him, catching James Fitzthomas, the Sugane Earl, hiding in a cave, and arresting Florence MacCarthy with a not untypical lack of principle. The province was almost completely subdued. Aguila's prospect of success depended, therefore, in the first place on strong and speedy aid from the

[1] C.S.P. Spain, 1587-1603, p. 692; Polentinos, p. 70.

northern lords, and in the second on reinforcements from Spain. He wrote at once to Tyrone and O'Donnell, urging them to march south, bringing with them horses, his chief need. Meanwhile he did not feel himself strong enough to do more than hold Kinsale, a walled town, but small and not very well fortified. His inaction cannot be condemned.[1]

Much depended therefore upon which forces, those of the Lord Deputy or those of Tyrone and O'Donnell, first reached the scene. The Lord Deputy was there in person, but without many troops, and he knew only too well that Tyrone and O'Donnell could not be prevented from marching through Ireland. He had, however, two great advantages on his side. In the first place, a large proportion of his reinforcements were coming by sea, and the winds proved kindly for a change. In the second, his organization was superior to that of the Irish. His regimental and company commanders, even the Irish among them, would require no long notice and would march quickly. Tyrone, who was overlord of a great part of Ulster, would have to deal with subordinates who were not his officers but inferior chiefs and would in all probability take longer to get on the move. Into the bargain his habit was to be leisurely and dilatory.

Mountjoy had in fact no difficulty in anticipating the Ulster forces. Shipping with stores and ordnance arrived at Cork on 23 October, and on the 28th two culverins were landed. By this time the army numbered nearly 7,000 foot and 600 horse. Aguila had occupied two castles outside the walls of Kinsale, Castle Ny Park, on a peninsula in the Bandon estuary, and Rincurren, on the left or eastern bank. Mountjoy determined to take these strongholds because they were a threat to shipping, and Rincurren first. He handed over the job to Carew. The fighting was sharp but short. Aguila twice tried to relieve or reinforce the castle with boats, and when that failed sent out five hundred men in an equally unsuccessful attempt to reach it by land. Meanwhile he bombarded the camp with guns to which extra range was given by hoisting them into little castles on the walls and others boldly brought outside the nearest town gate. That

[1] C.S.P. Ireland, 1600-01, pp. 369, 389; Falls, p. 288. The arrest of MacCarthy while under protection is discussed here.

evening, 31 October, the Spanish drums at Rincurren beat a parley. Mountjoy and Carew agreed that, battered though the castle was, it would cost many lives to storm. They therefore decided that it would pay them best to offer the Spaniards their lives and a promise of return to Spain if they would lay down their arms. The Rincurren garrison surrendered on 1 November.[1]

O'Donnell was the first of the two great Ulster lords to move. He marched through Sligo and Roscommon, was ferried across the Shannon at Shannon Harbour, and then advanced into Tipperary. He camped north of Templemore and ravaged the countryside to teach the people not to submit to the English. A council of war decided that an effort should be made to intercept him, and Mountjoy ordered Carew to go. The President did not like the undertaking, well knowing how often the Irish had marched round the English. In this instance the Irish were favoured by a sudden sharp frost, which made a track over the Slievefelim Mountains practicable for pack horses, whereas before it had been impassable after heavy rain. O'Donnell outmarched Carew and finally halted on the upper Bandon with some 3,000 men. Carew could only return to the camp, arriving on 25 November, having been absent since the 7th.[2]

Noting the weakness of the besiegers in Carew's absence, the Spaniards made a sortie on 10 November. They lined some trenches in the hope that the English would charge them frontally. Mountjoy instead sent a body of musketeers to outflank the trenches. The enfilade fire was so hot that the enemy could not abide it and had to draw back hastily to the gate. The English got a report that Aguila was deeply angered with the leader of the sortie, whom he accused of lack of judgement and resolution.[3]

On this day Mountjoy learnt that Lord Thomond, stirred from the Court by the Spanish invasion, had been blown out of his course and entered Castlehaven, 30 miles west of Kinsale Harbour, with 1,100 troops. The other half of this contingent of 2,000 foot and 200 horse was arriving at Waterford. This left

---

[1] Carew C., 1601-03, p. 180; Moryson, Vol. III, pp. 16-19.
[2] *Pacata Hibernia*, Vol. II, pp. 374-8.
[3] Moryson, Vol. III, p. 31; Carew, C., 1601-03, p. 159.

only 2,000 more troops to come with the royal fleet. That reached Cork on 12 November, and the Admiral, Sir Richard Leveson, and Vice-Admiral, Sir Amyas Preston, at once came to visit the Lord Deputy. The fleet reached Kinsale on the 14th. The troops were so raw and sickly in the bad weather that Mountjoy sent Thomond's force straight to Cork for rest and training before they joined in the siege.[1]

The next step was the capture of Castle Ny Park, and this time the fleet was there to join in the bombardment. The anniversary of the Queen's coronation, 17 November, could not be allowed to pass without an attempt to perform an action of note, so it was resolved to storm the place on that day. A machine known as a sow—because men, like piglets, sheltered beneath it —was wheeled up to the wall, so that a breach could be prised with levers, but the Spaniards smashed the timber with stones dropped from the tower, and the assault was repulsed. The bombardment was therefore renewed, and on the 20th the remaining seventeen Spaniards in the castle surrendered after a gallant defence.[2]

So the outlying works had both been taken; the besiegers had been strongly reinforced; and the fleet had brought trained gunners, artificers, and munitions. On the day after the surrender of Castle Ny Park fire was opened on Kinsale with a cannon and a demi-cannon mounted on a platform. By 23 November nine guns were in action. Next day Mountjoy decided to sap forward and bring his parallels closer to the walls. Good progress was made during the night, though the moon shed unwelcome light and the ground was frozen. On Carew's return on the 25th, strengthened by some Irish forces from the Pale and Connaught which had joined him in Tipperary, his troops were placed in a new camp west of Kinsale to prevent the Irish from joining hands with the Spaniards. Thomond was put in command here because Mountjoy desired to keep Carew at his side. Later on two forts were built between Thomond's camp and the Bandon and connected by communication trenches. Mountjoy's own camp was covered by Oyster Haven, on which supplies could be brought up by boat, and lay astride the road which

---

[1] Carew C., 1601-03, p. 181; *Pacata Hibernia*, Vol. II, p. 382.
[2] *Pacata Hibernia*, Vol. II, pp. 384-6.

crossed it. In making his dispositions he had the advice of his
capable Trench Master, Josias Bodley, brother of the founder
of Bodley's Library.[1]

A summons to surrender brought the typical reply from Don
Juan that he was holding Kinsale, first for Christ, second for the
King of Spain, and would maintain it against all foes. He was not
having a happy time in so doing. His walls were already damaged.
He afterwards said that he had never been able to catch Charles
off his guard. His sallies had been beaten back. Beyond twice
hitting Leveson's flagship the Spaniards had achieved little
success of any sort, though from now on they were to find a
strong ally in the weather, one more effective than the Irish
proved to be.

The walls of Kinsale were none too strong. The experienced
Aguila realized that a practicable breach would inevitably be
made if he did not at once interrupt the cannonade. On 30
November the artillery bombarded the wall beside the eastern
gate to such effect that a length was knocked down, and on 1
December two thousand English troops approached this place.
If they had any intention of forcing their way in, which Mountjoy's secretary denies, they were deterred by the alert and firm
attitude of the defenders both within the breach and in a trench
outside it. One Spanish officer continually walked up and down
across the breach, while Sir Richard Wingfield cried out that he
would give twenty pounds to the man who brought him down.
Finally the English drew off.

This bold front had, however, done nothing to stop the
English from widening the breach at their leisure. On the
following night, therefore, Aguila made a great effort. The frost
had gone, and it was dark and raining when the Spaniards
poured out, in numbers reported, probably with some exaggeration, to be two thousand. They carried with them mattocks to
pull down the English gabions, shovels to fill in the trenches, and
spikes to "cloy" the guns on the east side. The main body rushed
the battery, putting three or more companies to flight—about
the only occasion during the siege on which English troops
behaved badly. Another body entered the fort on the west side.
Mountjoy hurried reinforcements to both points, and after a

[1] C.S.P. Ireland, 1601-03, pp. xvii, xxx; *Pacata Hibernia*, Vol. III, p. 390.

prolonged and fluctuating struggle the Spaniards were forced back into the town. English reports attributed to them by far the heavier loss. They claimed to have spiked two guns, but the English admitted one only.[1]

Pedro de Zubiaur sailed again from Coruña on 26 November and reached Castlehaven on 1 December—a speed which sounds almost incredible, but his papers have been preserved. His squadron consisted of a Spanish store-ship, in which he flew his flag, and eight hired or requisitioned French and Scottish, most of them very small. Three of these parted company with him in hard weather. One which had not been ready to sail with him later on entered Kinsale Harbour, where its Scottish skipper handed over to the English the eighty Spaniards aboard. The reinforcements brought by Zubiaur were thus reduced to 650 men, but he also carried a considerable amount of food. On 5 December Leveson sailed for Castlehaven with four of the Queen's ships of war and a couple of small craft. Next day a fierce action began in the narrow inlet, the English warships pounding the Spanish merchantmen with their much more powerful guns, but being themselves galled by the fire of Spanish and Irish musketeers ashore, while the Spanish Admiral, who was over sixty years of age, himself laid and fired a cannon mounted on the jetty. One Spanish ship was sunk and another driven ashore, but Leveson was bottled in by a contrary wind and suffered severely before he was able to warp out on the 8th.[2]

The effect of the arrival of this small Spanish reinforcement proved to be out of all proportion to its strength. For the first time serious opposition revived in south-west Munster, and this was increased when shortly afterwards Tyrone arrived to join O'Donnell. The Irish handed over to the Spaniards the castle commanding Castlehaven, two more covering the entry to the harbour at Baltimore, 12 miles to the south-west, and Dunboy Castle at the head of the great inlet of Bantry Bay. The five guns and the stores landed by Zubiaur were valuable. Though they could not be sent to Kinsale, they could be handed over to the Irish field army and put into the castles. The harbours and their castles created some anxiety in the mind of Mountjoy because,

[1] Falls, p. 299; Moryson, Vol. III, p. 53; C.S.P. Ireland, 1601-03, p. 219.
[2] Moryson, Vol. III, p. 58; Polentinos, pp. 123-5.

whereas he had invested and blocked Kinsale, he could not be sure of keeping Spanish reinforcements from the other harbours. It would be necessary to divide the fleet, keeping part to guard Kinsale Harbour and the store-ships—in which he had to keep his munitions and victuals, having no means of establishing magazines ashore—while part patrolled the coast. He urged that Leveson should be strengthened and that more supplies should be sent, as at present he had enough only to last until 20 January.

At the same time he was much troubled by sickness and desertion. The troops, and more especially the raw men from England, melted away, as was inevitable in a wet winter from which they were protected only by improvised shelters. Mount-joy was doing all he could for them within the limits of contemporary knowledge of sanitation. At Cork he had established a rest-house, where they were carefully looked after. In the camp the Chief Justice, Sir Robert Gardiner—who had stoutly accompanied the army as a representative of the Council—acted as, in modern parlance, chief welfare officer. Fifty pounds a week was subscribed by the officers to provide hot broth, meat, and other comforts for sick and wounded. As a result "a marvellous great number" were recovering, but the wastage remained high.

Mountjoy had enforced the death sentence against some deserters as an example. He relied, however, chiefly on men acting as police at Cork, Youghal, Waterford and even Wexford —over a hundred miles from Kinsale—to which the runaways had gone in hopes of stowing away on ships returning to England or bribing the masters to carry them over. He did not forget to point out to the Privy Council that the misery the troops were enduring merited compassion; for example, several men, fit and well when posted as sentries or standing to, had been found dead.[1]

It was not possible for Mountjoy to persist in his intention of storming Kinsale, though he had already made a large breach in the wall. He brought back his outlying artillery into the main camp lest it should be overrun by a combined Spanish-Irish attack. Yet with fine persistence he ran out guns by day and continued the bombardment, which never wholly ceased.

Now both sides were being put to the test. As a fortified town

[1] Moryson, Vol. III, pp. 63-72.

Kinsale was a poor little place, though the houses had good cellars which afforded the troops ample protection. The walls were crumbling after a bombardment which would not have been thought of much account in the Netherlands. In all his sorties, big and small, Aguila had achieved little or nothing, and certainly had not interrupted the siege. Worst of all, though he had now been just three months ashore, the Irish had made no attempt to join hands with him. He was consuming his provisions only too fast. He wrote reproachfully to Tyrone and O'Donnell, urging them to bestir themselves. He told them that the English were weary and had not the men to garrison half their trenches. He promised that, if the Irish would attack, he from his side would keep the besiegers fully occupied.[1]

Tyrone's problem was different. He had all the countryside at his disposal for supplies. There was no need for him to hurry. On the contrary, the longer he waited, the more hungry and depleted in numbers would the royal forces become. If he waited long enough he could hope at least to force them to raise the siege; he might reduce them to such a state that it would be easy to overwhelm them. To attack now involved a pitched battle on open ground. He could not look forward to that with confidence. The Irish had won successes in defiles. He himself had gained a brilliant victory by attacking a long column of regiments on the march and unduly strung out. This was another matter. He had had opportunity to learn the power of English pikes, musketeers, and horse under the leadership of Mountjoy. He must have felt an uneasy doubt whether the Irish, transformed from guerrilla fighters to regular soldiers, were as yet capable of facing them. On the other hand, the young and ardent O'Donnell was constantly urging him to attack for the honour of Irish arms. A more material consideration was the contingency that the Spaniards might come to terms with the besiegers if he delayed too long. For a soldier, Tyrone had the bad habit of balancing two courses of action overlong. At last he decided on the second course. He would take the offensive.

Mountjoy's plight was worse than that of Aguila or Tyrone. He was beleaguered as much as Aguila in Kinsale, except that he retained communication with the outer world by water, and

[1] *Pacata Hibernia*, Vol. II, p. 405.

since the arrival of Leveson's fleet there had not been a favourable wind from England. One essential commodity, fodder, had
been used up; if the Irish had delayed the advance a day longer
it had been the intention to order the cavalry to break out in
order to save the horses from starvation. The strength of the foot,
11,800 by the list, had sunk to 6,595. The Irish army sitting on
Mountjoy's back—which could be dealt with only if it chose to
attack—was about 6,500. Aguila had still over 2,000 Spaniards fit
to fight, besides a small Irish contingent.

Mountjoy took two more precautions. He fortified his main
camp on the north side and created a "flying regiment", 449
strong, of companies drawn from other regiments, and placed it
under the command of Sir Henry Power. It was relieved of all
siege duties, so that it would be immediately available in case of
an alarm. There was no more to be done for the time being. If
Tyrone continued to hang back Mountjoy considered the possibility of making a great breach and trying his fortune in a storm;
but he did not like the prospect and would await Tyrone a little
longer. The bombardment of the walls was continued largely to
induce the Irish leader to come on. He would rather fight
Tyrone's six thousand in the open than Aguila's much smaller
force in a breach.

The strength of mind and tenacity which inspired Mountjoy
need no flowers of rhetoric. He had his hooks into Aguila and
he would not let go. He was getting his sleep by day now and
staying up all night in his "house of turf".

XIII

CROWNING GLORY

O N 21 December the Irish appeared in force on the road to
Cork, north of the main English camp. Mountjoy at once
drew out two regiments of foot and most of his cavalry, whereupon the enemy fell back into a wood. The conclusion must be,
in default of information from Irish records, that Tyrone was
hoping to surprise the camp; but it looks an unwise action,
since his arrangements with the Spaniards had not yet been
made. Now comes a story of treachery in the Irish camp which
has been disputed but is founded on evidence as good as any on
which the historian has to rely. Brian MacHugh Oge MacMahon
of Monaghan was Tyrone's son-in-law, but had once been on
friendly terms with the Government, so much so that his son had
gone to England as Carew's page. On 22 December he sent a boy
to Captain William Taaffe, a cavalryman, to tell him that he had
run out of whiskey and that he hoped Carew would send him a
bottle. It is to be noted that the date was 1 January, 1602, according to the new style, which the Irish followed, and that Christmas
had already been celebrated by them, "feasting and rejoicing
together", doubtless drinking all their store of liquor, and
leaving none with which to celebrate New Year's day. The
whiskey was sent. In reply MacMahon next night sent his love
and thanks to Carew and bade him stand upon his guard because
the Irish intended to assault before daybreak and the Spaniards
had agreed to sally out simultaneously from Kinsale.[1]

It is manifestly a boon to a commander to be informed when
his enemy intends to attack. Yet the theory that this warning
decided the Battle of Kinsale will not hold water. Mountjoy was

---

[1] *Pacata Hibernia*, Vol. II, p. 414; Mangan: *The Irish Sword*, Vol. I, No. 3,
p. 222.

now experienced as well as alert by nature. The approach of the Irish on the 21st had already revealed to him that they were likely to attack, though without indicating the date and time. He had other intelligence to this effect. He had already formed his flying regiment. Now he ordered Power to station it outside and to the west of the main camp and close to the main guard of the cavalry, as soon as the moon went down. He also strengthened the guards and directed the troops other than the flying regiment to hold themselves in readiness, but not to stand to their arms. He wisely decided not to fatigue them unduly.[1]

We may suppose that Charles comforted himself with the tobacco he was so much addicted to as he waited through the night. All was quiet but for the noise of a high wind and occasional claps of thunder. Christmas Eve came in. No alarm had sounded when, in the darkness but only half an hour before first light, he walked across to Carew's hut to confer with him and Wingfield. In the midst of their council a trooper rode up and called from the doorway: "My Lord, it is time to arm; for the enemy is near unto the camp!" A little after daybreak a messenger arrived from Sir Richard Graeme with the report that the cavalry could see the lighted matches of the Irish musketeers. The enemy was advancing from the west.

Mountjoy first ordered the whole army to stand to arms. Next he rode forward with Wingfield and, after going a short way, sent him on to the outpost line. The Marshal came back to report that the enemy had halted. Mountjoy's next moves were governed by what he saw and the reports he received. His first thought was to fight a defensive battle. He had a suitable position ready in Thomond's fortified camp, the fort south of it, and a trench connecting them, which he had ordered Thomond to man. He sent back the Sergeant-major, Sir John Berkeley, to bring up two more regiments of foot, those of Sir Henry Folliott and Sir Oliver St. John, to the support of Power's flying regiment.[2] However, the Irish did not attack. Finding the Queen's army on the alert and ready to fight, they drew back across a "ford"—apparently a causeway across boggy ground—

[1] *Pacata Hibernia*, Vol. II, pp. 411, 415.

[2] St. John had recently been sent to England to report the situation, which must have appeared none too good to the Queen and Privy Council, and his regiment was commanded by his lieutenant-colonel.

though the three English regiments numbered only 1,500 men and two of them were still some way behind Power. The retreat hid the Irish from the Deputy's view behind rising ground, but Wingfield could see them, and he sent back word that they were somewhat disordered.

Mountjoy gave the order to follow up the enemy. It was an exceedingly bold decision. He was moving away from his supports and yet was unwilling to withdraw from the camps more than the three regiments of foot and some four hundred horse. If the Spaniards came out in strength, considerable strength would be needed to hold them. He was actually leaving over three-quarters of his infantry for that purpose and marching after the Irish with less than a quarter. And the Irish foot numbered four times that which he was sending against it. If, therefore, the Irish attacked him he was likely to be pinned down by the superior strength of their infantry and to find retreat very difficult. It may be divined that he was obeying a reasonable intuition. Why had Tyrone halted? Because he had counted on surprise and was confused in mind when he found he had missed it. Why had he then drawn back? Because he was nervous and undecided. If so, it would be still more obvious to his troops than it was to the opposing commander. Therefore push forward and seize whatever chances occurred. Mountjoy rode on, but he sent Carew back to take supreme command of the investing forces.

Let us leave him for a moment and turn to the other side to find out how far he was right in his surmises. Here the evidence is less precise, but there is small doubt about the main facts. Tyrone, as has been suggested, rather assented to than initiated the offensive. The plan agreed upon was that the Irish should advance about midnight against the main camp and that the Spaniards should sally out and attack that of Thomond. To begin with a childish quarrel took place about precedence, no chief being prepared to allow another to lead the advance. Then O'Donnell, commanding the rear, lost his way, and the rest of the army had to wait for him. Even as it was he and his force were not present when the Irish advanced. Armies of the time moved with the foot in three bodies known by the old titles of "van", "battle" or "gross", and "rear", the horse preceding the van. They were drawn up to fight in line, van on the right, battle in the centre, and rear on the left, with the horse normally on the flanks. The titles were retained even when they were in order of battle, so that a historian is more likely to say that the enemy attacked "our rear" than "our left". The Irish van was commanded by Tyrrell, the gross by Tyrone, the rear by O'Donnell. The gross was made up wholly of Ulstermen; the rear of Ulstermen and some from Connaught; the van from other parts, including about a thousand Munstermen and a Spanish force of two hundred from Castlehaven. The horse numbered 600; the foot 6,000, perhaps rather more.

It would seem that Tyrone's state of mind was in fact what it appeared to be from Mountjoy's point of view. He had some loose form of supreme command, in an enterprise which he disliked and into which he had been led only by the urgent demands of O'Donnell. His withdrawal was made because, having failed to achieve surprise, he now preferred to fight on the defensive, at least to begin with, and therefore chose ground better suited to such tactics than that which he reached in his advance. His action was likely to have an unsettling effect on emotional troops, and, as will appear, this was not his last withdrawal. In Kinsale Don Juan waited. He had at first thought that Tyrone had called off the operation because the Irish had appeared so late. According to a journal of the operations at Kinsale kept by or for Carew, the latest intention had been to pass Tyrrell and eight hundred of his best troops, including the little Spanish contingent, into the town and fight the decisive battle next day. This does not square with other accounts, but, if true, it would furnish an additional reason why the Spanish commander should hold his hand. In any case, the light had been good enough for him to see from the walls the infantry force which Mountjoy had drawn out, and it seemed to him impossible that the English should attack against such odds. It has been suggested that he did not hear the musketry fire which followed. This seems improbable because the battle took place only about a mile and a half from the town, though out of sight from it. The account of the battle will show, however, that there can have been little musketry, hardly enough to suggest a big engagement and what noise there was may have been blanketed by the hills. No cannon were employed on either side.

We now return to the English. The cavalry, under the direct command of Sir Henry Danvers and accompanied by Wingfield, rode after the enemy. Mountjoy ordered Power's flying regiment to follow—the other two regiments of foot had not yet appeared on the scene. Almost at once the three great bodies of Irish foot marched off to the rear, covered by their horse. Mountjoy asked men who knew the country what it was like and was told it was a "fair champaign", that is reasonably flat and without obstacles, just what he wanted. Yet there was one obstacle at all events. After the cavalry had advanced a mile it found the enemy standing behind a boggy stream which could be crossed only by another ford. Spanish officers could be seen marshalling the force in order of battle, but to Wingfield's eye it seemed confused. He sent back a messenger to Mountjoy asking leave to try a charge. Immediately afterwards Clanrickarde, who had been riding with the Marshal, rode up to Mountjoy and begged him to fight. He did not balk these eager men. He gave Wingfield leave to use his discretion and himself led on the foot as fast as they could march.

When Power with his flying regiment had closed up on the cavalry Wingfield ordered him to take out a hundred musketeers and drive back an Irish rearguard defending the ford. A sharp but short fight followed. The Irish counter-attacked and drove back the English musketeers, but when the latter had been reinforced they shot to such effect that they broke down the resistance. The passage was open. Wingfield rode over with the troops of horse of Graeme—whose reputation has before been mentioned—Taaffe, and Fleming. On his command the lean horses were spurred into a gallop, perhaps only a canter, towards Tyrone's, the central body of Irish foot. The Irish couched their their pikes and stood firm.

Though some accounts have it that the charge was repulsed, the truth is that it was not pressed home. Cavalry could not hope to ride over a superior body of pikemen prepared to receive them, unless there were already gaps in its ranks or it flinched in anticipation of the shock. In accordance with accepted tactics when the enemy did not give way, the cavalry wheeled and returned, to the accompaniment of an Irish yell of exultation. It was then joined by Danvers with two more troops, one Mountjoy's own led by Godolphin, the other Carew's. The total strength was still little if any more than five hundred, but Wingfield decided to try again. By now not only the flying regiment but the other two regiments of infantry had crossed the bog and were ready to support him. He, Clanrickarde, and Danvers put themselves at the head of the cavalry and charged.

This time, first the Irish horse, then Tyrone's battle, broke at sight of the advancing English horse. The cavalry rode right into the infantry mass, hacking and stabbing. Tyrrell then began wheeling to his left to aid Tyrone. Mountjoy immediately sent St. John's regiment to attack him in flank, whereupon Tyrrell, seeing that the centre had now dissolved in flight, drew back to a neighbouring hilltop. Here, however, he made no stand worthy of the name when Mountjoy threw in his attack. The Irish troops had been so mishandled by their leaders and the wings so discouraged by the flight of the horse and of the centre that they could not be kept in hand. Tyrrell's men, already disordered, also broke and fled from the field. O'Donnell's force on the Irish left did the same thing, though it had not been attacked. Only the Spanish contingent with Tyrrell made any real resistance, and it too was soon broken by Mountjoy's troop of horse. After about half had been killed, the commander, Alonzo del Campo, and forty-seven others surrendered. Some sixty Spanish fugitives reached Castlehaven.[1]

Except for the Spaniards, the troops of the Irish wings for the most part escaped, and in fact O'Donnell can have lost hardly a man, because the English cavalry was pursuing the flying centre. Almost all the slaughter occurred in this body. The English claim to have counted 1,200 dead, though this may have been an exaggeration. The Irish chroniclers, the Four Masters, assert that the loss was not great. It would have been heavier had not the cavalry been unable to continue the pursuit on its half-starved horses for more than a mile and a half. Yet it

---

[1] C.S.P. Ireland, 1601-03, p. 241; Moryson, Vol. III, pp. 76-80; Carew C., 1601-03, pp. 192-4; *Four Masters*, Vol. VI, pp. 2281-9; Falls, pp. 304-7; C.S.P. Spain, 1587-1603, p. 700. The map is somewhat speculative as regards movements and the site of the fighting, since it is difficult to transfer features of the highly imaginative Elizabethan map of the modern survey.

was not an army that escaped from the battlefield or evaded the pursuit but an unarmed mob. The wings, like the centre, threw away their weapons in great numbers. About two thousand of these were found, together with all the powder, the drums, and nine ensigns or company colours. The English losses were trifling. One officer, Graeme's cornet, was killed; Danvers, Godolphin, and Crofts, the Scout-Master, were wounded, the first two but slightly. The heaviest loss was in horses.

After the retreat had been sounded, Mountjoy rendered thanks to God for the victory. He then knighted Clanrickarde for his valour. After returning to Kinsale, he drew out the whole army and once more gave thanks to God. At the end of the service a volley was fired to celebrate the victory.[1]

The volley was taken by the Spaniards as a sign that Tyrone was at last attacking. They therefore issued forth from the gate to join in. When, however, they saw the English cavalry waving captured colours, including Spanish, they fell back into the town.

Such was the victory of Kinsale. It was won so easily, with scarcely any fighting or loss to the victors, that it is sometimes belittled. Yet it is surely not discreditable, but rather the reverse, to win a battle without loss. Mountjoy accepted serious risks—risks such as perhaps only the Queen's Viceroy could have taken—and his boldness was rewarded. It is not in the light of knowledge after the event but by the situation as he faced it that his achievement should be judged. The story goes that a lady, who had heard of several people to whom the victory of the Marne was due, asked Marshal Joffre who really won it, and that he replied: "I do not know, madame, but if it had been lost I know who would have lost it". The loss of the Battle of Kinsale might have been the starting-point of widespread disaster.

"Never any general in this Kingdom", wrote Carew, "had a more fortunate day, or in his own person and direction has better deserved; for the dice was cast, the Kingdom being ready to sway on that side that proved victorious".[2]

[1] Moryson, Vol. III, p. 81; *Pacata Hibernia*, Vol. II, p. 421. The first authority describes the thanksgiving as on the battlefield, the second as on return to the camp. It would be natural that it should take place twice, first for the victors, then for the whole army, the latter probably taking the form of a religious service conducted by a chaplain.

[2] C.S.P. Ireland, 1601-03, p. 242.

The defeated Ulster troops went home at top speed. Tyrone's flight was marked by dead men and horses, and some of those whose houses he had burnt on his march south now took their revenge by throwing stragglers into bog-holes and treading them down. O'Donnell himself sailed to Spain in one of Zubiaur's ships to press Philip III for another expeditionary force. He handed over his troops to his brother Rory, who led them back through Connaught.

Although the Irish army had been dispersed, neither Mountjoy nor Carew was yet altogether easy in mind. Kinsale remained unsubdued and Don Juan and his garrison still in fighting form. On 25 December, the English Christmas Day, they made two sallies from the west gate, on the second occasion maintaining the fight from 9 to 11 p.m. On the 26th they again came out after dark and drove off with loss the defenders of a new trench close to the wall; but, being met by a volley when they approached the fort, withdrew into the town. As before the battle, they could be held; but the prospect of a storm was not inviting. According to the evidence of Spanish prisoners, reinforcements were expected, and Castlehaven, Baltimore, and Berehaven lay open to them, all defended by castles and none easily accessible to the English, Berehaven in particular being very hard to reach. True, only some four hundred Spanish troops were distributed among them, but they had been reinforced by Irish. The English fleet was nearing the end of its provisions and the cavalry horses were still without oats in a countryside eaten bare.

These points were brought out in the despatches sent home on 27 December. Mountjoy entrusted them to his friend Sir Henry Danvers because the bearer of tidings of victory is traditionally rewarded with high favour and this mission might be expected to disperse the cloud under which Danvers had lain since his brother Charles had been executed for his leading part in the conspiracy of Essex. In a private note to Cecil accompanying the official letters Mountjoy excused himself for its brevity. He was, he said, exhausted; he had caught a cold and his head was splitting. It would seem that he was never to recover all that Kinsale had taken out of him.[1]

Suddenly the scene changed. On 31 December Aguila offered

[1] Moryson, Vol. III, pp. 83-7.

a parley. The messenger, accompanied by the drum-major, brought a letter to Mountjoy, with the suggestion that an English officer should come into Kinsale to negotiate, while a Spanish officer of similar rank should stay in the English camp as a pledge for his safety. Mountjoy sent Godolphin. Aguila told him that he held himself relieved of any obligations to the Irish and did not think it to be in the interests of his master to exert himself further in their support. He was, therefore, ready to deliver Kinsale and the other places held by the Spaniards. The terms, however, must be honourable and such as could be entertained by men who were prepared to bury themselves in the ruins rather than accept base conditions.

The proposition so well suited both sides that agreement was virtually assured from the first. It was, however, preceded by some bargaining. Mountjoy demanded that Don Juan should leave behind his treasure, artillery and munitions, and should hand over the Queen's natural subjects in his army—that is, some two hundred Irish volunteers, who would almost certainly have been hanged. Aguila indignantly refused, very honourably where the Irish were concerned, and stated that if such conditions were again mentioned Mountjoy would have to depend on the sword because the previous offer would be withdrawn. The Lord Deputy and his Council did not persist. Norris's storm of Crozon Castle and the fearful loss suffered was ever in his mind. Most of the Spanish treasure was spent already, and it mattered little that the guns were not captured so long as they were removed from Ireland. Though Aguila knew Mountjoy was in trouble, he did not know how bad it was. The army had only six days' food left, was short of powder, and could mount only a single battery. The greatest inducement of all was that of obtaining without a fight control of the castles commanding the three harbours. Within forty-eight hours terms were drawn up, on 2 January, 1602.

The Spanish forces were to be shipped to Spain, all at once if possible, in two echelons if not, Aguila in that case waiting for the second. Aguila pledged himself that they should not bear arms against the Queen, even if reinforcements arrived before they had sailed. If the ships were driven into any English or Irish harbour they were to be treated as friends and allowed to buy provisions. If any English ships encountered the transport fleet on its voyage, they would allow it to go free; similarly the English ships carrying the troops would be well treated in Spanish ports and allowed to return as soon as possible. That afternoon Aguila came out and dined with Mountjoy. Next day Carew, Leveson, and Godolphin dined with Aguila in the stinking, battered town, bringing back three captains who were to be kept in English hands until the shipping returned from Spain.

The Spanish army was to remain at Kinsale, but Aguila and some of the senior officers rode to Cork with Mountjoy on 9 January. On the 14th Mountjoy sent home his despatch on the composition, the bearer being Sir Richard Moryson, chosen for the same reason as Danvers had been, as a follower of Essex who had been out of favour and could profit from bearing good tidings. Since the Spaniards at Kinsale retained their arms, the possibility of a reinforcement arriving before they had gone gave cause for reflection. Cecil, who was far from scrupulous, writing to his friend Carew, who resembled him in this, hinted that the pledge to the Spaniards should be broken and took it for granted that preparations had already been made to secure the Spaniards "so suddenly (though with breach of some formal article) as no new descent shall make these spiders dare to crawl". By the time this mean advice arrived the last of the Spaniards had gone home.

From Cork Mountjoy issued orders for his forces to disperse into garrison towns. He also directed a force to go by sea and take over from the Spaniards the castles of Castlehaven, Baltimore, and Berehaven. Westerly winds held it up, so that Castlehaven could not be reached until 10 February nor Baltimore until the 26th. As for Dunboy in Berehaven, the companies allotted to it were overwhelmed by sickness on shipboard and the crews so weakened that they could not face a spell of bad weather and had to return to Baltimore after very heavy loss of life. This delay in occupying Dunboy was to give Carew much trouble.

Mountjoy was still pretty fully occupied with collecting shipping and provisions for the repatriation of the Spaniards, dealing with civil affairs which had long been neglected, and breaking up weak companies of which the men were then distributed among others. He was itching to turn over Munster once more to Carew and prosecute the war in Ulster to a finish. He could not, however, leave Munster or withdraw troops from it until the Spaniards were gone. He had intercepted a number of letters to Aguila landed from a Spanish ship which entered the Kenmare River, including one from King Philip III and three from the Duke of Lerma. Some of these had been written before news of the Irish defeat had been received, some after the arrival of Zubiaur and Hugh O'Donnell at Coruña; but all promised Spanish reinforcements and provisions.

It was maddening that the wind should prevent the concentration of shipping because the arrival of the Spanish force in Spain would be the best insurance against any further action by the Spanish Government. Don Juan told Mountjoy that as soon as he reached home he would do all in his power to prevent the sailing of another expedition, and that there was not an officer in the force but would use his influence against it. They all felt disillusioned about Ireland, and in particular about Tyrone and O'Donnell. Meanwhile the ball was at the feet of the latter, who had been received by the King, treated with high consideration, and listened to when he pressed for reinforcements. One Spanish ship which captured an English boat's crew off the Old Head of Kinsale on 4 January did take back news of the surrender, and this is said to have caused preparations at the Spanish ports to slacken.[1]

On 20 February the first Spanish contingent, 20 officers and 1,374 soldiers, sailed from Kinsale. Mountjoy's expectations proved true. At Coruña the English crews of the transports were well treated and some Spanish vessels in the harbour, previously destined for Ireland, were unloaded. Before the second contingent sailed unpleasant news arrived from Berehaven. The owner of Dunboy Castle had originally handed it over to the Spaniards for the sake of the cause. He was, with some reason, infuriated that it was now proposed to deliver it to the English. To prevent this he surprised the Spanish garrison—a matter of little difficulty seeing that he and his people were treated as allies—sent it to Baltimore, seized its guns and ammunition, and

[1] *Pacata Hibernia*, Vol. II, pp. 445, 464-81.

put in an Irish guard. When Aguila received the report at Cork he took it for so great an affront to his honour that he proposed to go to Berehaven with the Spanish companies not yet embarked to regain the castle and deliver it to the English. Mountjoy and Carew, eager to be rid of him, told him not to trouble himself and that Carew would reduce the place after the rest of the Spaniards were gone. On 8 March the wind turned favourable and Aguila went aboard, only for the wind to change again. The fleet could not put to sea until the 16th, but Mountjoy did not await its sailing. He began his journey back to Dublin, via Waterford, on 9 March.

About 3,200 Spaniards, not counting the Irish troops who accompanied them, were shipped back to Spain, out of a total of over 4,400 who had landed at Kinsale and Castlehaven. Over 200 had been captured. Thus over a thousand had been killed or had died of sickness. The proportion of English losses was heavier. To crown all woes, a wave of fever, which would seem to have been a very violent type of influenza, carried off many who had survived the siege, so that the final death-roll amounted to several thousand. To fill the depleted ranks two thousand reinforcements had been sent. When he reached Waterford, Mountjoy found that five companies had already arrived, with provisions and munitions.

Mountjoy, accompanied so far by Carew, rode on to Kilkenny. It was exactly six months since he had sat in council there with Ormonde and received the tidings of the Spanish landing, and in that interval the fate of Ireland had been decided. Then he caught the malady, but nevertheless set out for Dublin. Next day he became so ill that he had to make the rest of the journey in a horse litter. Carew was also stricken, but, equally eager to get back to his post, returned to Cork by easy stages.

Fynes Moryson had a more agreeable journey than his master. He rode and gossiped with the Spanish hostage for the English ships, Don Pedro Morijon, and learnt that this was the dare-devil who had walked to and fro in the breach of Kinsale under the fire of all who could shoot at him. He was also informed that the Spanish officer's name had been originally the same as his own and that he was descended from an Englishman who had warred in the service of the Emperor Charles V and been granted an estate in Spain.

Mountjoy had much to reflect upon, as his fever died down. He was worried because of bitter complaints from captains whose companies he had broken up and whom he had sent home. He had naturally kept his old officers whom he knew well, but the return of the new-comers had caused resentment among their patrons in England. He thought it possible that Spain would send another expedition. He was perturbed by the enormous rise in prices, partly a normal effect of war, partly that of the devastation practised by himself and his subordinates, partly through the debasement of the Irish currency which he had been compelled to carry out in 1601 with the object of lessening the Queen's expenditure.[1]

He was not in a victor's mood even before the influenza gripped him because he was already under the influence of reaction from an effort which had tried his body and spirit to the utmost. Presently there would come to him—and to England—realization that he had been responsible for one of the greatest military achievements of the Queen's reign. He had been well served, notably by Carew in the siege and Wingfield in the battle, and the men of the old companies had fought magnificently; but it was his leadership, his handling of reserves during the Spanish sorties, his defiance of adversity, his boldness in battle, that had created the victory. Every decision and action of importance had been his. He had snatched triumph out of what might have been disaster.

He reached Dublin on 28 March. The Council and the chief citizens greeted him warmly, but those who accompanied him had no part in their joy. He took to his bed, but slept badly and lacked all appetite. He must have appeared very ill; for Sir Oliver St. John wrote in a letter to Cecil: "I fear me he will grow worse and worse". This was another way of putting it that his survival was doubtful.

[1] Moryson, Vol. III, pp. 124, 133-8, 142; Bagwell: *Ireland under the Tudors*, Vol. III, p. 395.

XIV

EST MODUS IN REBUS

THE Lord Deputy lay for some time too weak and ill to do business. On 28 April, 1602, he and his Council wrote to the English Privy Council advocating the building of a fort and magazine at Cork, the repair of those at Waterford (Duncannon) and Limerick, and new ones at Kinsale, Galway, and Carlingford. He had ever in his mind the danger of the Spaniards seizing one of the ports. He declared that he was now in better health. However, in a private letter to Cecil written some three weeks later, reporting that he had sent his forces northward, he mentioned that he was still not strong enough for any great business and was suffering from headaches. The letter is a holograph, and the writing is that of a sick man; in fact, only after careful examination can it be identified as his.[1]

On the whole, the landing of the Spanish expeditionary force and the unopposed march of O'Donnell and Tyrone through Ireland to join it had proved less harmful than might have been expected. The Pale and Leinster generally had remained reasonably quiet throughout the winter, so that there could be little cause for anxiety about the province now. In Munster there had been fairly extensive relapses, but only in the south-west corner were they likely to trouble George Carew. Connaught remained much as before, but hitherto Mountjoy had been able to make no serious effort to pacify it, as he now intended to. In Ulster the effects of the Spanish landing had cut both ways. Numbers of Irishmen fell away, including certain active allies of Docwra, the worst case being that of a leader of kerne in the Queen's pay who murdered all the English section of the garrison of his post. Chichester had to deal with a revolt

[1] S.P. Ireland, Vol. CCXI, 34. (Undated but written about 21 May).

by his protégé, Con O'Neill, in Clandeboye. Yet the departure of Tyrone and Hugh Roe O'Donnell to Munster with the best Irish forces of the province restored the freedom of movement of the English commanders. In December, 1601, Docwra penetrated to the lower Erne, which he had been directed to seize, as a barrier between Ulster and Connaught, at his first coming into Ireland. He could not take Ballyshannon Castle without artillery, and the cannon sent round by sea from Lough Foyle did not arrive until March, 1602. On the 25th of that month he secured the castle, at last. Now the Ulster troops had returned; but the vigorous Hugh Roe O'Donnell was in Spain—where he died later in the year—and his brother Rory was not of equal calibre; Tyrone was crestfallen and had suffered in prestige; their followers were dispirited and had lost thousands of fire-arms. Hard fighting was perhaps at an end in Ulster, but the last phase of rounding-up would be arduous and grim.[1]

Though a number of companies had been cassed, 4,000 more men had been sent, so that by the list the army stood at the very high total of 1,487 horse and 16,950 foot. Narrators and correspondents too seldom record strength by the poll; Carew mentions that a force nominally 2,500 strong which he placed under the orders of Lord Thomond was actually half that strength. Taking into account desertion—generally worst in England before the troops sailed—and sickness, at least one-fourth must be deducted from all figures. The list strength in Munster at the disposal of Carew was 325 horse and 4,400 foot. For the first time a considerable force was available for Connaught: 112 horse and 1,650 foot. In the detail of the foot is an item typical of contemporary finance: "Void for the Judge's pay, 100", meaning, of course, that this company existed only on paper and that its cost was appropriated to the Judge's salary. The Lord Deputy's field army numbered 506 horse and 3,650 foot, including a considerable proportion drawn when required from the nearer Ulster garrisons. The remainder were in Ulster —the bulk under the command of Docwra—and Leinster, where Ormonde would take over command when Mountjoy went north. They were disposed so that they could support one another, if necessary moving from one province to another.[2]

[1] Docwra: Relation.   [2] Moryson, Vol. III, pp. 146-51

The Queen had been informed of certain feelers towards peace made by Tyrone soon after his defeat, also that Mountjoy had allowed an officer to visit him, but with instructions to speak of nothing but unconditional surrender. Sir Oliver St. John had brought back a letter from her commending his handling of the matter and his preservation of his dignity, and hers through his. She had declared she would await another overture before giving instructions. Tyrone's offence, however, appeared so heinous as to make her still favour "the plain way of perdition". If mercy were to be exercised it should be rather to his vassals than to the overlord.[1]

Though Mountjoy was still low in health, he was gay in spirit, as is shown by a round of banter between him and Carew. When Aguila was waiting at Cork he had been on good terms with the Lord President. From Spain he sent him a friendly letter, with a present of wine, oranges, and lemons. Carew was on the Dunboy expedition when they arrived, and they were delivered in error to Mountjoy in Dublin. He forwarded the letter, but said he meant to keep the present until the title had been decided. Carew wrote back in the same vein, having just taken Dunboy: "When your Lordship hath taken your pleasure of it I hope to receive the rest". Unfortunately, the wine had been spoiled and the fruit was rotten. Mountjoy declared that this was a judgement for keeping what did not belong to him.

"Once before I had a ship, and victualled her out in the laudable traffic of piracy, and lost all my charge and in the end my ship; which I took to be God's will to discourage me in seeking to thrive by other men's goods. And since this last cozenage doth thrive so evil with me I will from henceforth forswear all dishonesty".[2]

Nothing is known of this venture on the part of Mountjoy, but it was customary for syndicates, or individuals who possessed the capital, to fit out privateers or expeditions to prey on Spanish trade. Many must have failed like this.

Before setting out for Dundalk the Lord Deputy addressed to the Privy Council a despatch which contained a full record of what he had accomplished. It was in a way an apologia, not for

[1] Moryson, Vol. III, p. 131.
[2] Carew C., 1601-03, pp. 235, 248, 250.

failures, but for the slow progress made. It was, however, generally convincing. It paid a tribute to the Irish, whom, he said, he had found on his coming over, "far from being naked people, as before times", to be better armed and to make better use of their weapons than the English army. It showed the connexion between the great expense, so much disliked at home, and the inevitable policy of ruining the herds and agriculture of the rebels, a policy impossible to carry out unless the army were liberally provided with food from home and extra transport to move it.

Once more Charles rode through the Moyry, undefended and deserted. On 14 June he was at Armagh, where a depot had been formed. Then on to the Blackwater. At sight of his approach the Irish on the far bank made off into the woods, Tyrone himself and his family hurrying up the west side of Lough Neagh to Moneymore, in what is today County Londonderry, this region being then covered by the most impenetrable forest in the north. Charles crossed the river at a point he had carefully marked down the previous year. He at once began the construction of a bridge and of a fort to cover the passage. He named the spot Charlemount, from his own names, and left Captain Toby Caulfeild to hold it with his company. It is Charlemont today, and Charlemont is the territorial title of the Caulfeild viscounty. Dungannon, a group of Irish cottages about Tyrone's castle, had been left in flames by the Earl, and from it Mountjoy wrote to Sir George Carey, whom he liked better than most of the Castle officials: "We have drunk your health in Dungannon. Tyrone is turned wood-kerne". On 26 June Docwra arrived from Omagh, a centre of communications in the heart of Tyrone, into which he had put a garrison as he passed. Next day Chichester crossed Lough Neagh, and for the first time the three met in conference. "The axe was now at the root of the tree", says Docwra.[1]

It was true; but some obstructions to swinging it remained. Mountjoy built a second fort, on the shore of the lough. Forts needed victuals, and he decided to move into Monaghan, where there was also work to be done, while his wagons were refilled. Meanwhile Docwra and Chichester were to press Tyrone in his

[1] C.S.P. Ireland, 1601-03, pp. 416-22; Moryson, Vol. III, p. 166; Docwra, *Narration*.

fastness. Before he broke camp Mountjoy had letters from the Queen and Cecil, the latter's a gloss upon the former's. Elizabeth gave her Deputy a free hand, with one exception: he might temper justice with mercy as he chose, but he must not pardon the Arch Traitor. Cecil remarked that this must be Mountjoy's warrant, but added for his private ear, with some circumlocution, that if Tyrone's plea for mercy were abject enough the Queen might listen. Cecil had, after hard work, obtained from her the concession that Mountjoy might promise Tyrone his life, but no more. This was all he could say for the time being.[1]

On the march to Monaghan some little strongholds in the bogs were taken. A chance shot killed the Sergeant-Major, Sir John Berkeley, who was replaced by Sir Henry Danvers. Before the days of Kinsale Mountjoy would not have ventured to make such an appointment, but the black mark against the name of Danvers had been erased; his conduct in the battle had made a strong contribution to the victory and his selection to carry home the despatch had completed his rehabilitation. Finding the MacMahons in Monaghan in stiff mood, Mountjoy wasted their land. He planted the loyalist Maguire of Fermanagh, "the Queen's Maguire", on the border of his country, ready to seize it at the first chance from "the Rebel Maguire". Many submissions were made, including those of kinsmen of Tyrone. At the end of July Mountjoy returned to Newry, where he gave his troops a rest.[2]

Elsewhere matters were going equally well. In fierce and bloody fighting Carew stormed Dunboy Castle, after battering it with guns carried by sea from Cork. The conduct of this affair illustrates both the decisiveness of artillery against such castles as were built in Ireland and the difficulty of bringing considerable armed forces to remote places. Carew quitted Cork on 23 April, completed the mounting of his guns on 16 June, and stormed Dunboy on 17 June; he thus took fifty-four days to approach, entrench, and set up the guns, and one day to breach and storm the castle. Little more remained to be done in the province, but the last flicker of revolt was not stamped out until

[1] Moryson, Vol. III, pp. 169, 173.
[2] C.S.P. Ireland, 1601-03, p. 458.

the winter. In Connaught the new Governor, Sir Oliver Lambart, secured Sligo and bought a galley, to be manned by a crew of fifty with fifteen oars aside, to deal with the O'Malleys and O'Flaherties, once again showing signs of activity on the coast. The Irish gained their last success of the war—the only appreciable success they had won since Mountjoy arrived—in early August, at the very place in the Curlieu Hills where the Governor of Connaught had been defeated and killed in the time of Essex. The victims were Clanrickarde and Sir Arthur Savage, and their reverse was due to the old weakness of English forces in Ireland when assailed in column of march. The success of the Irish came too late to benefit their cause.[1]

One preoccupation of Mountjoy's was uncertainty about the policy of Spain. Carew received information that Philip III had ordered preparations for a new invasion to cease but had not disbanded the forces held ready. So worried did the Lord President appear that Mountjoy sent back to Limerick 1,500 troops whom he had withdrawn from Munster and proposed to employ in the north. He was anxious to make use of all possible means to end the northern nightmare, and on 29 July requested the Privy Council to give him an appreciation of Spanish intentions. Sir Geffrey Fenton went so far as to tell Cecil that Carew was becoming a plague because his fears of re-invasion were weakening the Lord Deputy. Cecil's appreciation took some time to arrive. It showed that Master Secretary was coming round to the view that there would be no more trouble with the Spaniards and that in no case could Spain raise and transport a force bigger than that led by Aguila. He also revealed that an English fleet had been cruising off the Spanish coast as the best of all precautions. His estimate was, as so often, correct.[2]

On 20 August Mountjoy advanced northward again. Tyrone had fled to Fermanagh. Rather than follow him, Mountjoy decided to waste his lands and destroy his harvest, then to direct all the inhabitants who submitted to move south of the Blackwater, where the land was not wasted. There they could graze their cattle and later on sow seed. Thus, when Tyrone returned he would find his country a complete wilderness, unpeopled but

[1] Falls, Chap. xxiii.
[2] Carew C., 1601-03, pp. 282, 317; C.S.P. Ireland, 1601-03, pp. 417, 477.

by the Queen's garrisons. Mountjoy left a guard at Dungannon to preserve the oats in its neighbourhood for his horses in the winter. At Tullahogue, seven miles to the north, where the paramount O'Neill chiefs were proclaimed on succession, he broke the stone chair used for the ceremony. Tyrone had not now to be fought, but to be caught. His opponent was depressed by his own handiwork and by the sight of corpses of those who had died of starvation as the result of his policy. The mood did not last. Back in Dublin in September, he wrote to Carew that the weather was fine and that he was going hawking.[1]

Yet Mountjoy was now an advocate of moderation. He must bring this war to an end. He would have liked to draw up terms which Tyrone could honourably accept. He was moved by pity, not for the man, whose throat he would cheerfully have cut rather than commit himself or the Queen, were the opportunity to occur, but for the innocent victims of the long struggle. He realized too that it would be to his personal interest to reduce expenditure quickly and drastically by bringing peace to Ireland. He had been forced to drop communications with the rebel because the latter was inclined to bargain, and in view of the Queen's attitude he could not permit that. He did not, however, abandon hope. Before returning to Dublin he had written to Lambart in Connaught, praising him for his hard hitting but expressing disquietude at reports that Lambart had threatened to dispossess the principal men of their lands and transfer them to the Queen. That, said Mountjoy, would be the surest way to make them fight to the last gasp. He was inclined to think that Lambart, though a good soldier, was politically not the man for the work, and anxiety on this score was one of the reasons why he decided to go to Connaught in person in November.[2]

For the most striking proof of this spirit of toleration and creditable compromise we may anticipate for a moment. On 20 January, 1603, on his way back to Dublin from his Connaught tour, he told Cecil that in his absence the Lord Chancellor, Archbishop Loftus, and part of the Council left with him, had imprisoned a number of Dubliners, including six aldermen, for failure to attend Protestant churches. He was loth to inter-

---

[1] Moryson, Vol. III, pp. 202, 205, 208; Carew C., 1601-03, p. 340.
[2] Moryson, Vol. III, p. 214; C.S.P. Ireland, 1601-03, p. 518.

fere with such proceedings, taken under a writ of *praemunire*, but he thought the consequences would be disastrous, and pleaded for Cecil's support in ending this persecution. One remarkable passage from the letter, written with his own hand to a recipient in whom he could now confide all his thoughts on matters political, merits full quotation.

"I am persuaded that a violent course therein will do little good to win men's consciences; but, howsoever, it is too soon to begin it; and it is most sure that it will breed a new war and, as I believe, make all the towns and nobility solicit Spanish aids. The bringing in of the Inquisition did lose the King [of Spain] the Low Countries, and when the Estates were almost possessed of all the provinces they had almost lost all with their too much violence in prosecuting the contrary religion. I am of opinion that all religions do grow under persecution. It is truly good doctrine and example that must prevail. But, whatsoever shall be thought best, it is fit for me to let you know that if this matter be not discreetly handled you must look for a new war, the which I am afraid too many would be glad of, but I beseech God deliver us from it."[1]

These words of a laic and probably sceptical theologian are not readily paralleled in their period. The Lord Deputy was not merely in advance of his time but a good century ahead of it. While awaiting a reply he took it upon himself to warn the Lord Chancellor to go easily and contrived to prevent the Dublin procedure from being followed elsewhere. The Privy Council agreed with his policy and enjoined moderation.

About 18 November Mountjoy set out for Connaught, going first to the seat of government at Athlone, where he lodged for some time in the castle. He decided that he had misjudged Lambart, who had done better than he had supposed. On 14 December the most powerful rebel in Ireland came in to make humble submission. Rory O'Donnell was now by the Irish view head of his house and chieftain of Donegal because news had been received of the death of his elder brother, Hugh Roe, in Spain. He was in a stronger position than Tyrone, since he had not been harried to the same extent, had not lost his herds, and had suffered nothing like the same loss by desertion. He was a

[1] S.P. Ireland, Vol. CCXII, 118.

plausible man still in his twenties. He asserted that it had been his intention to serve the Crown and that he had been forcibly prevented by his brother from so doing. Mountjoy and the two members of the Council accompanying him, the Bishop of Meath and Sir Richard Wingfield, professed to be moved to pity his case.

They were not disinterested in this judgement. They wanted Rory as a counter-weight to his cousin, Neill Garve, and expected the former to be the more manageable of the two. Mountjoy considered, and advocated to the Queen and Council, a partition of Donegal between the two O'Donnells. It was scarcely fair dealing because Neill Garve had been clearly promised the lordship of Donegal and had strengthened his right by many deeds of arms done after receiving the promise. He had been invaluable to the Lough Foyle force. On Mountjoy's side it can be urged that Neill Garve's ambition, insolence, covetousness, ill temper, and generally bad promise made him unsuitable as a paramount chief. Yet one would wish that the Lord Deputy had stuck to his word. With or without excuse, Neill Garve soon put himself out of court by having himself proclaimed "the O'Donnell", a forbidden Irish princely title. Docwra imprisoned him, but for the sake of old friendship did not put him in irons, with the consequence that he escaped. In the end he got none but his old lands. He served the Crown in the minor troubles of 1608, but was arrested for treachery, sent to the Tower, and kept there for the rest of his life.[1]

Mountjoy went from Athlone to Galway, the most remote of the major fortified ports of Ireland but also one of the most loyal of the cities. There he spent Christmas. The principal rebels remaining in Connaught came to him to make their submission. Each left in the hands of the Council a document in which he acknowledged Queen Elizabeth to be the absolute sovereign of the realm of Ireland, submitted himself and his lands to her mercy, renounced the authority of any other power or potentate, pledged himself to support her against all enemies whether foreign or domestic, and acknowledged that he would be deserving of extreme punishment and unworthy of the name of a Christian if he broke his oath. The only exception was

[1] Falls, p. 330.

O'Rourke of Leitrim, and Mountjoy arranged that he should be attacked from all sides. While in Connaught Mountjoy gave orders for the first considerable reduction of the strength of the army, to 1,000 horse and 12,000 foot.

He was back in Dublin at the end of January, 1603, and was then able to report that, except for O'Rourke in Connaught, a handful in Munster who were being chased and routed, and Tyrone himself in Ulster, no rebels remained. He had not yet got leave to deal with Tyrone as he desired. He did not think it worth while offering such a man his life and no more if he surrendered. Many would not value life if it were to be spent in prison, and Tyrone was less likely than most to take such a risk in order to save a life which he had in any case a good chance of saving by slipping away to Spain. At last the Queen, doubtless in part impelled by the gentle, unobtrusive, and discreet advice of Cecil, came round to Mountjoy's point of view. On 17 February she gave him leave to offer life, liberty, and pardon. However, Cecil also wrote a letter, which showed that the Queen's pride was still touchy. If Mountjoy could get submission with promise of life only, he was to do so. If promise of pardon were given, Elizabeth would prefer that it should be in some name other than that of Earl of Tyrone, which she had come to regard as ominous and odious: preferably in that of Baron of Dungannon, the Earl's second title. It was also desirable that his lands should be returned to him in diminished form.

Mountjoy took little notice of the first and second proposals, one of them for an unattainable object and the other petti-fogging. With the third he was in agreement, but he wanted a free hand rather than advice. After three years in Ireland these matters were clear to him. The important factor in any settle-ment with Tyrone would not be the size of the territory restored to him, but provision for those members of his own house whom he had oppressed and for the maintenance of the forts on his borders. Above all, he must pledge himself not to interfere with the "uriaghts" or subsidiary chiefs, such as O'Cahan of Coleraine and MacMahon of Monaghan, over whom he had a vague over-lordship as a Celtic Irish chief, but not as an earl holding his lands from the Queen. At Mellifont Abbey, near Drogheda,

¹ Moryson, Vol. III, pp. 237-9.

the home of Sir Garret Moore, Mountjoy received from Tyrone a humble letter in which he besought the Lord Deputy to receive him and to take compassion on him. On 25 March Mountjoy sent his host and Sir William Godolphin to meet Tyrone with a safe-conduct and bring him in.

These commissioners reached Charlemont on 27 March. Moore went on to see Tyrone, while Godolphin waited. (Moore knew Tyrone well and was a figure of dubious reputation whose relations with the enemy were obscure and whose estate escaped surprisingly when trouble occurred in its neighbourhood.) On the morning of the 30th Moore returned with Tyrone to Godolphin. The Earl dismissed his escort and, accompanied only by a few gentlemen, rode to Mellifont with the commissioners.

While they had been absent a curious drama had been played. Late in the night of 27 March the servant of one of the Lord Deputy's voluntary gentlemen, having ridden post from London and made an exceptionally quick passage, reached Mellifont and told his master that Queen Elizabeth was dead. The master brought him to Fynes Moryson. The secretary bade the man keep his mouth shut and advised the gentleman to go to Mountjoy's bedroom with the news, to inform him that it was being kept secret, and to pledge himself to follow his fortune in this doubtful time.

What was to be done? The truth of the report was not quite certain, but Mountjoy, who knew that the Queen had been seriously ill, could hardly doubt it. If it was true, then his commission had lapsed, and if Tyrone submitted to Elizabeth this would not bind the next monarch. If Tyrone heard the news he would perhaps delay his submission, so as to be able to boast that he had never made it to the Queen and in hope of better terms from her successor. The succession to the throne was traditionally marked by unrest in Ireland. Were he to keep quiet until Tyrone arrived, tell him that the Queen had died and that he must submit to James I and VI, and it should then turn out that the Queen had in fact survived—slight chance though it was—he would have been guilty of an act which she would never forgive. He made up his mind: Tyrone was to be allowed to come in and submit to Elizabeth and silence was to be observed until the report of her death had been confirmed officially.

Queen Elizabeth had in fact died on 24 March, the day before Mountjoy sent his messengers to seek Tyrone

It was three years since Mountjoy had seen her, but, apart from that period, he had never in his adult life been long absent from her presence Though she had, since he came to Ireland, constantly exasperated him by holding him responsible for the corruption of purveyors and others, she had treated him with unfailing kindness She had overlooked and hidden the least creditable action of his life. As he waited for Tyrone he must have had memories enough for company: the tilting, the golden chess queen, the festive days, the loud voice that so many feared but that had so often spoken friendly words to him, the rough, masculine humour, above all the redoubtable personality. It was indeed the end of an epoch.

Yet the truth must not be overlaid with sentimentality. Men were not unwilling to see the epoch end and were already looking forward with interest and enthusiasm to the next. Charles was essentially cool and calculating. His prospects on the Stuart succession were good and he would do his best to improve them. He might expect to be home very shortly to receive the honours that must surely come to him and to rejoin Penelope. He was later to admit to Cecil that in his last letter addressed to Queen Elizabeth there had been some fustian and to pray him not to show it to the new King.

Tyrone arrived on the afternoon of 30 March. He knelt on the threshold of the room in which the Lord Deputy sat in state to receive him and made humble and penitent submission. He was then bidden to approach. This time he knelt at the very feet of Mountjoy, as representative of the royal power, and made further protestations of repentance and loyalty. On the morrow he brought his written submission, and presented it to the Lord Deputy and Council, in the presence of a great assembly.

It ran:

"I Hugh O'Neill, by the Queen of England, France, and Ireland her most gracious favour created Earl of Tyrone, do with all true and humble penitency prostrate myself at her royal feet, and absolutely submit myself unto her mercy, most sorrowfully imploring her gracious commiseration and appealing only to her princely clemency, without presuming to justify my unloyal proceedings against her sacred Majesty. Only most sorrowfully and earnestly desiring that it may please her Majesty rather in some measure to mitigate her just indignation against me, in that I do religiously vow that the first motives of my unnatural rebellion were neither practice, malice, nor ambition; but that I was induced first by fear of my life (which I conceived was sought by my enemies' practice) to stand on my guard, and after most unhappily led to make good that fault with more heinous offences, the which in themselves I do acknowledge deserve no forgiveness and that it is impossible for me, in respect of their greatness, in any proportion, even with my life, to make satisfaction; I do most humbly desire her Majesty to pardon them, that as I have been already a sufficient argument of her royal power, having little left but my life to preserve itself, so it may now please her Majesty to make me an example of her princely clemency, the chiefest ornament of her high dignity. And, that I may be the better able hereafter with the utmost service of my life to redeem the foulness of my faults, I do most humbly sue unto her Majesty that she will vouchsafe to restore to me my former dignity and living, in which estate of a subject I do religiously vow to continue for ever hereafter loyal, in all true obedience to her royal person, crown, prerogative and laws, and to be in all things as far and as dutifully conformable thereunto, as I or any other nobleman of this realm is bound by the duty of a subject to his sovereign, or by the laws of this realm, utterly renouncing and abjuring the name and title of O'Neill, or any other authority or claim which hath not been granted or confirmed unto me by her Majesty, and that otherwise by the laws of this realm I may not pretend just interest unto : and I do religiously swear to perform so much as is above mentioned and the rest of these articles subscribed by my own hand, as far as shall any way lie in my power, and to deliver such pledges for the performance thereof as shall be nominated unto me by the Lord Deputy.

"I do renounce and abjure all foreign power whatsoever and all kind of dependency upon any other potentate but her Majesty the Queen of England, France, and Ireland, and do vow to serve her faithfully against any foreign power invading her Kingdoms, and to discover truly any practices that I do or shall know against her royal person or crowns; and, namely and especially, I do abjure and renounce all manner of dependency upon the King or Estate of Spain, or treaty with him or any of his confederates, and shall be ready with the uttermost of my ability to serve her Majesty against him, or any of his forces or confederates.

"I do absolutely renounce all challenge or intermeddling with the Uriaghts, or fostering with them or other neighbour lords, or gentlemen out of my country, or exacting any black rents of any Uriaghts (or bordering lords).

"I do resign all claim and title to any lands but such as shall be now granted unto me by her Majestys Letters Patent.

"Lastly, as the only being a subject doth include all the duties of a subject, so will I be content to be informed and advised by her Magistrates here, and will be conformable and assisting unto them in anything that may tend to the advancement of her service and the peaceable government of this Kingdom, as namely for the abolishing of all barbarous customs contrary to the laws, and for the clearing of all difficult passages and places, which are the nurseries of rebellion, wherein I will employ the labours of the people of my country in such sort and in such places as I shall be directed by her Majesty, or the Lord Deputy and Council in her name; and will endeavour for myself and the people of my country to erect civil habitations and such as shall be of greater effect to preserve us against thieves and any force but the power of the State, by which we must rest assured to be preserved as long as we continue in our duties."

The penitent also pledged himself to write to the King of Spain that he had now submitted to his lawful sovereign and to beg that his son, who had been sent to Spain, should be returned to him. This Tyrone did in Dublin, with dignity.

The Lord Deputy promised him pardon in the Queen's name. He assured him that his earldom would be restored and that he would receive new Letters Patent for his lands, excepting only "countrys" possessed by two kinsmen which had been promised them on their submission, and 300 acres each for the maintenance of the forts of Mountnorris and Charlemont.

The terms were easy. It should be noted that the renouncement of the name and title of O'Neill refers to the princely appellation already mentioned. Tyrone was not called upon to abandon his family name, by which he indeed described himself in his opening words, having no right to the title of Tyrone, except by the mercy of the sovereign. The proscription of fostering refers to the custom of putting out sons of chiefs to nurse with families of subsidiary septs and thus binding them with one of the most sacred of Irish ties. Apart from the abjuration of dependence on the King of Spain, the main safeguards of the oath lay in the last paragraph and especially in Tyrone's pledge that he would be governed by the advice of the magistrates of the Crown and aid them in its service.[1]

On 3 April Mountjoy, with Tyrone in his company, rode to Drogheda, reaching Dublin next day. On the 5th Sir Henry Danvers arrived from England with the official report of the Queen's death. With him was a gentleman named Leigh, of the family of Mountjoy's mother, who bore a gracious letter from the new King, written in Scotland. The decease of the sovereign automatically annulled Mountjoy's appointment. On 9 April the Council therefore appointed him Lord Justice or Justiciar, the title always accorded to the temporary representative or representatives of the Crown upon a vacancy or a visit of the Viceroy to England. However, authority for all officers to hold their places presently arrived. On Sunday 17 April, a new patent having been received, Archbishop Loftus proclaimed him from the pulpit of Christ Church and swore him Lord Deputy.

Tyrone, on being informed of Elizabeth's death, burst into tears. His own explanation, that he wept for sorrow for her loss, need not be dismissed. He had always respected her, had never joined in the vulgar abuse of her, common in Munster, and had protested that he had been wronged by her servants, not by herself. Fynes Moryson, however, decided that he wept for rage and regret. "There needed no Oedipus to find out the true cause of his tears; for, no doubt, the most humble submission he made to the Queen he had so highly and proudly offended much eclipsed the vainglory his actions might have carried if he had held out till her death". Besides, thought Moryson, if he had submitted only to James, he would have been able to claim that he had done so out of his affection for the new King and would have credited him with winning over at the moment of his accession a rebel whom the Queen had never subdued. At all events Tyrone now had to make a new submission. On the other hand, he put his signature to the proclamation of King James I,

[1] Moryson, Vol. III, pp. 290-302; C.S.P. Ireland, 1601-03, p. 584; 1603-06, p. 20; Tanner, p. 57.

below those of Mountjoy, the Lord Chancellor and Archbishop of Dublin, the Mayor of Dublin, and the Archbishop of Armagh.[1]

Mountjoy considered that he might now go home. Obviously he could not at a stroke disburden himself of responsibility for the Kingdom of Ireland, where much remained to be settled. He therefore propounded for the King's approval an ingenious plan. He would return and would be created Lord Lieutenant, with full superintendence of Irish affairs—this arrangement having the advantage that his reputation would lie directly behind English authority and the Irish would realize that a strong and skilful hand still held the sword. It was not his custom to neglect his own interests or underrate his merit, and he proposed that he should be paid two-thirds of the viceregal stipend. No Lord Deputy could possibly maintain himself on the remaining third unless he were otherwise well provided for, so Mountjoy suggested that this office should be given to Sir George Carey, a competent official with a substantial salary and perquisites as Treasurer at Wars.[2]

No objection was raised to this project, which was later in fact adopted except that Carey was appointed the King's Deputy, not Mountjoy's, as would appear to have been the original suggestion. Yet alas! Ireland, having held Charles in thrall over three years, was not so easily to relax her grip upon him. Penelope, the Court, the favour of a grateful sovereign, high rewards, fame at home, power at the centre, all might beckon. He could not obey the calls. Another task, unforeseen and unpalatable, stretched before him. He took it up calmly, efficiently, and in an admirable spirit of moderation. No hint of the impatience which he must have felt escaped his lips.

The new disturbers of the peace were not the former rebels but the hitherto reasonably loyal citizens of the towns. This curious throb of unrest would seem to have sprung from three distinct causes. First came the unsettling influence of the demise of the sovereign and the succession of another, an influence which had made itself felt before now, though little if at all on the accession of Queen Elizabeth. In the second place, the

---

[1] Moryson, Vol. III, p. 303; C.S.P. Ireland, 1603-06, pp. 43, 95; *Tudor and Stuart Proclamations*, Vol. II, p. 15.

[2] C.S.P. Ireland, 1603-06, p. 11; Moryson, Vol. III, p. 310.

debasement of the coinage—which, in fact, King James and Sir George Carey were shortly to restore—had created a steadily increasing resentment. By far the most important element was, however, religious. The Roman Catholic clergy, including missioners from Spain still in the country, thought they saw a golden opportunity and acted with daring and resolution.

The movement was not universal. The capital was untouched by it. Galway remained quiet. Drogheda was momentarily disturbed, but the local authorities scotched the trouble without the need of intervention from the Government. The outbreak was serious only in Munster and southern Leinster, bad in Waterford, and worst of all in Cork. It extended even to Ormonde's home town of Kilkenny, of which his former steward and confidential secretary, Richard Shee, was sovereign or mayor and one of the most determined of the brawlers.

Mass had been regularly celebrated in small chapels in the towns with the tacit assent of the Government. Now the priests led processions to the churches, smashed their way in when the doors were barred, and took them over for the old cult. In some places they forbade any further private celebration of Mass. Their propaganda was inconsistent, but no less effective for that: while one proclaimed that James could not succeed to the Kingdom of Ireland unless he were a Catholic and confirmed by the Pope, another took the line that he *was* a Catholic and therefore would restore full freedom of religion. The municipal authorities, though some of them misbehaved, were more moderate. They protested their loyalty even when they refused to obey the instructions of the Lord Deputy and Council. It seems clear that most of them were carried on a wave which they lacked the strength to resist. The Recorder of Cork, William Meade, however, advised the Mayor that the authority of the Commissioners for Munster, appointed on Sir George Carew's departure to England, had lapsed on the death of Elizabeth. This was perhaps legally true, but Mountjoy reappointed them at the first possible moment. The upshot was that Cork defied the Commissioners and that the senior, Sir Charles Wilmot, returning after making an end of the revolt in Kerry, was denied an entrance. Fire was actually exchanged between the troops and the citizens, who had seized the magazine and armed themselves. The excuse made to Mountjoy for keeping Wilmot outside the gates was that the majority of his troops were "mere Irish", a rich specimen of unconscious irony.

Mountjoy set out for the south on 27 April. He had told Cecil that if the towns returned to their duty he would not make much of the matter. He knew well that it was the walled towns, and especially the ports, which had preserved the kingdom. He kept his temper when to have lost it might have brought on a disaster with long-enduring effects. The letters he addressed to the disobedient mayors were courteous, conciliatory, and firm. Yet he was taking no risks. The list strength of his force was five thousand men, and he was prepared to move the greater part of the army into Munster if the need arose. While on this expedition he received letters from the King informing him that he had been chosen to be one of his Majesty's Privy Council of England, had been accorded the title of Lord Lieutenant of Ireland, and licensed to come over to England, with authority to leave Sir George Carey to act as the King's Deputy during his absence. The King had done him particular honour by signifying that he was "to be holden and reputed as one of the Council", though he had not taken the oath.

It required only his approach to overawe most of the smaller inland towns. Ormonde met him in Carlow, at Leighlin on the Barrow, bringing with him the Mayor and four citizens of Kilkenny, who made humble submission. Thomastown, a little place, was punished for its offence by having troops lodged in it for a single night. Waterford was inclined to be insolent and would not provide boats, but Ormonde brought enough down from Carrick to ferry the force over the Suir. The authorities protested their allegiance, but the town in general remained defiant, so that he feared some would have to die. The chief men came to meet him, shamefacedly acknowledging that the people were out of hand. Outside the walls he had a curious theological argument with a Jesuit, Dr. White, on loyalty to the sovereign, in which the admiring Fynes Moryson represents him as triumphant. At last, on 3 May, the gates were thrown open. Mountjoy carefully occupied the points of vantage, rode in, and administered the oath of allegiance to the principal citizens. He arrested a few men known to have shouted: "We will not have a

Scot to be our King!" Brisk and firm though he always was in support of his own actions and judgement, he seldom boasted. Now he let Cecil know how proud he was to have brought his "poor army" to Waterford—perhaps then the richest town in Ireland after Dublin—"from the hungry north" and kept it there a day, without its taking away the value of a penny. His farewell words, however, were sardonic. Since he had found the citizens so weak, he said, he would leave a garrison with them. Fynes Moryson's brother, Sir Richard, was given the command, with the governorship of County Wexford.

The offence of Cork was more serious. Its people had seized the munitions of the Crown, bombarded Shandon Castle—in which Lady Carew was living, undismayed—and set about demolishing the uncompleted castle then being built outside the south gate, in which outrage they had been interrupted by Sir Charles Wilmot and driven back into the city. Wilmot, who was short of munitions, had been bidden to maintain an investment but otherwise to hold his hand, and a sort of truce had been arranged pending the arrival of the Lord Lieutenant. On 12 May, with Ormonde and other members of the nobility beside him, Mountjoy listened to the excuses of the citizens. He told them that he would leave censure to the King's pleasure. However, to forgo all punishment in this case would have been weakness. Three men were hanged after trial by martial law, almost certainly ringleaders in the armed opposition. The Recorder, William Meade, was left in confinement, though Mountjoy knew that no Irish jury was likely to convict him. Meade ended his life as a pensioner in Spain.

Cork was to receive a garrison a thousand strong. On 15 May Mountjoy marched towards Limerick. On the way he received a letter from Tyrone reporting that the Privy Council had accorded him authority to accompany the Lord Lieutenant to England, and that he would await him in Dublin. Limerick had offended in no way but by the public celebration of Mass, and its people gladly took the oath of allegiance. However, Mountjoy ordered the re-fortification of the castle, which would serve at need for repression as well as for defence. Then he returned to Dublin.

He said that he had extinguished the trouble, and it was

true. In most cases of the kind the work done is too optimistically regarded and in almost all some ugly aftermath crops up when the man with the scythe has passed on. Nothing of the sort occurred in southern Ireland. Let it be admitted that none of the towns, with the possible exception of Cork, had been rebelliously minded in the true sense. That fact had made the work of Mountjoy far easier than it would otherwise have been. Yet the serenity, clemency, tolerance, and understanding which he exhibited throughout makes this episode rank among the brightest ornaments of his career. His conduct was all of a piece with his dealings with Tyrone. He sought in Ireland a settlement of the best possible kind, from the English point of view. His action was typical also of his frame of mind. He did not believe in extremes or in pushing men too hard.[1]

At Dublin the King's ship *Tramontana* awaited him. She had a long connexion with his life. She had been a unit of the Channel Fleet under Lord Henry Seymour in which he had fought against the Spanish Armada fifteen years back. Six years ago, when with Lord Thomas Howard he had braved the gale which drove back the rest of the fleet and had reached the Spanish coast, it was the *Tramontana* that had carried back the Vice-Admiral's report to the Earl of Essex. She had done him good service on the coasts during his viceroyalty and had in the late crisis been ordered to Waterford in case her guns should have been needed. Now she was to take him home. He went aboard with his gentlemen, his household servants, the contrite Earl of Tyrone, and Neill Garve O'Donnell. On 29 May, 1603, they sailed.

[1] Moryson, Vol. III, pp. 312-35; C.S.P. Ireland, 1603-06, pp. 17, 20, 24, 27, 32, 36, 39, 43, 45, 55, 65; Bagwell, *Ireland under the Stuarts*, Vol. I, pp. 2-12.

QUEEN ELIZABETH I

In this portrait, painted by an unknown artist in her later years and now in the
National Portrait Gallery. The Queen is shown standing on a map of England.

PEACE CONFERENCE, SOMERSET HOUSE, 1604

Reading from the far end of the table. For Spain: the Duke of Frias,
the Count of Villa Mediana, Alessandro Rovida; for the Archdukes:
the Count of Aremberg, the President de Richardot, the Secretary
and Audienciary Verreykin.

PAINTING ATTRIBUTED TO MARC GHEERAEDTS THE YOUNGER

Reading from the far end of the table. For England : The Earl of Dorset, the Earl of Nottingham, the Earl of Devonshire (Mountjoy), the Earl of Northampton, Lord Cecil of Essendon (who was created Viscount Cranbourne for this affair).

The pourtraicture of the
Right Honorable the Lord
M D sculpsit Munjoy Blunt &c Tho Ienner exu

Mountjoy's eldest son, later Earl of Newport, from an old print.

XV

HOME AND BEAUTY

F AIR weather and a clear sky threatened no danger to the
voyage. Early in the morning of 30 May, 1603, the *Tramontana* sighted the Welsh coast. An hour later dense fog descended,
but Captain Floyd did not shorten sail. Suddenly the ship was
surrounded by screaming gulls. Jerked to attention, an officer
caught sight of a "hideous great black rock", off the Skerries,
straight upon which they were running. He roared: "Aloof
(luff) for life!" The helmsman instantly obeyed. With the aid of
the tide the ship just slipped along and past the flank of the
rock, but so close that the boat hanging in davits in the stern
dashed against it. It would have been a curious ending to die in
a calm sea on a May morning almost in port after having been
constantly under fire for over three years. At noon the
Tramontana entered Beaumaris Bay and put her passengers
ashore.

Mountjoy rode with Tyrone towards London. Recruitment
for the Irish wars had generally been heaviest in the west, as had
that for continental expeditions in the east, and Wales had
suffered a full share of the casualties of the former. Not even
respect for the Lord Lieutenant who had achieved victory and
peace prevented women bemoaning husbands and sons lost in
Ireland from throwing stones and dirt at Tyrone.

From Dunstable on 5 June Mountjoy sent on a courier with
a letter to Cecil. He announced that he was taking Tyrone in
the first instance to Wanstead and protested that nothing, save
the honour of serving King James, afforded him greater pride
than the love of his correspondent, which he would try to
deserve. Cecil already had in his possession a recent letter from
Penelope, Lady Rich, thanking him for his noble favours to "his

209

absent friend" and to herself. Penelope was enjoying still higher favours. On 2 May she was one of six noblewomen who set out from London to meet Queen Anne of Denmark on her way from Scotland and wait upon her. Penelope might appear an odd choice for this honour as having been involved in her brother's revolt, to say nothing of the fact that she was openly living apart from her husband. King James, however, was not bound by his predecessor's policy or disapprobation; in fact, he seems to have taken pains to disavow them in his treatment of the Essex faction, for example, in his immediate release of Henry Wriothesley, formerly Earl of Southampton, from the Tower.[1]

Charles could not have received a warmer welcome from the new King. He was at once sworn one of the Privy Council. On 17 June he was granted £200 a year old Rent of Assize out of the Exchequer and Duchy of Lancaster lands of similar value. In Ireland he received the district of Lecale in Down and lands in the Pale due to fall to the Crown on the death of the Dowager Countess of Kildare without heirs male of her body. The Letters Patent stated that these rewards were for his notable services in expelling the Spaniards from Ireland and his zeal in publishing "our right to the succession of this our Crown of England and quieting of great tumults begun in Ireland since our coming to the Crown", thus laying emphasis on his service to James since his accession.

His great day was 21 July. At Hampton Court, where the new King rewarded the faithful, Charles Blount, Lord Mountjoy, was created Earl of Devonshire; Henry Wriothesley was created anew Earl of Southampton; and Sir Henry Danvers was created Lord Danvers of Dauntsey. Where could we find a more fortunate trio? The second had lain under sentence of death and the brother of the third had been executed. The risks run by the first have been discussed at some length. It need hardly be said that his deserts were far superior to those of his companions in honour. The title of his earldom was based in all probability not only on his lands in Devonshire but also on the

---

[1] Moryson, Vol. III, p. 335; Salisbury, Pt. XV, pp. 87, 111, 123; Gawdy, p. 129. It has been stated that Mountjoy sailed for home on 2 June, the date given by me in *Elizabeth's Irish Wars*. Yet his first letter to Cecil, from Beaumaris, is dated 30 May, and he had reached Dunstable, little over 30 miles as the crow flies from London, by 5 June.

fact that the first Lord Mountjoy, his great-great-great-grand-father, had received forfeited lands of the Courtenays, Earls of Devonshire.[1]

It has already been stated that Charles, as Lord Lieutenant, was to receive two-thirds of the Irish viceregal emoluments. He did a good deal of work for them. All Irish affairs passed through his hands. The correspondence of the Lord Deputy, Sir George Carew, and that of his successor, Sir Athur Chichester, who succeeded him in the office in February, 1605, was addressed to the Lord Lieutenant. The King was accustomed to write "to the Earl of Devonshire . . . or in his absence . . . to Sir George Carey", maintaining a kind of fiction that the former was from time to time in Ireland. General policy, defence, appointments, finance—all were Charles's province. He remained the overlord of Ireland until his death.

The King was crowned on 25 July. Charles was one of the fifteen earls, wearing tabards of crimson velvet lined with ermine, crimson velvet hoods hanging over their tippets like stockings, caps of the same material with filets of ermine, and coronets, who unrobed the King before his anointing and after the coronation ceremony took the oath covered. The Venetian Ambassador informed the Doge and Senate that the handsome young Earl of Pembroke actually kissed the King's face, instead of his hand, at which the King laughed and gave him a gentle cuff. Dignity was not included in the list of James's virtues.[2]

On 13 August the Earl of Devonshire was appointed Master of the Ordnance, with supervision of the armament and muni-tions of the kingdom, thus, without lifting a finger, obtaining a high office for which Essex had had to toil, hunger, and wait. Four days later it was Penelope's turn. A licence was issued to Lady Rich, descended from the Bourchiers, Earls of Essex, to take precedence accordingly, that is, to have "the place and the rank of the ancientest Earl of Essex, called Bourchier". Lord Rich was the holder of a modern barony, but his wife now took precedence of all baronesses and of all daughters of earls except the Countesses of Oxford, Arundel, Northumberland (her own sister), and Shrewsbury. Her star was high in the heavens.

[1] Moryson, Vol. III, p. 336; Stopes, p. 269; C.S.P. Dom.,1603-10, pp. 16, 23, 31.
[2] C.S.P. Venetian, 1603-07, pp. 74, 77.

Jealous elders commented bitterly on the favour shown her by the Queen. She wore one dress after another, to the ravishment of beholders, though perhaps not of the older peeresses.[1]

Tyrone was kindly received by the King, who pardoned him and confirmed the promises made to him by Charles. Rory O'Donnell was created Earl of Tyrconnell, and poor Neill Garve had to be content with his original possessions. Sir John Harington expressed forcibly to the Bishop of Bath and Wells his disgust at the treatment of Tyrone. "I have lived", he wrote, "to see that damnable rebel Tyrone brought to England, courteously favoured, honoured, and well liked. Oh, my Lord, what is there which does not prove the inconstancy of worldly matters? How I did labour after that knave's destruction! I was called from my home by her Majesty's command, adventured perils by sea and land, endured toil, was near starving, ate horseflesh in Munster; and all to quell that man, who now smileth in peace at those that did hazard their lives to destroy him . . . and now doth Tyrone dare us old commanders with his presence and protection". Harington attributed undue importance to his services. If Devonshire, after fighting against Tyrone for four times as long, could stomach his restoration to rank and lands, Harington need not have felt the alleged dishonour so acutely.[2]

Still, Tyrone was not keeping the best company at Kingston, where he lodged while the Court was at Hampton. Evidence sworn before a Justice of the Peace was brought to Devonshire that Father James Archer, S.J., had been seen dismounting at Tyrone's door and was acting as his "massing priest". Moreover, dressed sometimes as a courtier, sometimes as a farmer, he was frequenting other Irishmen in England, including some who had been lodged in the Tower. It was natural that Tyrone should have a chaplain in his company, but Archer was a bitter opponent of the English and had been instrumental in the kidnapping of Ormonde soon after the beginning of Charles's term as Lord Deputy. The report must have made an unfavourable impression on the latter.[3]

[1] Rawson, pp. 267-9; C.S.P. Dom., 1603-10, p. 32.
[2] *Nugae Antiquae*, Vol. II., p. 149.
[3] C.S.P. Ireland, 1603-06, p. 80.

The love affair of Charles and Penelope was resumed. Indeed, it had never been broken off, though the parties had been separated by the Irish Sea for three and a half years. Now they were reunited. Since she had performed the graceful act of going down to Leighs to nurse her husband in his illness in the autumn of 1600, Penelope had lived apart from him. According to her own account, he abandoned her on the execution of Essex, not having ventured to while her formidable brother lived. There is no hint of any other woman in Charles's life. Rumours of two great matches are mentioned: first, while he was in Ireland, with Lady Elizabeth Butler, Ormonde's heiress daughter, and, secondly, with the Lady Arabella Stuart, the King's first cousin and a potential pretender to the throne; but both stories were probably mere gossip.[1]

Charles and Penelope had now come to the border-line between youth and middle age. The year of her birth is uncertain, but it was probably 1563. If so, both of them reached the age of forty in the year of the accession of James I. In general, women aged faster three and a half centuries ago than now, but Penelope continued to be a beauty in the eyes of her friends and of the group of poets who admired her. The great world accepted the two as lover and mistress as freely as in the former reign, though their relationship must have been even more obvious in view of his rise in station and his life at the centre of affairs. As has been already stated, there exists no evidence about the length of the liaison, except the vague words of Heylin, who may have been guessing at the facts: "But long she had not lived in the bed of Rich then the old flames of her affection unto Blount began again to kindle in her . . . they afterwards converst more openly and familiarly with one another than might stand with honour unto either". Peele's punning on her name dates from 1590, but they may well have been lovers for more than thirteen years, even as long as twenty.[2]

Even more important than the Irish affairs which continued to engage the attention of Devonshire was the business of the Spanish treaty. James I and VI had not, as Scottish sovereign, been engaged in war with the King of Spain. He did not regard

[1] Manningham, p. 59; Gawdy, p. 145.
[2] See p. 58.

the Spanish war as his war. It was his pride to be considered a man of peace. He proclaimed the end of active operations against Spain and set himself to bring about a formal peace with the least possible delay. In this policy he had the full support of the Lord Treasurer, Lord Buckhurst, and, what was still more important, that of Robert Cecil, Secretary of State, whom he had created Lord Cecil. Spain wanted peace, as had been rendered clear by advances made by Aguila to Devonshire.

The war had become lifeless, but for the Spanish expedition to Ireland, and that was a single experiment which had failed and was most unlikely to be repeated. As between the two states, little now remained to justify further hostilities. One important factor had, however, to be considered. Peace between England and Spain would be very unwelcome to the Dutch States General. They—and a large element in English opinion—would regard it as a betrayal. James was not to be deterred by this consideration. He did ask the States whether they were prepared to become a party to a peace treaty, but they answered that they would not on any terms.[1]

At the end of August, 1603, Don Juan de Tassio, Count of Mediana—always known to the English as "Taxis"—arrived in England as envoy of Philip III, but without powers to sign a treaty. The plague being in London and the King at Woodstock, he came to Oxford. On 2 September, Devonshire met him at Henley, to attend upon him during the last stage of his journey. The Ambassador is reported to have taken this as a particular honour because Devonshire was now more talked of in Spain than any other Englishman and was the one he most desired to meet. Villa Mediana was received by the Vice-Chancellor and lodged in Christ Church.

Not until 20 May, 1604, did the peace commissioners meet for the first time in London. On one side of the table sat the English: the Earls of Dorset (the former Lord Buckhurst), Lord High Treasurer; Nottingham, Lord High Admiral; Devonshire, Lord Lieutenant of Ireland; and Northampton (the former Lord Henry Howard), Lord Warden of the Cinque Ports; and Lord Cecil, Principal Secretary of State. Facing them were, for Spain, the Count of Villa Mediana and Alessandro Rovida,

[1] Gardiner, Vol. I, p. 206.

Senator of Milan; for the Archdukes, the Count of Aremberg, Councillor of State; the President de Richardot; and the Secretary and Audienciary Verreykin, all Netherlanders.

Sixteen years earlier Aremberg and Richardot had tried to reach peace with English representatives at Bourbourg, while Philip II was preparing the Invincible Armada. They had better luck this time, but not without a struggle and not altogether on such terms as they would have desired. Charles and his colleagues were aware that they were playing from a pretty strong hand because peace was even more to the interest of Spain than of England. Maurice of Nassau was showing his mettle in the Low Countries, with the admirable aid of the Vere brothers, Francis and Horace, and their English contingent, which had since 1598 been wholly in the pay of the States. The Archduke Albert had suffered a number of rebuffs and in 1600 a heavy defeat at Nieuport. The genius of his new general, the elder Spinola, had as yet barely been revealed, though he was to take Ostend in mid September. Just before the treaty was signed the Dutch took Sluys, from which the younger Spinola's galleys had played havoc with their shipping. The composition with Maurice of Nassau was made on the night of 9 August. On the 10th the place was occupied by the Dutch. On the 11th Devonshire wrote to Cecil from Wanstead that he was glad to hear of the Dutch success and felt that England still had a great interest in their fortunes. That he should have got the news so early is astonishing and affords proof of careful arrangements to keep himself informed.[1]

The business took six weeks, a reasonably short time in view of the magnitude of the issues. The relative position of England and Spain was made clear when Rovida proposed an alliance between them and it was coolly rejected. The Spaniards proposed a clause binding England not to permit her troops to serve against Spain or for her rebellious subjects. James refused to prevent voluntary enlistment in the service of the States General but engaged himself to make no levy. He also promised blandly not to stop enlistment in the service of the Archdukes. The Spaniards and the Archdukes' envoys had to put up with this compromise, which was the essence of neutrality in theory

[1] Salisbury, Pt. XVI, p. 221.

but in practice gave the States many more volunteers than the Archdukes. The latter did obtain some English Roman Catholics and a larger number of Irish.

Cecil gave way over a clause very dear to the Spaniards, which bound each of the contracting parties to throw open the blockaded ports of the other. It did not amount to very much. As Cecil remarked, England had no intention of keeping a fleet at sea for the purpose of making war on the Dutch. On the Spanish side a pledge was given that where there was no public scandal the King would recommend the Holy Inquisition not to question the beliefs of merchants trading with Spain. On one point the Spaniards, to the deep disappointment of mercantile England, proved immovable: they refused absolutely to permit trade with their possessions in the New World. The English Commissioners had to give up the struggle. They were mostly less pacific than the King, but like him they considered it futile to maintain a European war for the purpose of insistence on the right of merchant adventurers to trade in the Indies. They expected these men to defend themselves, which they had in the majority of cases proved themselves able to do.

By 16 August a copy of the treaty had been prepared for engrossment on parchment. The Duke of Frias, High Constable of Castile, had arrived with full powers and been lodged in Somerset House, where he was attended by the King's officers and servants in great pomp. There were sixty-four dinner-tables, and the King was anxious to conclude the business as soon as possible on account of its cost, said to amount to £300 a day. He also wanted to get back to the country. On 19 August Devonshire, with a retinue of fifty mounted gentlemen, splendidly clad, conducted the Constable and the others to Whitehall. The King swore to the treaty and feasted the Ambassadors. Next morning he came at six o'clock to bid the Constable farewell, and then rode to Ware.

Peace with Philip III, King of Spain, and Albert and Isabella, Archduke and Archduchess of Burgundy, was proclaimed at the gates of the Court and in the City. In the latter case it was received in gloomy silence. Yet the best English historian of the period is not unjustified in describing it as "just and honourable". It was not to be long before the States General concluded that it was to their interest also to seek peace with Spain, and they did so as equals.[1]

It may be surmised with confidence that the chief part in the negotiations had been played by Cecil. Devonshire had little of his experience in statecraft. At the same time, he now took rank as the foremost authority on military matters. Cecil regarded him as a close friend and respected his judgement. He assuredly played a valuable role in the business. He had been given also the decorative role of attending the Spaniards, experts in protocol and procedure, because he had the presence and the gifts required for it.

The work accomplished together was a new link with Cecil. On a date unknown, but probably a short time before the treaty was signed, Sir George Home, a Scottish follower of the King's who had been made Chancellor of the Exchequer, wrote to Cecil on the subject of their relations and what he considered should be made of them. The King, he said, had expressed to him his pleasure that Cecil and Devonshire "were so great as he saw you were". For the future, Home's advice was as follows: "And now, my Lord, since you are come to a good point with His Majesty, let a secret course be kept with him in his weightiest affairs by you four, and let his general errands be done by his own Council". Home added that the Queen was going to Wanstead and that the King, who had been feeling "melancollyowsse" about the attitude of the Puritans in the House of Commons, hoped to go too.[2]

The four who were to manage with the King the affairs that mattered were undoubtedly Dorset, Cecil, Devonshire, and Northampton. And this was reality, not mere courtliness or a flight of imagination on the part of Home. We may recall the remark of Fynes Moryson that Charles had originally looked forward to a quiet life in the country and had little relish for affairs of state but was led by ambition to engage in them. Ambition had carried him far, and fast.

One unpleasing fruit of the Spanish treaty confronts us. The Constable had brought with him money—eight or ten thousand

---

[1] Gardiner, Vol. I, pp. 209-14; H.M.C.: *The Family of Gawdy*, p. 94; C.S.P. Venetian, 1603-07, p. 178; *Tudor and Stuart Proclamations*, Vol. I, p. 115; C.S.P., Syllabus of *Rymer's Foedera*, Vol. II.

[2] Salisbury, Pt. XVI, p. 254.

crowns, reported the Venetian Ambassador—to be bestowed on the five nobleman who had arranged the peace. This was proper and in accordance with custom. But Mediana, who remained as Ambassador, was far more lavishly provided with funds, and acceptance of annual allowances from the King of Spain through his agency was another matter. Cecil, now Viscount Cranborne, accepted one of £1,500, a vast sum in relation to the purchasing power of the pound in those days. Dorset, Devonshire, and Northampton accepted pensions of £1,000. Suffolk (the former Lord Thomas Howard) refused, but his Countess did not. Monson, Devonshire's old companion in arms, took £350.

The best to be said of these transactions is that, while they were disapproved of by contemporary judgement, they did not involve a tithe of the ignominy with which they would be loaded in modern times; also that they were common. It may be added that Cecil's policy never became pro-Spanish. Charles undoubtedly loved money, and needed it to keep up his present state and hospitality. There the matter must be left.[1]

The activities of Charles in the Jacobean Parliament have already been briefly described, including his membership of the Lords' Committee which conferred with the Commons on Union with Scotland. On the discovery of Gunpowder Plot he was directed to pursue the conspirators who had fled from London. Cecil, who had by November, 1605, received another step in the peerage and became Earl of Salisbury, did not believe his services would be needed, being persuaded that "this faggot would be burnt to ashes" before he had ridden twenty miles on his way. As so often, the Secretary's estimate was correct. Charles received a commission as General and left London to take command of a force, reported by the Venetian Ambassador to consist of 1,200 gentlemen; but the plotters were dealt with locally before he could intervene. He was later appointed one of the seven Commissioners, all Privy Councillors, who attended the examination of prisoners. He wrote a courtly letter to the King, as his military adviser, urging him to guard himself better and ending: "God preserve you ever, and be not too careless of yourself, since God hath shown himself so careful for you".[2]

[1] Gardiner, Vol. I, p. 215.
[2] Winwood, Vol. II, p. 170; C.S.P. Venetian, 1603-07, pp. 292, 301; Rawson, p. 275.

He received further honours and emoluments. On 6 January, 1604, he was granted the office of Captain of the Town, Island, and Castle of Portsmouth, the appointment given to him by Queen Elizabeth ten years earlier, almost to the day. On 30 March he and Southampton received a joint commission of the Lieutenancy of the County and Town of Southampton and of the City of Winchester. On 5 February, 1605, he was one of seven lords granted the office of Earl Marshal in commission, this being an office too great to be entrusted to any single subject.[1]

One of his best services to the Irish Government was his choice of the brilliant young lawyer—and delightful poet—John Davies as Solicitor General. He cut down the military establishment to the lowest level reached for many years, 234 horse and 880 foot, roughly one-twentieth of that at the height of Tyrone's rebellion; but his view that such an economy could safely be made was justified by events. His policy was to make the Irish realize that the reduction of the army was due to the King's confidence in their loyalty, which allowed him to ease the people of their burdens. This was true enough and there was no reason why the Lord Lieutenant should call their attention to the other side of the medal, his desire to ease the King of his burdens.[2]

He engaged in one business transaction. He purchased the reversion, for seven years, of the farm or lease of customs' duties on imported French and Rhenish wines and then conveyed this reversion, doubtless at a profit, to a syndicate, which in due course succeeded to it. In 1613 the duties were sequestrated by order of the High Court of Chancery on some flaw in the lease. There was, however, no dishonesty in the transaction, and when the syndicate made a better offer for the farm the Crown struck a bargain with it.[3]

Ireland, foreign affairs, the Ordnance, the Privy Council, the House of Lords—it was a full life. Small wonder that the old headaches continued to torment Charles.

[1] C.S.P. Dom., 1603-10, pp. 64, 89, 192.
[2] C.S.P. Ireland, 1603-06, p. 442.
[3] Sackville, Vol. I, pp. 299, 307.

XVI

PENELOPE

LIFE was not all work, though nearly. A single record remains of Charles's enjoyment of the sport in which he delighted. In March, 1605, he stayed with Cecil, then Lord Cranborne, at Theobalds, together with the Earls of Northampton, Cumberland, and Southampton, and they went hawking together. Cranborne wrote on that occasion that on the 10th they would all go home to school. Such facts are rarely set down, and it may be supposed that this interlude of sport did not stand alone and that at least sometimes Charles accompanied the most enthusiastic of hunters and hawkers, King James I, in his country pleasures. In March, 1606, Charles's absence from the House of Lords was excused on the ground that he was attending on the King's person, doubtless away from London.[1]

He also contrived to be often at Wanstead, though he took work there and his head might be full of Irish affairs. He found the air a sovereign remedy for the bouts of sickness which had vexed him off and on for a number of years and with increased weight since the Kinsale campaign.

It can be assumed that when possible he was present at Court entertainments. Interested as he was in plays, he is unlikely to have missed the occasion in 1604 when Richard Burbage, finding no new play that Queen Anne had not already seen, revived an old one, *Love's Labour's Lost*, which he was confident would please her by its wit and mirth.[2]

Charles certainly witnessed the masques in which Penelope appeared and may be taken to have been an actor in the small

---

[1] C.S.P. Dom., 1603-10, p. 203; *Journals of the House of Lords*, Vol. II, p. 392.

[2] Salisbury, Pt. XVIII, p. 415.

role allotted to men. He was at Hampton Court when King James spent his first English Christmas there and Samuel Daniel wrote for the occasion *The Vision of the Twelve Goddesses*. It was performed on 8 January, 1604. The King sat in state with the new Spanish Ambassador, Mediana, and the Venetian beside him. The Queen took the part of Pallas. Penelope, as might be supposed, played that of Venus, in a mantle of dove-colour and silver embroidered with doves and a scarf of divers colours.

> *Then lovely* Venus *in bright majesty*
> *Appears with mild aspect, in dove-like hue,*
> *With the all combining scarf of amity,*
> *To ingird strange nations with affections true.*

Daniel dedicated the masque to Lucy Countess of Bedford, and that enterprising blue-stocking was probably its instigator. It is even more likely that she chose her own part, that of Vesta, and the costume which went with it. This astonished a male onlooker, who commented that it made clear the fact that women had legs as well as feet, which, he said, he had not known before. The spectacle and the dancing were the essence of these shows, and in this case the plot was even simpler than usual. The twelve masquers danced their measures alone; then the Graces sang a song; finally the masquers chose partners among the lords and danced with them.[1]

An even greater occasion was that of the performance of the first of the Queen's Masques by Ben Jonson. This was *The Masque of Blackness*, presented at the Court of Whitehall on Twelfth Night, 1605, with Penelope again one of the masquers. Queen Anne had desired the poet to give her and her ladies the parts of Negresses, a request which a modern critic rather unaccountably finds typical of her vulgarity. Ben constructed a plot to satisfy her. The theme was the visit to England of twelve nymphs, daughters of the Niger, "called Nigritae, now Negroes; and . . . the blackest nation of the world".

Jonson is one of the greatest writers of masques, and he had as partner a man of equal genius in his own sphere, Inigo Jones. His work in mounting the masque was far more than the designing of backcloths and costumes; he used also his mechanical skill in the construction of engines and shifting

---

[1] Sprague, p. xxiv; Grosart's Daniel, Vol. III, p. 187.

scenes. On these the beauty, the novelty, and the surprises of the performance largely depended. The masques composed and produced by these two in concert were a combination of comedy of the type of *The Tempest* and *The Faithful Shepherdess* with more modern forms of entertainment: the ballet and the pageant. Yet they were essentially Court shows, not for the popular eye and ear. The descriptions given by Ben Jonson, though full, are somewhat obscure, but the impression is generally favourable. Inigo Jones was unlikely to fail.

The daughters of Niger were grouped in six pairs. Each pair had its badge or symbol, painted on the fans. They were the Queen and the Countess of Bedford, as Euphoris and Aglaia; Lady Herbert and the Countess of Derby, as Diaphane and Eycampse; Lady Rich and the Countess of Suffolk, as Ocyte and Kathare; Lady Bevill and Lady Effingham, as Notis and Psychrote; Lady Elizabeth Howard and Lady Susan Vere, as Glycyte and Malacia; Lady Wroth and Lady Walsingham, as Baryth and Periphere.

The voyagers reached the English shore from an artificial sea in the banqueting hall, "in a great concave shell, like mother of pearl, curiously made to move on those waters and rise with the billow; the top thereof was stuck with a chevron of lights, which, indented to the proportion of the shell, struck a glorious beam upon them, as they were seated one above another". Beside the shell swam six huge sea-monsters, carrying on their backs twelve torch-bearers, the daughters of Oceanus.

The masquers were dressed alike in azure and silver. On forehead, ears, neck and wrists they wore ornaments "of the most choice orient pearl", the best setting for the black. The torch-bearers wore sea-green, waved with gold and silver on their skirts; their hair loose and flowing, garlanded with "sea-grass" into which were stuck branches of coral.

Ben Jonson was enthusiastic about the effect. A disinterested and cynical spectator was less so. Sir Dudley Carleton thought there was too much fish and too little water. He admitted that the ladies' dress was rich, but considered it "too light and courtesan-like" for the great ladies of England. Jones's sketch of one of the nymphs does not confirm this impression, but the conventions of his day and ours differ, and the complaint is of transparency rather than scantiness. Carleton also commented unfavourably on faces and arms painted black. He admitted that paint was an effective substitute for masks and made it hard to recognize the ladies, but found that it "became them nothing so well as their red and white".

Niger asked Oceanus what was the land his daughters now saw. Oceanus answered:

> *This land, that lifts into the temperate air*
> *His snowy cliff, is Albion the fair;*
> *So call'd of Neptune's son, who ruleth here:*
> *For whose dear guard, myself four thousand year*
> *Since old Deucalion's days have walked the round*
> *About his empire, proud to see him crown'd*
> *Above my waves.*

The daughters of Niger came ashore, chose partners from the men of England, represented by the noblemen and gentlemen of the Court, and danced with them. Pretty songs filled intervals of rest. Finally, the visiting nymphs returned to their shell to continue their voyage. Jonson speaks of "the singular grace of music and dances".[1]

Charles had been throughout his adult life "a patron to the learned and a prop", in the words of John Ford. He was the object of a number of dedications, beginning with that of Thomas Nashe's *Anatomie of Absurdities* in 1589. Among others are those of Gervase Markham's *The Most Honorable Tragedy of Sir Richard Grenville, Knight; The Courtiers Academie* by J. K.; Thomas Bastard's *Chrestoleros* (and seven of the indifferent epigrams in it separately dedicated); and Nicholas Breton's *The Honour of Valour*. Among poems addressed to him are a sonnet by Henry Lok and Latin verses by the epigrammatists John Owen and John Stradling. The last-named is addressed, "Ad illustrem Carolum Blunt, D. Montioy, Hiberniae proregem; De Victoria in Tironum ad Kinsale", and celebrates his achievements against the Irish and the Spaniards. It is characteristic of the poets' attitude to him that he appears so often in the role of courtier. The connexion between the words "courtier" and "courtesy" had not disappeared in the first Elizabethan age, and for it "courtier" often meant all that a well-

---

[1] Jonson: *The Queen's Masques*; Winwood, Vol. II, p. 46; Gotch, p. 29.

bred man would desire to be. As courtier and in courtesy Nashe, for instance, saw in Charles the successor to Philip Sidney.[1]

He was in a special sense the patron of Samuel Daniel, who dedicated an early edition of his *Civil Wars* to him and wrote the funeral poem already quoted. The patronage was of a practical and generous nature. It would seem that he supported the poet so that he might engage in this long and arduous piece of work.

> *And thou, Charles Mountjoy, born the world's delight,*
> *That hast receiv'd into thy quiet shore*
> *Me tempest-driven, fortune-tosséd, wight*
> *Tir'd with expecting and could hope no more:*
> *And cheerest on my better years to write*
> *A sadder subject than I took before;*
> *Receive the work I consecrate to thee,*
> *Born of that rest which thou dost give to me.*

At one moment their relationship was strained. Daniel's play *The Tragedy of Philotas*, performed on 3 January, 1605, was held to recall too vividly the career and fate of Essex. It was accordingly suppressed, and the author was summoned to appear before the Privy Council. He pleaded that three acts had been written prior to the revolt of Essex and that he had read part of the play to the Earl of Devonshire. Charles was annoyed. He did not want any fresh links established between himself and the Essex tragedy. Daniel apologized humbly. He said that he had no other friend to whom he could refer and that Devonshire's displeasure had more shaken his heart than he had thought any fortune could. It was little more than a trifle and can have done the poet no harm, since four editions or reprints of the play appeared in the next seven years. For the patron, however, it was an unwelcome echo from the past.[2]

Penelope had her share of poets' praise. John Florio linked her with her niece, the Countess of Rutland, in a dedication of his *Montaigne*. Thomas Campion epitomized her amatory history in two Latin lines:

> *Penelope, Astrophili quae vultu incendit amores*
> *Olim, et voce ducem dulci incantabit Hybernium.*

(Penelope, who kindled the loves in the face of Astrophel and

[1] Buxton, p. 214.
[2] Michel, pp. vi, vii, 37-9.

with her dulcet voice betwitched the ruler of the Irish.) A Breton poet and musician, Georges Tessier, brought her another dedication. Henry Constable addressed to her a number of sonnets, of which the following is one:

> *O that my song like to a ship might be,*
> *To bear about the world my Lady's fame;*
> *That, chargéd with the riches of her name,*
> *The Indians might our country's treasures see:*
> *No treasure they would say is rich but she;*
> *Of all their golden parts they would have shame,*
> *And haply, that they might but see the same,*
> *To give their gold for naught they would agree.*
> *This wishéd voyage, though it I begin,*
> *Without your beauty's help cannot prevail:*
> *For as a ship doth bear the men therein,*
> *And yet the men do make the ship to sail,*
> *Your beauties so, which in my voice appear,*
> *Do make my verse and it your beauties bear.*

This is more than agreeable, though one may regret the persistence of the old pun on the name. Constable also wrote a sonnet to Nicholas Hilliard "upon occasion of a picture he made of my Lady Rich". Would that it could be found!

In November, 1605, Robert Lord Rich and Penelope were divorced before the Court of High Commission. We now approach the final tragedy, but this approach has an element of comedy. "My Lord Archbishop chid my Lord Rich very much" —so far, so good—"and gave my Lady great commendation"— one must ask, for what? Had the Archbishop of Canterbury fallen under the spell like the rest? Perhaps yes, in some degree, but there was another reason. Dismissing Lord Rich, the Archbishop bade him "go amongst his Puritans". Rich was the leader of the sect in Essex and Archbishop Bancroft had no love either for Puritans or for their liberal ideas on divorce. So Penelope won commendation once more, but according to the accepted story for the last time.[1]

Charles at once acted. In 1603 a new chaplain named William Laud had entered his household. Charles now used the strong influence which their respective positions assured to him,

[1] H.M.C. 7th Report, App., p. 527.

allied with his own and Penelope's persuasive charm, to induce Laud to marry them.

The chaplain did not agree all at once. The generally accepted view was that divorce in the ecclesiastical courts was only *a mensa et thoro* (from board and bed) and that the remarriage of a divorced person was not permissible; but there was no definite code dealing with the subject. Charles and Penelope both informed Laud that a pledge of marriage had passed between them before her marriage to Rich. This was obviously without legal significance, but of some, thought Laud, in "a court of conscience". He is said to have examined the ecclesiastical authorities and found three opinions touching the legality of remarriage. The first was that it was lawful for neither party: the doctrine of the Council of Trent and of the Roman Catholic Church. The second was that it was lawful for the wronged party only: the doctrine of some Calvinists and some ancient writers. The third was that it was lawful for both the innocent and the guilty: the doctrine of most Calvinists and Lutherans and of certain Catholic doctors. This is all very well, but we cannot avoid the feeling that Laud was moved strongly by more mundane considerations: the advantage of having a powerful patron behind him to back the abilities of which he was fully conscious, the prospect of preferment in the Church. His early biographer owns that this may have been the case and adds, in terms which may make a not unsympathetic appeal to the honest and unprejudiced, that, if such motives prevailed, "they may with charity be looked on as the common incidencies of human frailty, from which the holiest and most learned men cannot plead exemption". At all events, on 26 December, St. Stephen's day, Laud performed the ceremony.[1]

What followed is a matter of evidence the precise validity of which is difficult to weigh. It is said that the King was deeply offended and that the remarriage caused a scandal, that the world which had smiled on a liaison was shocked by a marriage ceremony of doubtful legality and turned its face away from the parties. The evidence comes from four sources: the account of Heylin, Laud's biographer; that of the Scottish annalist, Robert Johnston; a letter written by John Chamberlain after Devon-

[1] Heylin, p. 52.

shire's death; and the fact that Devonshire himself thought it necessary to defend himself in an elaborate "Apology". Heylin is not exact and both he and Johnston are in error over points of which we have full knowledge, while Chamberlain is a gossip who picked up news in conversation. Still, the combination deserves some respect. It is reinforced by Devonshire's tract, and by references to criticism in the obituary tributes of the poets Daniel and Ford. The conclusion must be that the King was in fact offended, that Charles and Penelope were blamed and perhaps by some treated coldly, but that the suggestion of their being sent to Coventry is almost certainly exaggerated.

Charles continued to go about his official business. The final Irish military establishment, already mentioned, was clearly drawn up by him after the marriage ceremony. A protest which he made to Salisbury about the appointment to the clerkship of the Ordnance of a man who was neither clerk nor good captain is also attributed to the year 1606. On 21 January he was appointed a member of a Committee of the House of Lords to consider laws for the preservation of religion. On 3 February he appears as a member of another committee to consider an act of attainder of various offenders in "the late most detestable and damnable treason"—Gunpowder Plot. On 10 March his absence from the Lords was excused on the ground that he was in attendance on the King, which would seem to reduce the weight of the royal displeasure and the social obloquy to relatively small proportions. On 17 March he attended a meeting of the Privy Council and signed a letter to Sir Charles Cornwallis in Spain, informing him that a Spanish proposal for an alliance—a repetition of that put forward during the negotiations in England—could not for the time being be entertained. He still wrote on friendly terms to Cecil.[1]

"A Discourse or Apollogie. Written by Sr Charles Blount Lord Mountjoy & Earl of Devonshire in defence of his marriage with the Lady Rich. Año dmi. 1606" is a notable piece of casuistical argument, forcible and pregnant.[2] The writer made

---

[1] Salisbury, Pt. XVIII, p. 83; Winwood, Vol. II, p. 201; *Journals of the House of Lords*, Vol. II, pp. 360, 367, 392. Unfortunately, the Journal is not reliable. It states that he was present on 3 April, the day of his death.

[2] The heading of the Bodleian copy. That in B.M. Stowe omits the word "apology".

use of his long study of the Scriptures and of the Fathers, as well as of legal knowledge.

He began with the statement that God was infinite in His being and in its attributes: wisdom, power, and goodness. He created the world for man, and both world and man for His glory. He saw that it was not good that man should be alone and therefore created an assistant or helper, which was the woman.

Because marriage was both a sacred and a civil contract, it had to be considered in the light of the word of God, the law of nature, and so much of the law of the country as was not contrary to the word of God or the law of nature. It could not be doubted that the contract *de jure* ought never to be broken. The question was whether *de facto* it might be broken in face of the rule that no man should put asunder whom God had coupled together. To argue that this rule denied that the contract might ever be broken could be likened to concluding that no man might kill because of the Commandment, "Thou shalt not kill". On the contrary, "the magistrate may both kill an offender and justly kill him; yet it is not to be said that he, but Justice, killeth him, and the offender is guilty of his own death, and not the magistrate". So, if two married people should, contrary to the objects of marriage, instead of being "comfortable helps", become continual torments to each other, and if one or other should become one flesh with another, there was no danger in the magistrate announcing that the contract was broken, since by the fault of the offender it was indeed broken. And it was clear from the Scriptures that divorce was permitted among the Jews, that it dissolved the bonds of marriage, and that both parties might remarry. There was nothing in the first institution of marriage by the law of God which made the bond of marriage so fast but that in some cases it might be dissolved.

Having proved to his own satisfaction that divorce was permissible, he passed on to the problem of remarriage. Christ had said that he who married a woman who had been divorced was committing adultery, yet he had also allowed that a man might put away his wife for fornication, thus sanctioning divorce, but not remarriage. Yet, says Devonshire, on the question of legality there could be no doubt of the right of a man to marry a woman lawfully put away. If she had been put away unlawfully she was still the wife of the man who claimed to put her away, but if lawfully, then she was now no man's wife. Therefore she could marry again. As for the partial divorce which did not allow remarriage, that called *a mensa et thoro*, it was an emendation, an error of the Canon Law, "which in many things but especially in this of marriage hath so many errors". Once again, "if we grant a separation from the bond of marriage we must yield that it is lawful for both parties to marry again".

This argument would have been unanswerable had the institution of civil marriage existed. It is not now denied by "the law of the country" where the institution now exists, as in the United Kingdom, though the Church may refuse to solemnize a marriage where one or both of the parties have been divorced. Yet even should the Church direct the clergy not to solemnize such a marriage, this will not invalidate a marriage solemnized in due form by a clergyman.

The above is a brief summary of a long thesis. It omits numerous quotations from the Fathers of the Church and is confined to what appear to be the essential points. Though the writer was a student of theology, the reasoning as regards remarriage is that of a secular logician. Charles desired to prove his right to marry Penelope, without any consideration of morals.

The moment of the divorce was untimely and it would seem that the position would have been stronger only a few years earlier. After the Reformation there was a tendency to reject divorce *a mensa et thoro* as a relatively modern invention. The reformers favoured divorce a *vinculis matrimoniis* (from the bonds of matrimony), a complete break, after which there could be no question of the legality of a remarriage which had been celebrated in due form. All their continental authorities agreed that an absolute divorce should be given for adultery and most of them would have permitted the clergy to remarry the innocent party. Calvin considered that both innocent and guilty should be allowed to remarry. English Protestants were more conservative, but they agreed that a man could put his wife away for unfaithfulness and marry again. Some would not allow as much for the woman, and John Hooper was criticized for demanding equal justice for the sexes in this respect.

In the year 1552 a commission appointed by Parliament had drawn up a code of ecclesiastical laws, drafted mainly by Cranmer. This was never put into force, but it exercised an influence on doctrine. It laid down that divorce *a vinculis matrimoniis* might be granted for faithlessness, desertion, and cruelty, but that only the innocent spouse might contract another marriage. A well-known historian considers that the custom of divorce followed by remarriage was under Elizabeth "ripening into law", though obnoxious to many, and points out that the Foljambe Case of 1602, though generally held to mark a change in divorce law, did show that remarriage went on up to the last year of the reign of Queen Elizabeth I. The Stuart era, however, gave the signal for reaction. Charles and Penelope were unfortunate in that their case came up in the atmosphere of the Canons of 1604.[1]

It may at first sight seem surprising how much abstract doctrine influenced Laud in his solemnization of the marriage and Devonshire in his defence of it. For example, if the divorce could be said with certainty to be only *a mensa et thoro*—a mere judicial separation and not a breaking of the marriage contract —then neither Laud nor Devonshire had the shadow of a case and remarriage was obviously impossible. On reflection, it will appear that these preoccupations with doctrine were due to the uncertainty of the law, one might say to the absence of it. Many contemporary divines considered such a marriage to be lawful.

Laud bitterly repented his action. He issued a refutation of Devonshire's arguments. He made the feast of St. Stephen into an anniversary fast, humbling himself each year on that day before God and craving pardon for his error. He composed a prayer containing the following passage:

"Lord, I beseech Thee for the mercies of Jesus Christ, enter not into judgement with me Thy servant, but hear His blood imploring Thy mercies for me. Neither let this marriage prove a divorcing of my soul from Thy grace and favour; for much more happy had I been if, being mindful of this day, I had suffered martyrdom, as did Saint Stephen the first of martyrs, denying that which either my less faithful friends or less godly friends had pressed upon me.

[1] Howard, Vol. II, pp. 53-85.

I promised to myself that the darkness should hide me, but that hope soon vanished away. Nor doth the light appear more plainly than that I have committed that foul offence. Even so, O Lord, it pleased Thee of Thy infinite mercy to deject me with this heavy ignominy, that I might learn to seek Thy name".

In his notes on his own life Laud wrote: "My cross about the Earl of Devon's Marriage".[1]

Yet as with the marriage, so with the regrets for it, a lurking suspicion of Laud's motives remains. It would seem that there existed some worldly tincture in his repentance, at least that he would not have repented so heartily but for the brake which he believed his action had put upon his progress in the Church. It is true that, by the standard of his vigour and brains, that progress was slow for a long time. He did not become a bishop until 1621—then only of a Welsh see—and King James lectured him about the old offence before he appointed him. Yet by 1633 he was the Archbishop of Canterbury and immensely powerful. By 1645 he was a martyr.

Penelope's former husband, Lord Rich, had the custody of the children by their marriage, of whom the eldest son was now eighteen years old. She had brought with her to Wanstead five other young children. The eldest of these, a boy named Mountjoy, was about eight years of age. The names of the other four were St. John, Charles, Penelope, and Isabella. These children were of course not legitimated by the marriage, even if it be accepted as legal, though Charles is said to have hoped that they might be.

What a fantastic picture it is! Here stood his mother, claiming to be the wife of one of the greatest men in the land, amid a whole brood of children all born out of wedlock, having passed on to the care of her former husband another brood as large, and having but two years since played the part of Venus before the critical eyes of the Court.

Perhaps the King and the Court are not to be blamed if they found it beyond the bounds of romance, so extraordinary and unconventional as to cause deep embarrassment. We may hold that errors of conduct are no more blameworthy if open to all eyes than if hidden from the vulgar; yet the Lord Lieutenant of

---

[1] Laud, Vol. II, pp. 81, 132.

Ireland, a Lord of the Privy Council, the Master of the Ordnance, and a Knight of the Garter must expect his visible actions to be subjected to a code rather different from that applied by easy-going people to people of no importance. However, the situation was very brief.

XVII

SUDDEN ENDING

IN relation to the number of letters from his hand after his return from Ireland which have been preserved, Charles's complaints of ill-health are frequent. Twice in 1604 he mentioned the subject, on the first occasion saying that he was in the grip of the old fury of the headache, and on the second that he was staying at Wanstead because he was in fear of "desperate sickness". In an undated letter, probably written in 1605, he reported that he was unable to come to Court owing to lameness, due to weakness in the leg in which he had received his "great hurt" at Arnhem, twenty years before. On 26 April of that year he declared that he was as weak as if he had suffered a year's sickness, but thanked God the pain was over. And on 1 October he sent apologies for being too ill to wait upon the King.[1]

Three months after his marriage ceremony he was attacked by what would appear to have been pneumonia. His last known letter, written about 27 March, 1606, was addressed to his friend Salisbury—who certainly had not deserted him—promising to meet him if well enough. Charles grew rapidly worse. The news of his plight got abroad. The shameless and vulture-like haste to tear the body before life had left it, which is one of the most unpleasant characteristics of the age, was illustrated by a letter from the Earl of Sussex, whose father Charles had succeeded as Captain of Portsmouth, saying that in the event of the holder's death he intended to apply for the post if Salisbury would favour his suit.[2] It is almost a pleasure to note that Salisbury evidently did not do so and that the appointment went

[1] Salisbury, Pt. XVI, pp. 236, 430; Pt. XVII, pp. 159, 588; C.S.P. Dom., 1603-10, p. 234.
[2] C.S.P. Dom., 1603-10, pp. 304, 307.

to a worthy character, Sir Francis Vere, prematurely worn with exertions and wounds in the Low Countries.

Fynes Moryson thus records his loved master's last illness:

"He was surprised with a burning fever, whereof the first fit being very violent, he called to him his most familiar friends, and, telling them that he had ever by experience and presaging mind been taught to repute a burning fever his fatal enemy, desired them (upon instructions then given them) to make his will, and then he said: let death look never so ugly, he would meet him smiling, which he nobly performed; for I never saw a brave spirit part more mildly from the old mansion than his did, departing most peaceably after nine days' sickness, upon the third of April, in the beginning of the year 1606."

Moryson is the only eye-witness who has recorded the scene— and he is so discreet that he never mentions Penelope at any point in his writings—but others have described it. The Jesuit John Gerard, who had tried to convert Penelope to Roman Catholicism at Leighs, had information on the subject. He states disapprovingly that with his last breath the dying man called upon his "angel", not upon his God. The Scot, Robert Johnston, writing in Latin, gives a somewhat similar account, though in his case one knows not where it came from. Charles, he writes, breathed his last as he lay in the arms of his dearest lady, who blessed him through her tears and kissed his mouth and hands. Then, overwhelmed, she lay night and day in a corner of the bedroom—*noctu, interdiu in thalami sui angulo, humi jacens.*

Daniel may have had his account from Moryson, for the description in his "funeral poem" bears a strong resemblance to that of the former, even to the phrase about meeting death smiling. Daniel could write fine verse, but here he is unfortunately at his worst:

> *He told his faithful friend whom he held dear*
> *(And whose great worth was worthy so to be)*
> *How that he knew these hot diseases were*
> *Of that contagious force, as he did see*
> *That men were over-tumbled suddenly,*
> *And therefore did desire to set a course*
> *And order to his affairs as speedily*
> *As might be, ere his sickness should grow worse:*

And as for death, said he, I do not weigh,
I am resolv'd and ready in his case.
It cannot come to affright me any way,
Let it look never with so grim a face:
And I will meet it smiling, for I know
How vain a thing all this world's glory is.

We are grateful for the information, written in the margin of the first edition, that the faithful friend was Sir William Godolphin. Perhaps he, and not Moryson, was Daniel's informant.

Finally, there is the heavily condemnatory letter of John Chamberlain:

"The Earl of Devonshire left this life on Thursday night last, soon and early for his years, but late enough for himself : and happy had he been if he had gone two or three years since, before the world was weary of him or that he had left that scandal behind him. He was not long sick, past eight or ten days, and died of a burning fever and putrefaction of his lungs, a defect he never complained of. He hath left his lady (for so she is now generally held to be) £1,500 a year and most of his movables, and of five children (that she fathered upon him at the parting from her former husband) I do not hear that he hath provided for more than three, leaving to his eldest son (as I hear) between three and four thousand pounds a year, and to a daughter £6,000 in money".

The writer then mentioned the offices to be disposed of and the fancied candidates, a matter of great interest to those like himself who loved to chat and speculate about the filling of vacant places. They were those of Lord Lieutenant of Ireland, Governor of Portsmouth, commander of a company of horse in Ireland, Warden of the New Forest, Master of the Ordnance.[1]

The first thing that strikes us about this judgement is that it is not moral but social. The scandal, not the conduct, was condemned. Then the interpolation, "for so she is now generally held to be", is important. Despite the questioning of the validity of the marriage, which had, as will appear, a repercussion at the funeral, Penelope was generally held to be Countess of Devonshire. And she has come down in history as such, though remembered as Lady Rich because she was celebrated under

[1] Moryson, Vol. III, p. 337; Johnston, p. 420; Winwood, Vol. II, p. 204.

that name, just as the Earl of Devonshire is remembered as Lord Mountjoy.

The distressing feature of the letter lies, however, in the coarse phrase, "fathered upon him" and the even uglier, "I do not hear that he hath provided for more than three". Of these words Penelope's one biographer wrote:

"When Devonshire's papers came to be opened, all the world knew that out of their five children, all illegitimate, he acknowledged but three. It is impossible to probe into this terribly painful story of conjugal difference. It is an ugly blot on the story, and remains a mystery. Nothing can palliate the slur which the Earl's will cast upon the lady. In the absence of all secret correspondence and family documents the matter eludes investigation. It were fairer to give the mother the benefit of the doubt."[1]

This wretched tale, based on the tattle of a gossip who did not claim to rely on more than hearsay, has been repeated again and again from the first telling until now. There must, one would have thought, have been some element of truth in it. There was in fact not an iota. It is entirely untrue and without relation to the facts. The proof of its falsity lies in the will, long and elaborate, which must have taken a considerable time to draw up and was signed by Charles on the day before he died.

He said that he desired an honourable funeral but without superfluous pomp and expense. He gave directions for the payment of his debts, for which sales would be necessary, beginning with those of Irish lands. He established a trust for vast English possessions—castles, manors, farms, rights, advowsons—widely spread in the counties of Devon, Dorset, Somerset, Leicester, Northampton, Southampton, and Worcester (some, in Northampton and Dorset described as lately bought, suggesting that he had not done ill out of the Irish wars even if he had had to pledge his credit). The trustees were his kinsman, Sir Edward Blount, Sir William Godolphin, Henry Berkeley, Joseph Earth, and John Wakeman—the two last probably stewards. He appointed another set of "overseers" or trustees, the Earls of Suffolk, Southampton, and Salisbury, the Lords Knollys (the former Sir William, "Mr. Controller") and Danvers, to apply

[1] Rawson, p. 298.

the proceeds of his estate for the maintenance of his "very dear and loving wife" for her lifetime.

On her death the estate was to pass first to his eldest son Mountjoy (described as "one of the sons of the said Lady") and to his heirs male, *then*[1] to a child in the womb, if a son, and his heirs male, *then* to his son St. John and his heirs male, *then* to his son Charles and his heirs male, *then* to his daughter Penelope and her heirs male, *then* to his daughter Isabella and her heirs male, *then* to the child in the womb, if a daughter, and her heirs male, *then* to the heirs female of Mountjoy, *then* to the heirs female of the child in the womb, if a son &c. . . . and finally in default of all such issues to the Lady Penelope and her assigns.

Out of the estate in the trust the annual sum of £500 was to be paid to Mountjoy for life and £300 each to St. John, Charles, and the child in the womb, if a son, as each attained the age of sixteen years. The elder daughter, Penelope, was to receive £5,000 as a marriage portion on attaining the age of eighteen, and Isabella and the child in the womb, if a daughter, £3,000 each. He was assured that his widow would maintain and educate the girls suitably while she lived, but on her death further sums of £15 annually for each would be provided till they were aged eighteen. He bequeathed £1,000 to his widow to distribute among his servants according to her discretion and their deserts. He bequeathed to her all his gold and silver plate, jewels, tapestries, household furniture, and all movable goods. The first three of the witnesses to his signature were Southampton, Sir Oliver St. John, and William Laud.[2]

It will be seen that there is here no disavowal, no unreasonable differentiation. It is true that "the child the Lady now goeth withal", if a boy, comes next in succession to the eldest son. This may have been because the father considered that this child's legitimacy could be established. It will be observed, however, that, if this unborn child were a girl, she would fare less well for her marriage portion than Penelope, the first-born daughter. What of this child? If a boy, he cannot have lived, or an effort to establish his right to the earldom would have been

---

[1] In this summary the word *then* is used in each case for "in default of such heirs".

[2] Copy in the Library of Exeter College, Oxford.

made and recorded. Another female name has been mentioned, as though an alternative to one of those given; but it may have been that of this child.

The size of the annuities and dowries provided for this large family and the long roll of manors and farms—though acreages are not given—are evidence of great wealth. If Charles had been given to "greedy gathering" he had done it to some effect. With peace in Ireland, land and fisheries were already rising rapidly in value.

It must be rare, if not unique, in English history for a woman not of royal blood to be the mother of three earls, two of them earls by creation. This was the case of Penelope. Her first husband afterwards became Earl of Warwick, and their eldest son, Lord High Admiral for the Parliament in the Civil War, succeeded him in that title. Another son was created Earl of Holland; he was beheaded by the Roundheads, thus following Penelope's brother, Essex, and her step-father, Sir Christopher Blount, in the family tradition. Her eldest son by Charles, Mountjoy Blount, was created Earl of Newport. Her blood is widely spread in the peerage.

Whatever small degree of truth may have been embedded in the story that Charles and Penelope were given the cold shoulder after the marriage at Wanstead, this does not apply to her after her lord's death. She was daily visited by the greatest in the land. She had, however, to endure one other painful ordeal. A dispute arose among the heralds about the propriety of empaling her arms with his at the funeral. In these cases the negative argument is more likely to succeed than the positive, and so it was here. Charles was buried in state in Westminster Abbey. He did not lack arms, without those of his widow. His hearse was adorned with fourteen escutcheons besides his own, including those of the Spanish family of Ayala, of Beauchamp, and of Leigh of St. Oswalds, the family of his mother: all within the Order of the Garter. The rites were marked by the tributes of the nobility and the sympathy of the populace—*funus maerore procerum et charitate plebis celebratum*. The Earl of Southampton was the chief mourner.[1]

No trace of the tomb remains and the register does not cover

[1] Croke, Vol. II, p. 251; Rawson, p. 292; Johnston, p. 420.

the burial, but there survives a voucher of May, 1606, "for a rail in the Church at the funeral of the Earl of Devonshire".[1]

The Mayor and Burgesses of Portsmouth expressed their grief at the loss of their very good Lord and High Steward, and begged Salisbury to accept their choice of himself for the office. From France the Comte de Beaufort wrote that King Henry IV had expressed his great sorrow at the news, both for Devonshire's own merits and still more on Salisbury's account, being well aware of their affection; Beaufort added his regrets for the death of this "brave and gallant cavalier". From Ireland Chichester wrote on 25 April, having only just got the news, that the death of the Lord Lieutenant was very grievous, in respect both of the office he had held and of his kindness to the writer. John Davies said that he had lost a noble patron, who had sent him to Ireland. Sir Geffrey Fenton, whom the dead man had often blamed, bemoaned his loss. The Earl of Tyrconnell floridly described his grief as "intolerable". A great change in Irish administration was now inevitable. Chichester pointed out that he had always addressed the news and the papers to Devonshire, with such advice as he had thought suitable; he wished that Salisbury now had all the papers, since he hardly knew the rest of the Council. On its side the Council informed him that, Devonshire's experience and merit being what they were, his Majesty and his Privy Council had interfered little in Irish affairs; now they must revert to the practice of former times.[2]

Let the last words on Charles come from the poets, who had given him so much pleasure. The elegy of Samuel Daniel is notable for providing as good a study of the subject's character as can be found. Charles appeared to the eulogistic poet as he appeared to the more critical and less idealistic secretary, Fynes Moryson.

> *Mild, affable and easy of access*
> *He was, but with a due reservedness:*
> *So that the passage to his favours lay*
> *Not common to all comers, nor yet was*
> *So narrow but it gave a gentle way*
> *To such as fitly might or ought to pass.*

[1] Westminster Abbey Muniments, 41089.

[2] Salisbury, Pt. XVIII, pp. 102, 117, 140; C.S.P. Ireland, 1603-06, pp. 456, 457, 460, 463.

The Lord Deputy is shown at Kinsale answering the advisers who urged him to abandon the siege and withdraw his army from the risk of being taken in front and rear by Irish and Spaniards simultaneously.

> *Let us not now our travails disappoint*
> *Of the honour which doth thereunto belong.*
> *We cannot spend our blood more worthily*
> *Than in so fair a cause, and if we fall*
> *We fall with glory, and our worth thereby*
> *Shall be renownéd and held dear of all.*

On another note are the lines on the passage of the great to the tomb,

> *Where all attendance and observance ends,*
> *Where all the sunshine of our favour sets,*
> *Where what was ill no countenance defends,*
> *And what was good the unthankful world forgets.*

The last two lines look forward to Alexander Pope.

John Ford was not, like Daniel, under the patronage of Charles—he was at this time scarcely out of his teens and at the start of his poetic career—but he was a warm admirer. The story of Charles and Penelope had evidently fascinated him. Extreme passion in love was a subject that attracted and stirred him deeply—witness the emotion, the tenderness, and the sensuous beauty of his depiction of the incestuous love of Giovanni and Annabella in his most famous tragedy. He would also seem to have relished a tilt at convention. He was at this stage uneven like Daniel, but could be absurd, whereas the elder poet was at worst dull. In Ford's *Fame's Memorial* a few fine things are surrounded by poverty and tawdriness. It is, however, original and spirited.

> *Linked in the graceful bands of dearest life,*
> *Unjustly termed disgraceful, he enjoyed*
> *Content's abundance; happiness was rife,*
> *Pleasure secure; no troubled thought annoyed*
> *His comfort sweet; toil was in toil destroyed.*
> *Maugre the tongue of malice, spite of spite,*
> *He lived united to his heart's delight.*

240

Sheath up the sword of war, for Mars is dead;
Seal up the smoothèd lips of eloquence,
For flowing Mercury is buried;
Droop wisdom, Numa's grave intelligence
Is vanished, African's stout eminence
    In Devonshire lies obscur'd, for he alone
    Exceeded all, they all died in him one.

He was more fit for heaven than to survive
Amongst the chaff of this unseasoned age,
Where new fantastic joys do seek to thrive
By following sensual toys of folly's rage,
Making the gloss of vice true virtue's badge:
    He saw their shame, which misery begun it,
    Seeing he did it scorn, and scorning shun it.

Hence sprung the venom of impoisoned hate,
Poor malediction's sting, who did despise
Bright honour's stamp, which in his bosom sate,
For that he could not brook to temporize
With humours maskèd in those times' disguise.
    But let dogs bark, his soul's above their anger;
    They cannot wound his worth with envy's slander.

"African" stands for Scipio Africanus. Much of the significance of these verses lies in the fact that the youthful poet saw nothing attractive in the atmosphere of the new reign, into which the great men, including Devonshire himself, had entered with so much hope and zest. He felt himself an Elizabethan. Those who survived that age had passed into a world of chaff, a time of decadence, and Devonshire was fortunate to have survived in it for so short a period. The poet's eye saw at least a measure of the truth.

Two more glimpses of Penelope, "his heart's delight", are left. The first sight of her, living her life alone, is charming and should bring pleasure to all who have followed her career, since it shows her once more lively, energetic, no longer the poor creature who had crouched in a corner of her bedroom. Now, apparently, she was finding some happiness, perhaps living in a gleam of vespertine sun. This picture also shows the kindness characteristic of her and her friendship for Lord Salisbury. The second picture will appear edifying, at least to some.

Her mother, we must recall, had been successively Countess

of Essex, Countess of Leicester, and Lady Blount. On her marriage to Sir Christopher Blount she had gone to live at Drayton Basset, in Staffordshire, and there she remained, thrice a widow, after his death on the scaffold. Penelope had gone to stay with her. The two women had passed through tragedy upon tragedy. Lady Blount had seen two husbands carried away by disease in the flower of their years, a third executed as a traitor; her elder son had suffered the same fate; the younger had been killed in battle when hardly more than a boy. Lady Devonshire had lost her two brothers and now her husband. Letitia Blount was the more resilient of the two, as she was to prove by living well into the reign of Charles I, passing the age of ninety, and taking a walk of a mile in her park almost up to the end. On this occasion both had enjoyed themselves in the company of the young, one of them being Lord Cranborne, Salisbury's boy.

Hearing that Salisbury was ill, Penelope had hurried on her journey back to Wanstead. Either at the house or from a messenger on the road she learnt that he was better. She at once wrote to express her pleasure at this news. The letter was delightful.

"Noble Lord. The rumours of your sickness I confess have made me haste to this place, where I might receive better satisfaction by the knowledge of your health and had the good fortune this day to meet with the messenger you sent to my Lord Clanrickarde, whereby I was assured of your safe recovery, beseeching your Lordship to believe that no friend you have living doth participate more of your grief or joy than myself, whose affection you have so infinitely obliged with your constant favours. While I was at Drayton with my mother, the young hunters came very well pleased, until your servant came with your mission to guide my Lord of Cranborne to my Lady of Derby, which, discontented for fear of parting three days, made them all lose their suppers, and they became extreme melancholy till it was concluded that their train should stay at Drayton and they go together with two servants apiece. I fear nothing but their riding so desperately, but your son is a perfect horseman and can neither be outridden nor matched any way. My mother, I think, will grow young with their company; so, longing to hear of your safe and perfect health, I remain,

Your Lordship's most faithful to do service,

P. Devonshire".

The letter is undated. No difficulty, however, exists in discovering the date to be towards the end of the first week in September, 1606, and fitting the whole incident into its place. On 27 August Salisbury wrote to Sir Charles Cornwallis that he was newly recovered from sickness and on 3 September the King congratulated him. On 1 September Edmond Casse, Cranborne's tutor, wrote to the boy's father that they were just leaving Drayton to visit his cousin, Lady Derby, in Lancashire. The poor man was evidently finding it a strain to keep up tuition in the midst of the social and sporting occasions. "We speak Latin both travelling and hunting", he reported to Salisbury, "yet the sound of it is so harsh amongst a cry of dogs as it comes not with a wonted facility". Lady Derby wrote to her uncle, Salisbury, that Cranborne's companions were the fifteen-year-old Earl of Essex and his brother, Harry Devereux, Penelope's nephews and Lady Blount's grandchildren.[1]

Now for the other glimpse, the last. Father John Gerard, the proselytizing Jesuit, then living in Brussels, had not forgotten the great lady who had escaped him when he was bringing so many converts into what he held to be the only sure fold. About this time, he tells us, a girl who had been one of her ladies crossed to Belgium to become a nun—the English intelligence confirms him by reporting the presence at the English Convent in Brussels of a certain Mistress Deacon who had previously "attended on the Lady Rich". Gerard questioned this girl, who said that her former mistress often spoke of him. She also told him that Penelope's interest in Roman Catholicism appeared to have revived and suggested that he should write to her. He was in the act of composing a letter, doubtless skilfully imbued with the propaganda of which he was a master, when he learnt that she had died of fever. Another source gives the date of her death as 7 July, 1607. Gerard had the satisfaction of learning that she had been received into the Church of Rome by one of his colleagues.[2]

No reason exists for doubting the truth of this report. If we trust Gerard, who was completely sincere, if disconcertingly subtle and diplomatic, Penelope had stood upon the brink of

[1] Salisbury, Pt. XVIII, pp. 263, 271, 273, 394; Rawson, p. 309.
[2] Gerard, p. 35.

this decision some fifteen years before. Charles was no longer at hand to pull her back. His loss may very well have impelled her forward in her search for a high, spiritual, consolation, promised her in the arms of the Roman Church, a consolation which she had found unattainable in the less ecstatic atmosphere and more humdrum doctrine of the Church in which she had lived. So she goes by, having achieved, it may be hoped, what she was seeking, whatever this may have been.

BIBLIOGRAPHY

MANUSCRIPTS

State Papers, Ireland
British Museum, Stowe MSS.
Carnsew Diary
Lansdowne MSS.
Bagot MSS.
Westminster Abbey Muniments
A Discourse or Apollogie ... by ... Lord Mountjoy (Bodleian
    Library)
Will of the Earl of Devonshire (Exeter College Library)

CALENDARS AND COLLECTIONS

Calendar of State Papers, Domestic
Calendar of State Papers, Foreign
Calendar of State Papers, Ireland
Calendar of State Papers, Spain
Calendar of State Papers, Venice
Calendar of Patent Rolls
Calendar of Ormonde Deeds
Syllabus of Rymer's Foedera
Tudor and Stuart Proclamations
Calendar of State Papers, Carew
Acts of the Privy Council
Return of Members of Parliament
Journals of the House of Lords
Historical MSS. Commission, 7th Report
—— De Lisle and Dudley Papers
—— The Family of Gawdy
—— Rutland Papers
—— Sackville Papers
—— Salisbury Papers

Sydney (Sidney) Papers (Collins)
Tanner Letters, edited by Charles McNeill
Letters of John Chamberlain
Purchas His Pilgrimes. The Fourth Part
Monro, Cecil: Acta Cancellariae or Selections from the Records
of the Court of Chancery
Dugdale: A Perfect Copy of all Summons of the Nobility to the
Great Councils and Parliaments of this Realm

WORKS AND ARTICLES

Abbott, Edwin A.: Bacon and Essex
Alexander, J. J.: Berealston as a Parliamentary Borough
(Devonshire Assoc., Vol. XLI)
Allen, P. S.: Opus Epistolarum des Erasmi Roterdami
Aubrey, John: Letters written by Eminent Persons . . . and
Lives of Eminent Men (Ed. 1813)
Bagwell, Richard: Ireland under the Tudors
,,   ,,   Ireland under the Stuarts
(Bastard, Thomas): Seven bookes of Epigrames written by T.B.
(1598)
Birch, Thomas: Memoirs of the Reign of Queen Elizabeth
Boas, Frederick S.: Christopher Marlowe
Buxton, John: Sir Philip Sidney
Camden, William: The History of the Life and Reign of that
Famous Princess Elizabeth (Trans. of Vol. II of "Annales")
Chambers, R. W.: Thomas More (Bedford Historical Series)
Cheyney, Edward P.: A History of England from the Defeat of
the Armada to the Death of Elizabeth
Clowes, William Laird, etc.: The Royal Navy, Vol. I.
Constable, Henry: Diana. Edited by William Carew Hazlitt
(1859)
Corbett, Julian S.: Drake and the Tudor Navy
,,   ,,   The Successors of Drake
Croke, Sir Alexander: The Genealogical History of the Croke
Family, originally named Le Blount
Daniel, Samuel (see Grosart, Michel, and Sprague)
Devereux, Walter Bouchier: Lives and Letters of the Devereux

D'Ewes, Sir Simonds: The Journals of all the Parliaments during the Reign of Queen Elizabeth (1682)

Dictionary of National Biography

Docwra, Sir Henry: Relation of Service done in Ireland (Celtic Soc. Miscellany)

Duro, Cesario: Armada Española desde la Union de los Reinos de Castilla y de Aragón. Tomo III

„   „   La Armada Invencible

Essex, Vol III (Royal Comm. on Historical Monuments)

Falls, Cyril: Elizabeth's Irish Wars

„   „   Neill Garve: English Ally and Victim (The Irish Sword, Vol. I, No. 1)

Feiling, Keith: A History of England

Ford, John: The Works of John Ford. By William Gifford. A new Edition . . . by the Rev. Alexander Dyer

Foster, Joseph: Alumni Oxoniensis, Vol. I, Early Series

Four Masters, Annals of the

Fox Bourne, H. R.: Sir Philip Sidney (Heroes of the Nations)

Froude, J. A.: Life and Letters of Erasmus

Gardiner, Samuel R.: History of England from the Accession of James I to the Outbreak of the Civil War (Ed. 1900)

Gawdy, Philip: Letters of. Edited by Isaac Herbert Jeayes

Gerard, John: The Autobiography of an Elizabethan. Translated from the Latin by Philip Caraman.

Gotch, John: Inigo Jones

Grosart, Rev. Alexander: The Complete Works . . . of Samuel Daniel

Heath, Sidney, and Prideaux, W. de C.: Some Dorset Manor Houses

Hemingway, Joseph: History of the City of Chester

Heylin, D. D.: Cyprianus Anglicus, or the History of . . . William (Laud) Lord Archbishop of Canterbury (1671)

Howard, George Elliott: A History of Matrimonial Institutions

James VI of Scotland, Correspondence of, with Sir Robert Cecil and Others in England (Camden Soc.)

Johnston Robert: Historia Rerum Britannicarum

Jones, the Rev. Frederick M.: The Destination of Don Juan del Aguila in 1601 (The Irish Sword, Vol. II, No. 5)

Jonson, Ben: The Queen's Masques

Laud, Archbishop: Works (Ed. 1853)

Laughton, John Knox: The Defeat of the Spanish Armada (Navy Records Soc.)

Leicester: Correspondence of Robert Dudley, Earl of, during his Government of the Low Countries (Camden Soc.)

Lilley, Henry T., and Everett, Alfred T.: Portsmouth Parish Church

Lodge, Edmund: Illustrations of British History, Biography, and Memoirs (1791)

Mangan, Henry: Del Aguila's Defence of Kinsale (The Irish Sword, Vol. I, No. 3)

Manningham, Diary of John, 1602-1603 (Camden Soc.)

Michel, Lawrence: The Tragedy of Philotas. By Samuel Daniel

Monson, Sir William: Naval Tracts, Vol. II (Navy Records Soc.)

Moreau, M.: Histoire de ce qui c'est passé en Bretagne durant les Guerres de la Ligue

Moryson, Fynes: An Itinerary (Ed. 1907)

Murrell, Richard, and East, Robert: Extracts from Records . . . of the Borough of Portsmouth

Naunton, Sir Robert: Fragmenta Regalia (Arber's English Reprints)

Neale, J. E.: Elizabeth I and her Parliaments, 1559-1581
    „   „   The Elizabethan House of Commons

Nugae Antiquae (Harington Papers) (1779)

Nichols, John: The Progresses and Public Processions of Queen Elizabeth, Vol. II (1788)

Parliamentary History of England, Vol. I, 1066-1625 (1806)

Peele, George: The Works of. Edited by A. H. Bullen, Vol. II (Polyhymnia & Anglorum Feriae, England's Holidays)

Polentinos, Conde de: Epistolario del General Zubiaur

Pollard, Alfred: Sir Philip Sidney's Astrophel & Stella . . . Edited from the Folio of MDXCVIII

Rawson, Maud Stepney: Penelope Rich and her Circle

Richmond, Admiral Sir Herbert: The Navy as an Instrument of Policy

Smith, Preserved: Erasmus

Spedding, James: The Letters and Life of Francis Bacon

Sprague, Arthur Colby: Samuel Daniel, Poems and a Defence of Ryme

Stafford, Francis: Pacata Hibernia (1810 Reprint of Ed. 1633)

Stopes, Charlotte Carmichael: The Life of Henry, Third Earl of Southampton

Strachey, Lytton: Elizabeth and Essex

Stow, John: Annales, Augmented . . . by Edmund Howes Gent (1631)

Vere, Sir Francis: Commentaries (1657)

Wallace, Malcolm William: The Life of Sir Philip Sidney

Winwood, Sir Ralph: Memorials of Affairs of State (1725)

Wood, Antony: The History and Antiquities of the Colleges and Halls of the University of Oxford

Worcestershire Archaeological Soc., Vol. XIX, New Series

Wotton, Sir Henry: Reliquiae Wottonianae (1685)

References are made under the author's name only, except when the bibliography contains more than one work by the same author; in this case the title follows the author's name.

The dividing line between "collections" and "works" is obviously narrow, sometimes hardly existing. In principle, collections where the editorship has appeared important and which are not official have been listed above under "work".

Well-known abbreviations such as "C." for Calendar, "S.P." for State Papers, "C.S.P." for Calendar of State Papers, "A.P.C." for Acts of the Privy Council, and "H.M.C." for Historical MSS. Commission, are used in references.

INDEX